STATISTICAL QUALITY CONTROL

USING EXCEL

Second Edition

Also available from ASQ Quality Press:

The Desk Reference of Statistical Quality Methods
Mark L. Crossley

Improving Performance through Statistical Thinking
ASQ Statistics Division

The Handbook of Applied Acceptance Sampling: Plans, Procedures, and Principles
Kenneth S. Stephens

Glossary and Tables for Statistical Quality Control, Third Edition
ASQ Statistics Division

Innovative Control Charting: Practical SPC Solutions for Today's Manufacturing Environment
Stephen A. Wise and Douglas C. Fair

SPC Essentials and Productivity Improvement: A Manufacturing Approach
William A. Levinson and Frank Tumbelty

The Uncertainty of Measurements: Physical and Chemical Metrology and Analysis
S. K. Kimothy

Zero Acceptance Number Sampling Plans, Fourth Edition
Nicholas L. Squeglia

Statistical Process Control Methods for Long and Short Runs, Second Edition
Gary K. Griffith

To request a complimentary catalog of ASQ Quality Press publications, call 800-248-1946, or visit our Web site at http://qualitypress.asq.org .

STATISTICAL QUALITY CONTROL

USING EXCEL

Second Edition

Steven M. Zimmerman
Marjorie L. Icenogle

ASQ Quality Press
Milwaukee, Wisconsin

Stastical Quality Control Using Excel
Steven M. Zimmerman and Marjorie L. Icenogle

Library of Congress Cataloging-in-Publication Data

Zimmerman, Steven M.
    Statistical quality control using Excel / Steven M. Zimmerman
Marjorie L. Icenogle.—2nd ed.
        p. cm.
    Includes bibliographical references and index.
    ISBN 0-87389-566-5 (Soft Cover, Auto Bind : alk. paper)
    1. Quality control—Data processing. 2. Microsoft Excel (Computer
file) I. Icenogle, Marjorie. II. Title.

    TS156 .Z54 2003
    658.5'62—dc21   2002014684

10 9 8 7 6 5 4 3 2 1

ISBN 0-87389-566-5

Publisher: William A. Tony
Acquisitions Editor: Annemieke Koudstaal
Project Editor: Paul O'Mara
Production Administrator: Gretchen Trautman
Special Marketing Representative: David Luth

ASQ Mission: The American Society for Quality advances individual, organizational, and community excellence worldwide through learning, quality improvement, and knowledge exchange.

Attention Bookstores, Wholesalers, Schools, and Corporations: ASQ Quality Press books, videotapes, audiotapes, and software are available at quantity discounts with bulk purchases for business, educational, or instructional use.
For information, please contact ASQ Quality Press at 800-248-1946, or write to ASQ Quality Press, P.O. Box 3005, Milwaukee, WI 53201-3005.

To place orders or to request a free copy of the ASQ Quality Press Publications Catalog, including ASQ membership information, call 800-248-1946. Visit our Web site at www.asq.org or http://qualitypress.asq.org .

Printed in the United States of America

∞ Printed on acid-free paper

Quality Press
600 N. Plankinton Avenue
Milwaukee, Wisconsin 53203
Call toll free 800-248-1946
Fax 414-272-1734
www.asq.org
http://qualitypress.asq.org
http://standardsgroup.asq.org
E-mail: authors@asq.org

To my grandchildren Samantha, Arthur, Richard, and Elizabeth —S.M.Z.

To my nephew Brian, and nieces Talia and Kristin —M.L.I.

Contents

Preface

Statistical Quality Control (SQC) Using Excel

Statistical Quality Control (SQC) Using Excel® is for the *beginner* in both quality control and using Excel. Beginners in statistical quality control include inspectors, technicians, engineers, professionals, and managers who are looking for ways to implement quality control in the workplace. Beginners in using Excel include each group just identified, plus quality control experts who want to use spreadsheet programs for quality control procedures to improve the quality of products or services. SQC and Excel are not difficult to learn, and due to the graphic nature of both, Excel is an ideal tool for SQC.

If an individual has a background in either SQC or Excel, the learning process will be easier. Individuals with some background will be able to skip some of the basic material and move faster through the text.

For those of you who are intimidated by computers, we suggest that you work slowly through the book, one step at a time. If you have waited this long to learn to use a computer, there is no reason to rush. You can do it. Read the instructions in this text, as well as the instructions on the computer screen. This text includes step-by-step instructions for creating spreadsheets that will help you analyze quality control data. We selected the simplest and most direct methods for solving SQC problems.

Why Spreadsheets?

Statistical quality control ensures that goods and services are produced that meet and exceed customer expectations. SQC includes two general techniques: (1) acceptance sampling and (2) statistical process control. *Acceptance sampling* is the method of collecting data regarding lots or batches of materials, products, or services, and then using analytical tools or methods to make decisions regarding the lot(s), that is, whether to accept or reject the lot based on the quality of the items in the sample. *Statistical process control* includes methods of analyzing data collected from ongoing processes to make decisions about the processes in order to control the quality of the product(s). Both techniques are important for all types of business organizations. Spreadsheet programs offer effective tools for efficiently, accurately, and rapidly performing SQC analysis to improve quality.

Spreadsheet programs give the quality specialist control over the data analysis, graphics, and presentations. Spreadsheet programs help new users learn how to structure, solve, and present SQC problems by:

- Helping individuals learn to structure SQC problems

- Eliminating calculation errors

- Facilitating the creation of charts and graphs

- Facilitating the creation of attractive presentations

- Increasing the ease of problem solving

- Facilitating better and faster decisions

Selecting a Spreadsheet Program

There are three considerations for selecting a spreadsheet program:

1. Capability

2. Ease of use

3. Compatibility

Various spreadsheet programs may be used for solving SQC problems. We authored a text, *SPC Using Lotus 1-2-3*, which was published by ASQ when Lotus 1-2-3 was the most popular program used by quality control professionals. Currently, Excel is the most popular spreadsheet program in use, so that is what this text uses. A number of versions of Excel are available for Windows and Macintosh. Based on frequency of use, we have selected the latest version, *Excel xp* and *Windows xp*.

Every version of Excel has had the capability of creating SQC charts and analysis, and each new version has included changes that enhance the task of creating SQC charts. Our work is version-specific. That is, we detailed how to do things using Excel xp. If you are still using Excel 5 or Excel 2000, almost everything we did is consistent, except for the graphing.

The authors have found no Windows spreadsheet program that cannot be used to solve every SQC problem we have ever encountered. Today's spreadsheet programs have so many features that it is difficult to find applications beyond the spreadsheet software capabilities. Users who are familiar with other Windows-based programs will find Excel xp very easy to use because the options in the Excel menu bar and tool bars are similar to other programs.

Compatibility is the critical factor. In our opinion, the best spreadsheet program is the one the *user knows how to use*. Most beginners find that it is easiest to learn the spreadsheet program that co-workers are using because help is available. Since Excel xp for Windows is currently the most popular spreadsheet program, the authors believe it is the most compatible one. Compatibility increases the ease of file transfer and aids the learning process. Using Excel xp, it is very easy to move data among other Microsoft programs, particularly the programs that comprise the Microsoft Office Suite.

The key difference between Excel for Windows and Excel for the Macintosh is the keyboard design used on these two computers. A Macintosh user who is knowledgeable on the differences between Windows keyboards and Macintosh keyboards may use our text to create SQC applications on the Macintosh. In addition, spreadsheet files created in any version of Excel can be transferred to all versions of Excel and even to Lotus 1-2-3 for Windows or DOS.

Organization

The book is divided into five parts:

Part	Title
1	Starting
2	Fundamentals of Excel xp
3	Fundamentals of Statistical Quality Control
4	Statistical Process Control
5	Acceptance Sampling

Part 1 introduces the concepts of statistical quality control and explains how to use spreadsheets for quality control. These chapters provide the foundation for all the other chapters.

In part 2, basic Excel skills are reviewed, such as saving a file, opening a file, and so on. In addition, some of the more advanced features of Excel are presented. This edition includes a chapter that demonstrates how to link charts and graphs created with Excel into PowerPoint presentations.

Part 3 reviews the general concepts of statistics, distributions, outliers, and statistical quality control analysis that are needed to use SQC methods.

In part 4, the basic statistical process control methods are demonstrated, including the creation of specific spreadsheets for solving selected SPC problems: $\overline{X}$ and range control charts; $\overline{X}$ and sigma control charts; p and np control charts; c and u control charts; process capability; Pareto charts and fishbone diagrams; cumulative summation charts; individual, moving average, and moving range control charts; and exponential weighted moving average charts.

In Part 5, acceptance sampling methods are demonstrated, including binomial and hypergeometric distributions, operating characteristic and power curves, and average outgoing quality curves, and methods for comparing control chart performance are introduced.

Features

Jargon is the specialized language of a given field. SQC and Excel each has its own language. A large part of learning the language of SQC and Excel is learning the terminology. We have defined both the computer and SQC terms carefully. At first the terminology may slow you down, but mastering the terms will increase your rate of learning.

Within each chapter we have identified key terms. To minimize the importance of reading each chapter in order, key terms are defined where they occur in the text, even if they were listed and defined in earlier chapters. To further reduce the need to read the chapters in order, beginning in chapter 7, each chapter includes a section at the beginning that identifies knowledge from previous chapters that is required to successfully complete the chapter problems.

Many chapters in parts 2, 4, and 5 contain real-life examples of how the authors have used statistical process control techniques. These examples are offered to provide additional insight into the ways that SQC can improve quality in real organizations.

Chapters 10–22 have practice problems that require either the use or modification of spreadsheets from the chapters. The spreadsheets used throughout the text are available on the CD-ROM provided with the book. The user may simply load the spreadsheet from the CD to the computer and then modify the spreadsheet as needed, or the user may create the spreadsheet from scratch by following the steps in the book.

Appendices are included that contain many of the traditional quality control factors and some computer issues that do not fit neatly into any particular chapter.

Acknowledgments

We could not have reached the final stage of our project without the help of many people. We appreciate the opportunity of having our work reviewed and the kind help of our reviewers. We would like to thank Kendall Stockman for working through the entire book with diligence and patience. We would also like to give a special thanks to our spouses, Carol Zimmerman and Craig Cortright, who lived with us through the completion of this text.

Steven M. Zimmerman
Marjorie L. Icenogle

Part I

Starting

1

Introduction

Introduction

Statistical Quality Control Using Excel is a "how-to" text for learning:

1. The fundamentals of statistical quality control (SQC)

2. The use of Excel xp as a tool for solving SQC problems

This book is written for managers, engineers, professionals, technicians, physicians, nurses, and others who are interested in improving the quality of the products and services offered to customers, clients, or patients. The content was developed for readers who know little or nothing about SQC and spreadsheet programs, or readers who know a little about SQC but want to learn to use spreadsheet programs to help control the processes that are important to their businesses. Every effort has been made to keep the instructions basic so that beginners in SQC and beginners in computer spreadsheet programs can obtain maximum results. It is fun and exciting to be able to produce beautiful control charts for large data sets in a minimum amount of time so that time and effort may be spent analyzing and understanding the data.

Individuals working alone can use this book, or a trained instructor or professor may select this book for a course. Individuals learning on their own will be able to accomplish the objectives by working diligently through the book. We recommend that a person with little or no background in SQC work through each chapter and complete the exercises in Microsoft Excel. There are no shortcuts to learning a powerful program such as Excel to produce solutions to a large variety of problems.

If you have any background in either SQC or spreadsheet programs, you will be able to skip around and choose the material that interests you. If when skipping around you find that a particular section is difficult to use or understand, most likely you have skipped a little too far.

We have made every effort to keep the text and examples simple, always looking for the easy way to solve SQC problems, as well as to set up and use Excel. If you are looking for advanced Excel procedures, you should choose another text. SQC is a complex body of knowledge; Excel is a complex and powerful spreadsheet program. Only by selecting simple solutions were we able to combine these two areas and bring them to you in an easy, ready-to-use package.

What Is Statistical Quality Control?

Statistical quality control involves the activities associated with ensuring that goods and services satisfy customer needs. SQC uses statistical analysis based on measurements taken from a process or from a sample of products or services to make decisions regarding the quality of goods and services. *Quality* is the composite characteristics of a product or service, which includes aspects of engineering, manufacturing, design, and service. The level of quality determines the degree to which a product or service pleases customers.

The foundation of SQC incorporates statistical analysis, the concept of management by exception, and graphical analysis. The analytical methods of statistical quality control may be divided into two groups: statistical process control (SPC) and acceptance sampling. SPC involves monitoring and controlling processes operating in real time based on process data collected recently (nearly real time). Acceptance sampling involves the creation and utilization of a variety of plans for accepting/rejecting lots or batches of products. The purpose is to limit an organization's risk of purchasing or selling poor quality product.

What Is Statistical Process Control?

A primary task of a manager is to control a business (a process); a primary concern of an engineer is to control a project (a process); and a primary concern of a healthcare professional is to control a patient (a process). Professionals in all fields are responsible for controlling ongoing processes. Every project, company, organization, and institution behaves like a process in some manner. SPC may be used to help control almost all processes that can be monitored (measured) to ensure that the process performs within limits.

SPC is a decision-making tool, and change is the foundation of SPC. When a process changes (goes beyond established limits), SPC helps the quality specialist identify the change and decide if the change is good or bad.

1. If the change is bad, the reason for the change is identified and every attempt is made to eliminate the occurrence of the cause of the change

2. If the change is good, the reason for the change is identified and every attempt is made to make the occurrence of the cause of the change common practice

When some action is taken that should produce a change, and the change does not occur, then the action has not been effective. The lack of change when change is expected is important information in SPC. The significance of a change requires management, engineering, or clinical judgement. Only a person trained in the process can make the bad–good judgement. SPC shows when a change occurs; the professional determines why.

Three considerations are critical to effective SPC:

1. Selecting the correct characteristics or factors to measure

2. Obtaining precise and accurate measurements

3. Timing the measurements

A primary limitation on the use of SPC is the ability to select a characteristic that is useful for controlling the process. If a characteristic is selected that does not measure what we want to control, then all our efforts will be of no value or may actually produce a negative change in the process. For example, some patient vital sign data monitor characteristics that are easy to measure and do not cause great discomfort to the patient; however vital signs that are indicative of the patient's condition should be monitored. A particular vital sign may or may not be related to the patient's illness. We may not have the ability to measure a particular characteristic and if we cannot measure a characteristic, it cannot be used to control the process.

In addition to measuring the wrong characteristic, sometimes we lack the capability to obtain precise measurements, which can reduce the effectiveness of control charts. For example, if a customer demands that a component is produced to specifications within one-thousandth of an inch, and your equipment can only measure within one-hundredth of an inch, you will be unable to control your manufacturing process to meet the customer's specifications.

The timing of the measurements is also an important consideration in SPC. If the decision-making time horizon is in minutes, the data collection and recording rate should be matched. Consider that current clinical practice is to manually record one vital sign measurement each hour. Assuming a patient heart rate is 90 beats per minute, then there are $90 \times 60 \times 24$ or approximately 129,600 possible observations per day, so a single data point (average heart beat during one minute) does not seem adequate. Control charts based on the data recorded hourly may be useful; nevertheless, a volume of clinical data is missed between each recording.

What Is Acceptance Sampling?

Acceptance sampling is the procedure in which samples are taken from lots of material and evaluated. If the sample is found acceptable, then the lot is accepted, otherwise the lot may be rejected or other corrective action is taken. Often a rejected lot is sent back to the seller (supplier), or in some cases, the rejected lot may be subjected to 100 percent inspection. The exact action taken on the rejected lot is determined by the agreement between the supplier and the buyer.

Almost all businesses and organizations must purchase and/or receive material from other organizations. A procedure for accepting and inspecting incoming material is important. Even if a formal plan is not used, the concepts of acceptance sampling may be used for managing material purchases.

Why Use Spreadsheets?

The statistical and graphic nature of SQC makes Excel a useful tool for solving SQC problems because the Excel spreadsheet (worksheet) makes all of the calculations and graphing easy. SPC and acceptance sampling require many simple calculations that may be performed using the basic spreadsheet capabilities. Excel offers an easy way to perform these calculations.

Excel is a perfect environment for performing SQC calculations because once the spreadsheet is built, your computer easily completes the required calculations. It is simple to replace the data in one spreadsheet with a new set of data, and then to record the results under a new name. It is also simple to create a model—a template that may be used over and over to enter new data and to create new SPC charts or acceptance sampling evaluations. Excel makes solving SQC problems fun because it is more enjoyable to get analysis results quickly and to spend time increasing your understanding and using the results, rather than spending time learning and completing the detailed mathematical calculations required to get to a solution.

Proficiency in the use of Excel to solve SQC problems may help you earn a promotion. We have had many students who over the years parlayed their Excel–SQC skills into higher-paying jobs and professional advancement. One student was promoted from secretary to quality control engineer to a large extent because of her spreadsheet and SQC skills. The quality control engineers in her department were so impressed that she was able to create beautiful, complete SPC spreadsheet analysis in no time that they promoted her.

The typical SPC problem includes the analysis of data saved in a series of subgroups. The number of observations within a subgroup may vary from one to five, to 10, or 20. In our experience the most common subgroup size is five. Except for data collection situations where data are collected at a "high rate" we seldom use subgroup sizes greater than 10. Figure 1.1 is an example of an $\overline{X}$ and sigma worksheet using five observations in each subgroup.

How to Use This Text

This text is a hands-on text. We recommend that readers work through each chapter while sitting at a computer. If your objective is to learn Excel, then we recommend that you *do not* load the templates from the CD, but instead create your own worksheets by following the instructions in each chapter. Even though each step in the creation process is simple, you may need to complete each task more than once to understand the reasoning behind the instructions.

If you are familiar with Excel and want to learn about SQC, we recommend that you use our templates as software and focus on understanding the concepts of SQC. To use the templates as software, copy the templates

Figure 1.1 $\overline{X}$ and sigma worksheet.

to your computer's hard drive and put the master CD in a safe place. When you open the worksheets to complete the exercises, we suggest that you use the instructions in chapter 3 on "Opening a Copy of a Template." Opening a workbook as a template keeps the original worksheet intact and creates a copy for your exercises. After you have completed the exercises in the book, you may then replace the textbook data or the randomly generated numbers with your own "real" data and analyze the results.

The templates on the CD that is included with the text are not copyrighted. They were written for your use in solving the exercises in the book and to help you conduct your own quality analyses. You may publish the results and you do not have to give us or the American Society for Quality (ASQ Quality Press) any credit; however, we would not mind if you do reference this book.

Part 1 is an introduction to SQC and Excel. If you want, you can skip this material and go directly to the chapter that interests you. We have made each chapter independent of the other chapters.

Part 2 is a review of the fundamentals of Excel xp for Windows xp and some basic Windows concepts. In all Windows programs Save, Save As, Open, and many other basic activities are performed in the same or in a similar manner. If you have not used any version of Windows, this is a critical section. Work through these chapters carefully. If you have used Windows or Excel, you will most likely find this material extremely basic. If you are familiar with Windows programs, we suggest that you skim these chapters so that you are familiar with the content and can refer back to these chapters if you need detailed instructions as you complete the exercises. Excel has many exciting and unexpected capabilities. This section introduces a few of these capabilities and identifies some of the special features available that are not usually used for SQC problem solving.

Part 3 includes an overview of the fundamentals of statistics and SQC. SQC is based on statistical concepts and it is helpful to understand how to use these concepts in the Excel environment. This section also reviews basic SPC terms for the readers who need this material. A few of the exciting statistical add-ins are reviewed. The objective of this text is to cover the concepts associated with SQC.

Part 4 is the core of the SPC material. In this section you will find details on how to create and use the basic quality control charts: $\overline{X}$ and range process control charts; $\overline{X}$ and sigma control charts; p and np process control charts; c and u process control charts; cumulative sum charts; individual, moving average, and moving range control charts; and estimated weighted moving average control charts. In addition, you will find a chapter on process capability, Pareto charts, and fishbone diagrams.

Part 5 details acceptance sampling. This part of the text focuses on attribution acceptance sampling based on both the binomial and hypergeometric distributions. You will learn about probability functions, cumulative probability functions, operating characteristic curves, power curves, and average outgoing quality curves.

Organization and Features

The authors would have preferred to make each chapter totally independent of all other chapters; however, this was not practical. To minimize the amount of prior chapter readings, beginning in chapter 7 we have identified the prior knowledge required to complete each chapter. If you have a background in the material identified, it will not be necessary to go back and read earlier chapters. If you do not have a background in the required material, you can start the new chapter and if you have difficulty, you can refer to earlier chapters.

You will find key terms listed at the beginning of most chapters and defined when they are first encountered in the chapter. A term may be listed as a key term in more than one chapter. The key terms form the basic vocabulary of SQC and Excel and are included in a glossary at the end of the book.

Most of the chapters in parts 3 and 4 contain a "Real Life" section near the end of the chapter. These sections are based on the real-life experiences of the authors in using SQC. These examples illustrate the concepts presented in the chapter.

At the end of each chapter in parts 2, 4, and 5, you will find exercises that are helpful in developing your knowledge and skill in SQC. We recommend that you complete all of the exercises for each chapter.

Summary

This text is written for anyone who is interested in improving the quality of the products and services offered to customers, clients, or patients. *Statistical Quality Control Using Excel* is a "how-to" text for learning the fundamentals of statistical quality control (SQC) and for learning how to use Excel xp as a tool for solving SQC problems. The content is targeted toward readers who know little or nothing about SQC and little or nothing about using spreadsheet programs, or readers who know about SQC, but want to learn to use spreadsheet programs to help control the processes that are important to their businesses. Every effort has been made to keep the instructions basic so that beginners in SQC and beginners in computer spreadsheet programs can obtain maximum results. Learning about statistical quality control and Excel xp is a challenging assignment, but we hope you find this approach easy and fun.

2

SQC and Spreadsheet Programs

OUTLINE

Introduction

Statistical quality control (SQC) involves the activities associated with ensuring that goods and services satisfy customer needs. Calculations needed to perform SQC are usually simple and easy to do except for the numerous calculations required. Excel is a perfect environment for performing SQC calculations because once the spreadsheet is built, your computer easily completes the required calculations.

You are probably reading this book because you are interested in SQC. There are many things that one must learn in order to perform SQC in the Excel environment, but generally, the concepts are not difficult; however, learning to use Excel for solving SQC problems does require time and effort. We hope our work helps you to learn important SQC concepts that you can apply to your organization.

History of Quality Control

The foundation of quality control is built on the work of Shewhart, Dodge, Romig, Deming, and Juran, among others. The work of Walter Shewhart forms the foundation of all of statistical quality control thinking. Deming was the master salesman of quality thinking, whose concepts were based on the work he did as Shewhart's editor in 1929. Dodge and Romig developed the concept of the acceptance sample theory while working for the Bell Telephone Laboratories. Deming and Juran were among the early leaders who taught the world how to use and understand quality methods.

The combination of simple statistics, the concept of management by exception, and graphical analysis form the foundation of SQC. The graphic nature of SQC makes Excel a powerful tool for solving SQC problems because the Excel worksheet makes SQC calculations and graphing easy.

Statistical quality control: Activities associated with ensuring that goods and services satisfy customer needs.

Structure of SQC Problems

SQC techniques may be divided into two classifications:

1. Statistical process control (SPC)

2. Acceptance sampling

Statistical Process Control

Statistical process control utilizes statistical methods to control the performance of a process to ensure that the output meets customer needs. A process is an ongoing repetitive activity, such as producing paper, chemicals, or items that are mass-produced on an assembly line. Processes can also include customer services, production systems, administration activities, and physical processes of the human body.

Variation in a process may be stable or unstable. When a process is stable, only normal (random) variation is present. Just because a process is stable does not mean that the amount of variation is acceptable, given the objectives of the process. In situations where the variation is too great, quality control specialists may attempt to reduce or control the variation in the process. An unstable process has normal random variation plus variation due to outside forces. The milling machine that has just developed a loose bearing, the automobile driver who has consumed a large amount of alcohol, or the consumer who just ate a hamburger contaminated with botulism are all examples of outside forces creating variation in a process. Similarly, quality control specialists are responsible for identifying and eliminating the outside forces causing the unstable variation.

Quality control specialists can utilize statistical control charts to see if a process is stable or unstable. Creating SPC charts requires three primary steps: (1) entering process measurements (data) into a spreadsheet, (2) entering formulas to calculate averages and control limits, and (3) generating SPC charts that may be used to develop performance standards for averages and variations for future comparisons.

$\overline{X}$ and sigma control charts require 100 or more observations, which are usually collected in groups. The examples in this text frequently use groups with five observations in each. The spreadsheets illustrating the examples are routinely organized into 20 rows of data in five columns. Each row contains data for one group (five columns). For each group, an average and standard deviation (or range) is calculated.

In addition, SPC requires formulas to calculate the following statistics:

1. The average of the subgroup averages ($\overline{\overline{X}}$)

2. The lower control limit ($LCL_{\overline{X}}$) for $\overline{X}$

3. The upper control limit ($UCL_{\overline{X}}$) for $\overline{X}$

4. The average of the subgroup ranges ($\overline{r}$) (or standard deviation)

5. The lower control limit (LCL_r) for the subgroup range (or standard deviation)

6. The upper control limit (UCL_r) for the subgroup range (or standard deviation)

The third step is to generate the graphs of the subgroup measurements by defining the graphing ranges, selecting the chart type in the Chart Wizard, naming the chart scales, locating the chart in the spreadsheet, and editing the chart according to the user's preferences. Figure 2.1 illustrates the structure of an SPC spreadsheet.

Acceptance Sampling

Acceptance sampling is a method of taking samples from lots of material or products and inspecting the items in the sample to determine if the items meet customer requirements or product specifications. Each lot is accepted or rejected based on the number of defective items found in the sample. The purpose of acceptance sampling is to guide decision making concerning the acceptance or rejection of lots of materials. Acceptance sampling

Figure 2.1   Structure of an SPC spreadsheet.

allows the quality specialist to separate incoming lots of material according to whether the lots have a high probability of containing high-quality items or items of poor quality. Acceptance plans are created to balance the risks between the producer and the consumer. The producer's risk is the probability that good-quality lots will be rejected, while the consumer's risk is the probability that low-quality lots will be accepted.

When acceptance sampling is used for statistical quality control, the first step is to decide which items form a lot. Care should be taken to ensure that each lot contains only output from a single machine or a single process for a specific period of time. Carefully identifying the source of each lot allows the quality specialist to investigate and correct the sources of poor quality. Care should also be taken to ensure that all samples are drawn at random, meaning that every item in the lot has an equal chance of being tested.

The next step is to develop a sampling plan, which specifies the acceptable quality level, states the sample size, and determines the maximum number of defective items that will allow the lot to be accepted. As the sample is drawn from the lot, the number of defective items are counted. If the number of defective items in the sample is less than the maximum number acceptable, the lot is accepted. If the number of defective items in the sample is greater than the maximum number of acceptable items, then the lot is rejected.

Acceptance sampling problems require fewer measurement observations for input and output than process quality control charts. Acceptance

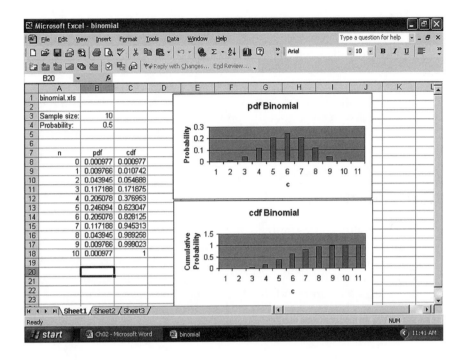

Figure 2.2   Binomial distribution.

sampling problems usually consist of the calculations that create operating characteristic curves or power curves. The operating characteristic curves help the quality control manager select sampling plans that provide the desired consumer (user of the product) and producer (manufacturer of the product) risks. An operating characteristic curve is a plot of the probability of acceptance of a lot versus different levels of incoming quality, given an acceptable quality level.

The type of problem seen in acceptance sampling usually does not lend itself to the type of calculations used in control charts, however the spreadsheets created in this text may easily be used as software for acceptance sampling problems. Figure 2.2 illustrates a spreadsheet for calculating the probability function (pdf) and the cumulative probability function (cpf) for the binomial distribution. Only the sample size and the probability of finding a poor-quality item in the sample or population are needed to perform the calculations for the graphs illustrated.

Acceptance sampling: The procedure of taking a sample of observations from a lot of product or material and making a decision about whether to accept or reject the lot.

Statistical process control: Using statistical analytical methods to measure the performance of a process to ensure that the output meets customer needs.

Using Spreadsheet (Worksheet) Templates As Software

The worksheet templates that are provided with this text may be modified by entering your own data (over the original data), and then examining the resulting control charts. It is recommended that you read the chapter associated with the worksheet you select. We have designed these worksheet templates to solve real-life problems. These designs may not match your situation exactly, but by using Excel you may revise the SPC worksheets to custom-fit them to your needs.

Editing the Templates

The ability to customize your own reports and evaluations is one of the magic features of using Excel (rather than a custom software package) for solving SQC problems. You can start with the worksheet template and then change it to fit your custom needs. If you have no background using Excel, we recommend that you spend time working through the examples in each chapter. As your understanding of the worksheet templates presented increases, you will find it easier to change the worksheet to match your needs.

Locking Worksheet Cells for Other Users

The templates provided on the accompanying CD were designed for editing to meet your needs. This means you have the capability to change the contents of every cell. As you create worksheets for other users, we recommend that you limit the new users' ability to change formulas or enter important data by protecting certain cells in the worksheet. This is accomplished by creating a protected worksheet that contains unprotected cells. The unprotected cells are most often the observation cells, which allow the user to type measurements from a manual data collection form into the worksheet.

The steps required to create a protected worksheet with unprotected cells are:

1. Define (highlight) the cell range you want unprotected (usually data observation cells).

2. In the menu at the top of the screen, select Format, Cells, Protection.

3. Clear the Locked check-box, as shown in Figure 2.3.

4. In the menu at the top of the screen, select Tools, Protection.

5. Click on Protect Sheet as shown in Figure 2.4.

6. Click on the Select Unlocked Cells check-box and be sure to clear the Select Locked Cells check-box as shown in Figure 2.5.

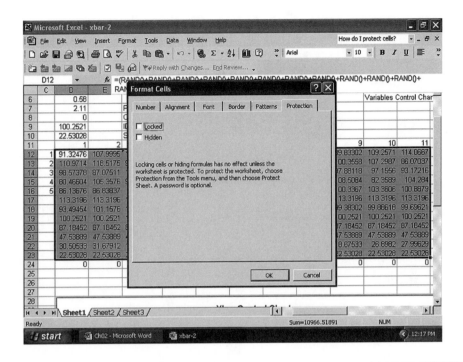

Figure 2.3   Unlocking worksheet cells.

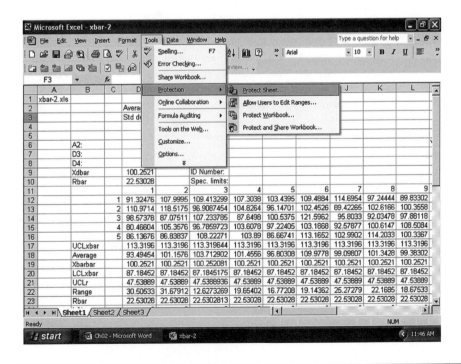

Figure 2.4   Tools, Protection, Protect Sheet option.

Figure 2.5   Password protection screen.

The screen shown in Figure 2.5 allows you to protect your worksheet by entering a password, which will limit any user's ability to remove the protection you are establishing. If you do assign a password, make sure you do not forget it. We know of no way to unlock a worksheet that is protected without the password.

Excel Capabilities

SQC uses many worksheet capabilities, but only a fraction of what is available in Excel. Excel has a large collection of built-in capabilities that may be of value to you. You may have preferred that we solve our problems using some of the more advanced capabilities. We suggest that you use the Help capabilities in Excel to explore the built-in capabilities that are not utilized in this text. The methods used in this text were selected to facilitate the reader's understanding of statistical quality control. We hope you enjoy learning how to use Excel for solving quality problems.

Summary

The purpose of statistical quality control (SQC) is to ensure that products and services meet customer needs. The techniques of SQC can be divided into two classifications: (1) statistical process control (SPC) and (2) acceptance sampling. A process is an ongoing repetitive activity. Quality specialists utilize SPC charts to determine if a process is stable or unstable. Acceptance sampling involves taking samples from product or material lots, inspecting the sample items, and either accepting or rejecting the lot based on the number of defective items found in the sample.

The templates created in this text are designed to analyze and solve real-life quality control problems. You can replace the example data with your own real data. Depending on your inspection plan, in some cases you can use the worksheet templates without changing the worksheet or you can revise the template to match your specific needs. Our objective is to demonstrate only a fraction of the capabilities available in Excel to help you improve the quality of your products and services.

Part II

Fundamentals of Excel xp

3

Microsoft Excel Basics

OUTLINE

What Are Worksheet Programs?

Worksheet programs are tools that solve mathematical and statistical problems by allowing the user to enter, edit, save, retrieve, calculate, and present the results of mathematical operations in charts and graphs. Worksheets facilitate decision making by providing the capability to organize data, complete many mathematical calculations, and summarize the results in meaningful ways. Electronic worksheets are organized by columns and rows, and resemble the paper worksheets used by accountants and engineers. Worksheets allow users to store and easily access very large quantities of information.

Worksheet programs are especially useful for statistical quality control (SQC). Quality specialists can enter inspection data and/or process performance measurements into a worksheet, calculate averages and control limits, and generate graphs and charts to illustrate how current measurements compare to base period data. Excel offers all of these capabilities and many more; however, the purpose of this text is to demonstrate how Excel can help solve statistical quality control (SQC) problems, not to demonstrate all the capabilities available in Excel xp.

The Excel skills needed to solve SQC problems include the ability to:

1. Perform basic functions such as save, open, print, copy, cut, and paste.

2. Use equations with relative and absolute addresses.

3. Edit and copy equations from one part of a worksheet to another.

4. Import data stored in a variety of formats.

5. Use Excel's add-ins features.

6. Use the Data-Analysis tools.

7. Create simple macros.

8. Use the Excel Help menus.

Most of these Excel skills will be reviewed as they are needed in the solution of an SQC problem. This chapter provides an overview of the basic Excel skills required to create worksheets. More advanced skills such as creating charts and graphs and importing data from other sources are covered in chapter 4.

Worksheet program: A program for creating, editing, calculating, saving, and opening computer files, and for graphing and printing worksheets using cells identified by their row and column position.

A model worksheet that is created and saved for future use is a template. Although Excel is available in versions for DOS, Macintosh, and Windows, the templates included on the text CD were developed and tested using only Excel xp and Windows xp. Many other programs can read Excel files, including versions of Lotus 1-2-3. Experienced Excel users are likely to have the knowledge to adapt these templates for use in other versions of Excel or other worksheet programs. The authors found that some worksheet programs can read some of the templates on the CD, but not others. If you are using a program other than Excel, the other program may fail to read the Excel template or may read the template with errors. An alternative method of making the files more compatible with other programs is to use the Save As option in the Excel File menu. Excel allows the user to save worksheets as text files, ASCII files, or as worksheet files for use in earlier versions of Excel, Lotus, Quattro Pro, or dBase.

Template: A worksheet model recorded on disk, CD, or tape for future use.

Warning

Chapter 3 is a lengthy chapter that covers many basic Excel skills. Everything presented in this chapter is used in subsequent chapters. We recommend that you read over this chapter without trying to memorize all the procedures. If you need more detailed instructions as you complete later chapters, you will know where to locate them. We recommend that you spend time at the computer working on the worksheets and performing statistical quality control activities rather than memorizing these details.

Operating in the Microsoft Windows xp Environment

Although Excel xp runs only in the Microsoft Windows xp, Windows 2000, Windows 98, or Windows NT operating environments, there is also a version of Excel that runs in a Macintosh environment. The primary difference between the Windows and Macintosh versions is the use of the keyboard. A Macintosh user who is knowledgeable about the differences between the Windows xp keyboard and the Macintosh keyboard may use this text to create SQC applications on the Macintosh. All Microsoft Windows operating systems are based on windows, which are display areas on the video screen that facilitate the operation of software programs. If you have used other Windows programs, you are already familiar with most of the common procedures, such as Open, Save, and Close files and Copy, Cut, and Paste. Although this text is written for novice Excel users, the text assumes that the reader has some familiarity with the Windows operating environment and has some minimal skill operating a mouse.

Using the Mouse

Table 3.1 contains a summary of the instruction terms that describe common actions associated with the mouse.

Understanding the Excel Operating Environment

Why Use Microsoft Excel?

The authors have chosen Excel xp to demonstrate SQC techniques, although other worksheet programs can perform many of the same functions. Microsoft Excel provides more statistical functions and greater computing power and flexibility than other worksheet programs. And currently, Excel is the most widely used worksheet program in the United States. Excel's compatibility with other Microsoft products such as Word, Access, and PowerPoint increases the program's usefulness for manipulating data and producing effective documents and presentations.

This text is for beginners in both Excel and SQC. The objective is to show how one can solve statistical quality control (SQC) problems using

Table 3.1   Basic mouse actions.

Instruction	Action
Point to	Move the mouse to position the arrow or icon.
Click	Press on the left mouse button once.
Double click	Quickly press twice on the left mouse button while holding the mouse still.
Drag	Press and hold the left mouse button as you move the mouse. Release the button when the mouse pointer is in the appropriate place.
Select	Point and press once on the left button.
Right click	Point and click once on the right mouse button.
Highlight text	Position the mouse pointer at the beginning of the text to be highlighted. Press and hold the left mouse button as you drag the mouse pointer across the desired text.
Select a range	Position the mouse pointer in a cell in a corner of the area to be selected. Press and hold the left mouse button as you drag the mouse pointer across the cells to be selected (highlighted).

the worksheet program Excel xp. Learning to use Excel is a means to an end and not an end in itself. Excel xp is an elegantly simple, yet powerful, program with capabilities to perform all basic SQC functions such as creating, editing, calculating, saving, opening, graphing, printing results, and programming (macros). In addition, Excel has the capability to import graphics and perform many statistical routines. We will use only a fraction of Excel's capabilities, that is, only those capabilities needed to solve SQC problems selected for this text. When given a choice between a simple or a complex solution, we have selected the simple solution.

Starting Excel

There are two ways to start the Microsoft Excel xp program: (1) use the Windows Start button or (2) use the Excel shortcut button.

To start the Excel program using the Windows Start button, click the Start button ▉ *start* in the bottom left corner of the screen, click on Programs, and then click on Microsoft Excel. The menus are shown in Figure 3.1.

If you have created a shortcut icon (button) for Excel, simply point to and click on the Excel icon to start the Excel program. Your Excel icon will probably look like one of the icons in Figure 3.2.

Closing Excel

There are two ways to exit Excel: (1) the Close button or (2) the Exit option in the File menu.

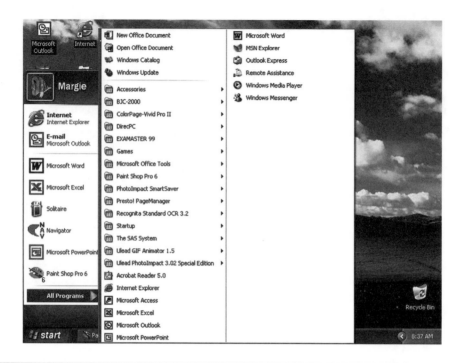

Figure 3.1   Windows Start menus.

Figure 3.2   Excel icons.

You may exit Excel by clicking once on the top Close button ![icon] in the upper right corner of the screen. The lower Close button simply closes the Excel Workbook.

To exit using the menu bar, click on File and then click on Exit. If you did not save your workbook since making changes, Excel will prompt you to save your work before you exit. When you save your work, you are recording your work on a disk.

Save: Windows term for recording a worksheet on a disk.

Shutting Down Your Computer

When you use Microsoft Windows xp, it is important to use the Start–Shut Down menu selection. We also prefer to shut down all Windows applications ourselves before starting the shut down routine. If you simply turn off your computer, your files may be damaged. The shut down procedure is:

1. Close each of your active Windows applications.

2. Click on the Windows Start button .

3. Click on the Turn Off Computer button .

4. Click on the next Turn Off button; if you forgot to save changes to files, Windows will prompt you to save your changes.

5. Do not turn your computer off until a message that you can safely turn off your computer displays or your computer automatically shuts down.

The Excel Window

Each Excel window displays graphic icons and menus that can be customized by the user. Consequently, the screen you see when you start Excel may not be identical to the screens displayed in the text. The appearance of the startup screen depends on the selections that were made as the program was installed and the options activated by the user. The primary components of the Excel window are shown in Figure 3.3.

There are more than 19 different toolbars available in Excel xp. To display selected toolbars, click on <u>V</u>iew and click on <u>T</u>oolbars to display the toolbar menu shown in Figure 3.4 and click once on the options desired. Only toolbars with a check are shown on the screen.

The Windows environment is based on a menu-driven system, which means that to initiate most procedures the user selects the appropriate options from a menu. The menu system is easy to learn and operate because all the program commands are stored in menus, submenus, and dialog boxes. The titles of the menus are displayed in the menu bar. Each menu contains four types of items:

1. *Commands with checks* are menu commands that toggle off and on as checks are added or removed.

2. *Commands with submenus* are commands with a triangle to the right of the command. As these commands are selected, a submenu cascades to the right.

3. *Commands with dialog boxes* are commands that require additional input or choices. Commands with three dots after the command have dialog boxes. Dialog boxes are described in the following section.

Figure 3.3 Excel window.

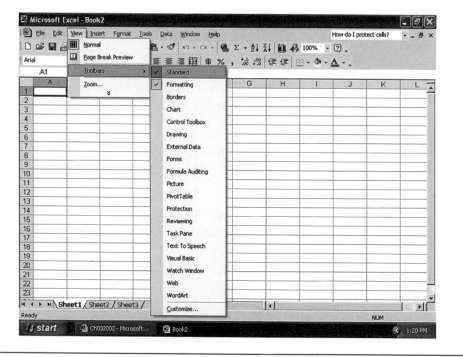

Figure 3.4 Excel toolbar menu.

4. *Commands with keyboard shortcuts* are executed as soon as they are selected. Keyboard shortcuts are the keyboard commands that can be used in place of the menu selection. Every menu item has a keyboard shortcut that requires the user to hold the control (Ctrl) key or the alternate (Alt) key and then press a letter.

   a. Capital letters with an underline indicate that the user must hold the Alt key and then the appropriate letter to execute the command or display a dialog box.

   b. Commands with Ctrl+letter indicate that the user must hold the Ctrl key and then the appropriate letter to execute a command or display a dialog box.

The four types of commands are shown in Figures 3.5, 3.6, 3.7, and 3.8.

Dialog box: An area on the screen that shows status information and allows the user to select among options and enter additional information.

Understanding the Dialog Boxes in Excel xp

Dialog boxes provide status information, offer options for completing Excel procedures, and allow users to enter new information required to complete a procedure. The Print dialog box in Figure 3.9 illustrates most

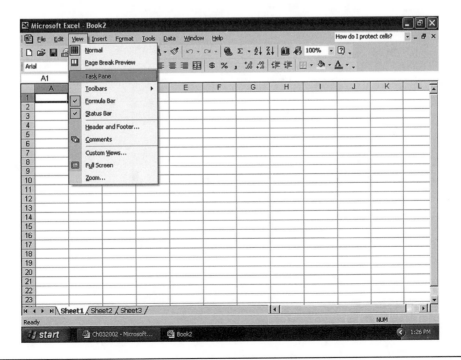

Figure 3.5   Menu commands with check boxes.

Figure 3.6   Menu command with a submenu.

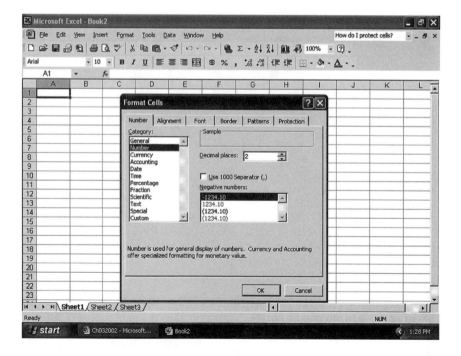

Figure 3.7   Menu command with a dialog box.

Figure 3.8   Menu commands with keyboard shortcuts.

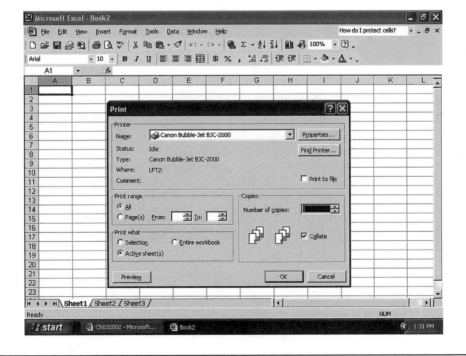

Figure 3.9   Print dialog box.

of the standard dialog box options. The Print dialog box contains the following elements:

1. *Click buttons* perform a function such as continuing or canceling a procedure. To activate the function described on the button, simply click the left mouse button while pointing to the button. The OK and Cancel buttons are click buttons.

2. *Check boxes* are activated when an X appears in the box. The Print to File and the Collate options are check boxes. Clicking once on the left mouse button while pointing to the check box toggles the option on and off.

3. *Option buttons* (radio buttons) present mutually exclusive alternatives. When one option is selected the other options are cleared. Select an option by pointing to the button and clicking on the left mouse button. Option buttons are shown in the Print What and the Page Range sections of the print dialog box.

4. *Drop-down list boxes* provide acceptable options from which the user must select. To activate a drop-down list, click on the arrow

   pointing down on the right side of the area ▼ , then click on the appropriate option. The printer Name: is an example of a drop-down list box.

5. *Spinner buttons* ▲▼ allow the user to change the values in the edit areas by clicking on the up arrow to increase the value and clicking on the down arrow to decrease the value. The user may also type in the value by pointing to and clicking once in the area to position the cursor for typing. Spinner buttons are found to the right of Number of Copies:, and in the Page Range From: and To: areas. Two other types of dialog features are found in dialog boxes, edit boxes, and tabs.

6. *Edit boxes* are small areas where the user can type in a value or edit the value that is displayed. Figure 3.10, the Find dialog box, prompts the user to enter the text or numerical expression to be found.

7. *Tabs* in a dialog box allow Excel to group a series of related dialog boxes together in one area. The Page Setup option in the File menu provides an example of four dialog box tabs as shown in Figure 3.11. To display the dialog box associated with each tab, point to and click on the tab.

Opening, Creating, Saving, and Closing Workbooks

All Excel xp worksheets are contained in workbooks. A workbook is an Excel document that contains one or more worksheets. Think of each worksheet as a page in a workbook. To move from one page to another simply

Figure 3.10 Edit box.

Figure 3.11 Tabs in a dialog box.

click on the Sheet tabs near the bottom of the screen. When worksheets that were created with earliest versions of Excel are opened in Excel xp, the old worksheet is opened as a workbook with one worksheet.

Worksheet: Another term for a spreadsheet.

Opening a Copy of a Template

To open the workbook templates on the CD that came with your text, we suggest that you open these workbooks as templates. Opening a workbook as a template opens a copy of the worksheet and keeps the original workbook intact. To open the workbook as a template:

1. Click on the Open Folder button (icon) 📂 in the menu bar. The Open dialog box appears.

2. Click on the down arrow ▼ in the Look in: area to display the options.

3. Click on the option that corresponds with the CD drive to access the templates on the CD.

4. When the templates are displayed in the window, click once using the left mouse key to highlight the template name.

5. Click on the Open button, as shown in Figure 3.12.

6. A read-only copy of the worksheet opens.

7. Save the worksheet to the subdirectory of your choice by using the Save <u>A</u>s option. (Note: If you save the revised worksheet using the Save option, Excel will save the worksheet using the file name *Copy of worksheet name* in the same directory as the template.)

Opening a Workbook

Open is the Windows term for reading a worksheet from a disk. Although there are several ways to open existing documents in Windows programs, the following instructions describe how to open the workbooks stored on a disk.

1. From the <u>F</u>ile menu, click on <u>O</u>pen.

2. To open a document stored on a disk in drive A, click on the arrow next to the Look in box ▼ and click on the 3½ Floppy (A:) option.

3. When the worksheets stored on disk are displayed in the window, click on the document that you want to open.

4. Click on the <u>O</u>pen button.

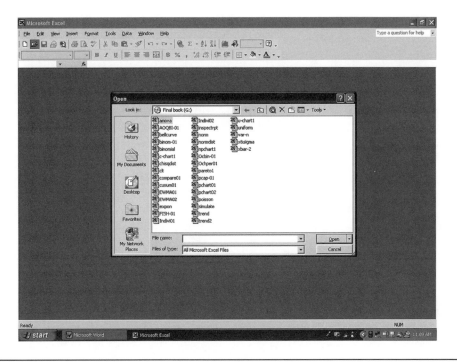

Figure 3.12   Open worksheet templates from CD drive.

Reopening a Recently Used Workbook

An alternative method for opening workbooks is to use the list at the bottom of the File menu. By default, Excel records the four most recently used Excel files. These files may be retrieved by pointing to the desired file and clicking the left mouse button, or by highlighting the names of the files at the bottom of the screen using the arrow keys and pressing the Enter key. When you open files with this method, Microsoft Excel remembers the path to the file. Figure 3.13 illustrates selecting a file from the list.

To change the number of files displayed at the bottom of the File menu, follow these steps:

1. Click on Tools.

2. Click on Options . . .

3. Click on the General tab.

4. Change the number in the Recently used files list box.

5. Click on the OK button.

Open: Windows term for reading a worksheet from a disk.

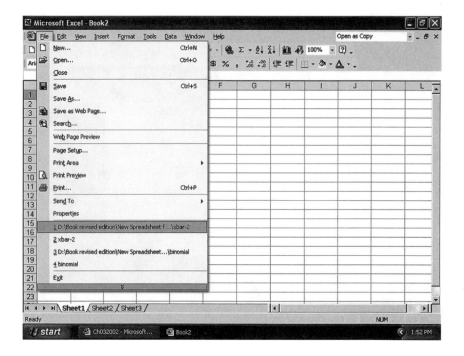

Figure 3.13   Opening a file from the list on the File menu.

Creating a New Workbook

To create a new workbook, click on the New option in the File menu or click on the New button 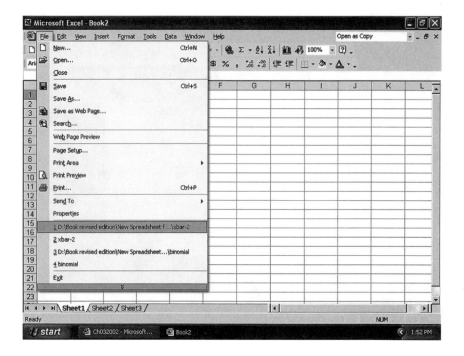 in the standard toolbar. Each new workbook is created with the number of sheets specified in the General Settings dialog box. Each workbook can contain hundreds of sheets, depending on the memory of your computer. Each worksheet may contain over 65,536 rows and 256 columns. The size of your workbook is limited only by your computer's memory capacity.

To change the number of pages that a workbook contains, follow these steps:

1. Click on Tools.

2. Click on Options . . .

3. Click on the General tab.

4. Change the number in the Sheets in New Workbook box.

5. Click on the OK button.

Saving a Workbook

One of the first things to know when learning a new program is how to save a file. The process starts in the File menu, as illustrated in Figure 3.14. Two options are available in the File menu: Save or Save As.

1. Click on File in the menu bar.

2. Click on the Save or Save As option.

If you are saving a file (workbook) for the first time, you may use either the Save or Save As option to achieve the same results. If you previously saved a workbook (file), the Save option merely resaves the file in the same location by replacing the previous version with the newest version. To resave a workbook in the same location, you may also use the Save button ![save icon] in the standard toolbar. If you wish to save the file using a new file name, or save to a disk, a tape, or a different subdirectory, you should use the Save As option. When you are saving a file for the first time and select either the Save or Save As option, or click on the Save button, the Save As window appears, as illustrated in Figure 3.14.

The purpose of the Save As screen is to name the file and identify where the file is to be saved. First, decide in which folder the file should be

Figure 3.14   Save As option dialog box.

saved. Workbooks and other documents are saved in file folders (sub-directories). The default subdirectory used by Excel is *My Documents.* Initially, you may wish to use this subdirectory rather than climb up and down the directory tree to another location. If you would like to change the default file folder, follow these steps:

1. Click on Tools.

2. Click on Options . . .

3. Click on the General tab.

4. Change the file folder name in the Default File Location box as shown in Figure 3.15.

5. Click on the OK button.

Windows xp is not limited by the file and subdirectory naming rules of Windows 3.x and DOS, which limit the number of characters in a name to eight. You may wish to refer to your Windows xp manual if you want to examine the new naming rules. If you are working with users limited by the naming conventions that require eight characters, a decimal point, and a three-character extension, we recommend that you stick with the old naming rules so you can transfer files easily between systems.

Figure 3.15   Changing the default file location.

Closing a Workbook

You may close a workbook using two options: (1) the Close option in the File menu or (2) the lower Close button in the upper right corner of the screen. To close a workbook click on the File menu and click on the Close option. If you have not saved the latest changes to a workbook, Excel will prompt you to save the workbook.

If you have more than one workbook open and want to close all the workbooks with one command, hold down the Shift key while you click on the File menu. The Close option changes to Close All. Clicking on the Close All option closes all the workbooks. If you have not saved the latest changes to any open workbook, Excel will prompt you to save the changes for each.

Entering Text, Numbers, and Formulas in Excel

Moving to a Cell

A worksheet is divided into columns and rows. A *cell* is the box where a column and row intersect. One cell is always active. Using the column-row location procedure, the cell in column C and row 5 is the cell identified as cell C5. The address of the active cell is displayed in the Name box above the column labels. Excel also allows you to use a row–column identification procedure where C5 would be R5C3 (where R = row and C = column). Column–row location is most common in computer applications, while the row–column location is most common in mathematics. Depending on your needs, Excel gives choices on how to locate a cell. The column–row location system is used throughout this text. Several methods are used to move around Excel worksheets.

If the target cell is on the screen, three options are available:

1. Use the mouse pointer to point to the cell and click.

2. Use the arrow keys to move the cursor to the desired location.

3. If the cell you want to move to is in the same row, you may press the Tab key to move the cursor to the right or hold down the Shift key and press the Tab key to move the cursor back to the left.

If the cell is not displayed on the screen, use the scroll bars on the right side and bottom of the worksheet to bring the cell into the display area, then point and click with the left mouse button or move from cell to cell with the arrow keys. Table 3.2 shows combinations of keystrokes that locate cells quickly and easily.

Table 3.2   Keystrokes for moving to an active cell.

Keystrokes	Active Cell
Home	First cell in a row
End, Enter	Last cell in a row
Ctrl + Home	Cell A1
Ctrl + End	Bottom right corner of the worksheet
End (with Scroll Lock on)	Lower right cell in the viewing window
Home (with Scroll Lock on)	Top left cell in the viewing window
Page Up	Up one viewing window
Page Down	Down one viewing window
Arrow keys	Up, down, left, or right one cell at a time

Another option is to use the Go To . . . instruction in the Edit drop-down menu.

1. Click on Edit in the menu bar.

2. Click on Go To . . .

3. When the Go To option box appears, type the cell address in the Reference area as shown in Figure 3.16.

It is also possible to select a *range* of cells. To select a *range* with the mouse, click a cell with the left mouse button and hold the button as you drag the pointer across the cells. When the appropriate *range* is identified (highlighted) release the mouse button. To select a *range* with the keyboard, hold the Shift key and press the arrow keys. When the correct *range* is identified, release the Shift key. The *range* of cells is identified by the address of the cell in the upper left corner, a colon, and the address of the cell in the bottom right corner, for example, A1:D27.

Entering Text and Numbers

Text may be entered into a cell or a text box. If we are entering single words or short phrases as column or row heads, we prefer to enter the text directly into a cell. Each cell can hold up to 32,767 characters; however, only 1024 are displayed in the cell, while all 32,767 will display in the formula bar. If you are entering a sentence or paragraph, we recommend a text box. Creating a text box is covered in chapter 4. If the characters in a cell do not fit within the width of a cell, the contents are displayed over the adjacent cells. The display is truncated if the adjacent cells to the right contain text or numbers.

To display the complete cell text within the width of the column (wrap the text), click on the Format menu, click on Cells, and click on the Alignment tab in the dialog box. Click on the Wrap Text check box and then click on the OK button.

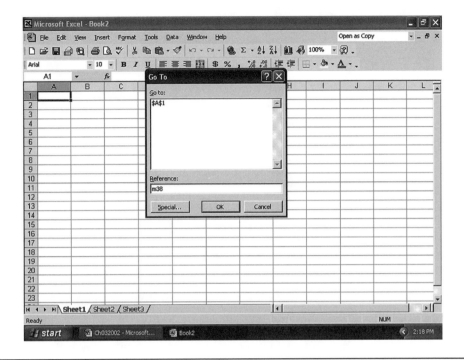

Figure 3.16 G̲o To window.

To enter text into a cell, highlight the cell by pointing and clicking with the mouse, or by using the arrow keys, type the desired text, then press the Enter key. If you make a mistake, press the F2 key to edit the contents of the cell or double click in the cell.

Entering Formulas

A *formula* performs calculations or mathematical operations. Formulas begin with an equal sign and may consist of numbers, functions, and references to other cells. After a formula is entered in a cell, the resulting value of the formula is displayed in the cell and the formula displays in the formula bar when the cell is selected. Excel supports the arithmetic operators in Table 3.3.

Excel performs operations in the following order: (1) %, (2) ^, (3) * and /, and (4) + and −. To change the order of operations, group operating expressions by inserting parentheses. The operations within the parentheses are conducted first. If operators are nested in with other parentheses, the innermost operations are completed first. Sample formulas are shown in Table 3.4.

A formula may be entered by typing in the cell address and the mathematical operators and then pressing the Enter key. Another common way to enter a formula is to type in the mathematical operator then click on the cell containing the value to be used, and then press the Enter key. If you

Table 3.3   Arithmetic operators.

Function	Symbol
+	Addition
–	Subtraction
/	Division
*	Multiplication
^	Exponential operation
%	Percent when placed after a number

Table 3.4   Example formulas.

Formula	Description
+A12	Copies the contents of cell A12 to the formula cell
11	A number is a formula equal to a constant
=(A10–$A$1)/$A$2	The contents of cell A1 are subtracted from the contents of cell A10 and the remainder is divided by the number in cell A2
=NORMDIST(A5,100,10,true)	Creates a value from a normal distribution with a mean equal to 100 and a standard devation of 10

need to enter a long formula, you may find it easiest to type the mathematical operator, click on the cell, type the next operator, and then click on the next cell until the formula is complete.

Understanding Absolute and Relative Addresses

An *absolute address* is like the address of your home, for example, 115 East State Street. A *relative address* is like giving relative directions from a point—two blocks south and one street east from Jose's home. When a formula with an absolute reference is copied, the formula always refers to the original cell. When a formula with a relative reference is copied, the formula always refers to a cell in the same relative position.

The notation *+$A$7* is an absolute address, which means the contents of the cell A7 are used in the formula, even if the formula is copied to other cells. No matter where this cell is referenced, the value that will be used is the exact value that is contained in cell A7. The address *+A7* is a relative address. If this formula is copied to other columns, the relative address will change to +B7, +C7, and so on, across the columns. If the content of the cell A7 is copied down the rows, the relative addresses will change to A8, A9, A10, and so on.

A *mixed reference* has one relative coordinate and one absolute coordinate. For example, in the address *B$7*, the B is a relative address and the 7 is an absolute address. If this formula is copied into other columns, the column address will change to match the worksheet column, but row 7 remains the same even if the address is copied to another row. In the address $B7, the B is an absolute address and the 7 is a relative address. If this formula is copied into other rows, the column address B remains the same and the row number 7 changes to match the row in the worksheet.

Using Excel Functions

A *function* performs a calculation or operation. Excel contains over 300 functions in a variety of categories including financial, date and time, mathematical, statistical, logical, and engineering categories. There are more than 70 statistical functions available. Lists and descriptions of all Excel functions are available using the Help option. Figure 3.17 shows the screen of statistical functions. The SQC problems in this text use only a few of these functions. To use a statistical function, select the cell where the function will be used. Then either click on the Function button ![fx] in the standard toolbar or click on the Insert menu and select the Function option. A dialog box containing the function categories is displayed in the left column. As each category is highlighted, a list of specific functions displays in the right column. To select a specific function, click the left mouse button on the function, and then click on OK. The examples in this text routinely use the average and standard deviation statistical functions and other functions such as sum, maximum, and minimum.

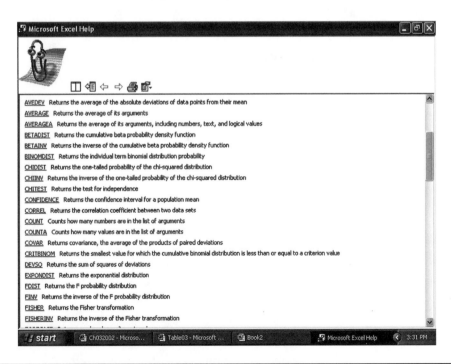

Figure 3.17   List of statistical functions.

Manipulating Worksheet Contents

Copying Cells

At times it may be necessary to move or copy text or formulas from one cell to another. SQC worksheets often contain a large number of calculations for creating control charts, operating characteristic curves, or for other types of graphical output. In most worksheets, one or two rows or columns are entered manually and then the formulas are copied into the remaining rows or columns. When you need to move or copy the contents of a cell or a range of cells, it is usually easier to cut and paste or copy and paste rather than to retype the contents. Edit, Copy or Cut, and Paste commands may also move material between programs, for example, from Excel to Microsoft Office programs, from Excel to other worksheet programs, or from other Windows programs into Excel worksheets.

There are three ways to copy data from one cell to another or from a range of cells into another range: (1) use the Copy option in the Edit menu, (2) use the shortcut buttons in the standard toolbar, or (3) use the cell fill handle to drag and drop the contents into adjacent cells.

The steps to copy data using the Edit menu are:

1. Click on the cell or identify the *range* of cells to be copied.

2. Click on Edit menu and click on Copy.

3. Locate the cell or identify the *range* where the data are to be copied.

4. Select the Edit menu again and click on Paste.

The steps to copy data using the shortcut buttons are:

1. Click on the cell or identify the *range* of cells to be copied.

2. Click on the Copy button ![copy button] in the standard toolbar.

3. Locate the cell or identify the *range* where the data are to be copied.

4. Click on the Paste button ![paste button] in the standard toolbar.

The steps to copy data using the cell fill handle are:

1. Click on the cell or identify the *range* of cells in a row or column to be copied.

2. Point to the fill handle at the lower right corner of the selected cell(s), as shown in Figure 3.18 (when you point to the fill handle, the mouse pointer changes into a black cross).

3. Press and hold the left mouse button as you drag the cross over the *range* where the data are to be copied.

4. Release the mouse button to copy the data into the highlighted cells.

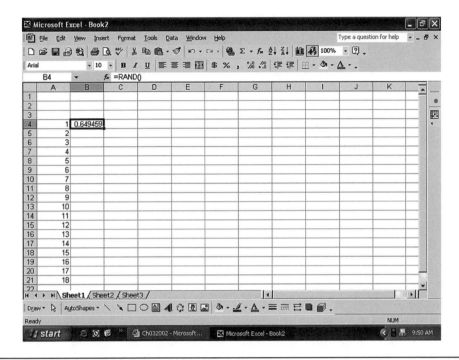

Figure 3.18 Cell fill handle to copy contents of cells.

Cutting and Pasting

The Copy command results in the cell being replicated with the contents of the original cell left intact. The Cut command is a *move* command—the original cell is erased after the command is executed. There are two options available for cutting and pasting the contents of a cell or *range* of cells: (1) the Edit menu or (2) the button icons on the standard toolbar.

To cut and paste the contents of a single cell or a range of cells using the Edit menu, follow these steps:

1. Highlight the cell or the cell *range* to be moved.

2. Click on the Edit option at the top of the window.

3. Click on the Cut option or use the arrow keys to highlight the Cut option and press the Enter key.

4. The border around the cell(s) is highlighted with a flashing border.

5. To locate the cell(s) that will receive the data, use one of the following three methods:

   a. Click on the cell,

   b. Use the Go To option in the Edit menu to identify a single cell, or

   c. Highlight the *range* of cells where the contents are to be moved.

6. Click on the Paste option in the Edit menu.

To cut and paste the contents of a single cell or a *range* of cells using the button icons, follow these steps:

1. Highlight the cell or the cell *range* to be moved.

2. Click on the Cut button ![cut icon] in the standard toolbar.

3. To locate the cell(s) that will receive the data, use one of the following three methods:

   a. Click on the cell,

   b. Use the Go To option in the Edit menu to identify a single cell, or

   c. Highlight the *range* of cells where the contents are to be moved to; click on the Edit option at the top of the window.

4. Click on the Paste button ![paste icon] in the standard toolbar.

Formatting Text and Numbers

Excel provides many options for improving the appearance of worksheets and reports. When you utilize the formatting options, you can draw attention to important data, improve readability, and generate professional-looking reports. The Format menu selection may be used to line up decimal points, specify the use or nonuse of commas, justify text, add borders to cells, or select fonts and font size. In general, formatting improves the appearance of a worksheet. The formatting dialog boxes are: Number, Alignment, Font, Border, Patterns, and Protection. Figure 3.19 shows the Format Cells dialog box.

Among the most important formatting options are the Number formats, which control how numbers are displayed in the cells. To control how numbers are displayed in the worksheet, follow these steps:

1. Select the cell or *range* of cells to be formatted.

2. Click on Format in the menu bar.

3. Click on Cells.

4. Click on the Number tab in the Format Cells dialog box.

5. Click on the Category in the left column.

6. Click on the correct format code in the right column.

Retaining Leading Zeros

In addition to the cell formats that are available in the menus, users may create custom formats by selecting the Custom category in the Number dialog box. A common formatting problem for numbers is instructing Excel to retain leading zeros in an entry, for example, a part number with leading

Figure 3.19 Format Cells dialog box.

zeros such as *00345*. To retain leading zeros, create a custom format by following these steps:

1. Select the cell or range of cells to be formatted.

2. Click on Format in the menu bar.

3. Click on Cells.

4. Click on the Number tab in the Format Cells dialog box.

5. Click on the Custom option in the Category window.

6. In the Type area, type one zero for each digit in the part number.

7. Click on OK.

Adjusting Column Width or Row Height

To adjust the width of a column or the height of a row, point to the cell border on the right side of the column or the cell border below the row. When the cursor becomes a double-sided arrow, press the mouse button and drag the cell border to the right to widen the column or to the left to decrease the column width, or drag the row border down to increase the row depth and drag up to decrease the row depth.

Column widths and row heights may also be adjusted by selecting Format in the menu bar, selecting either the Row or Column option, and then selecting the appropriate choice from the cascading menu.

Inserting and Deleting Columns and Rows

One of the wonderful things about using an electronic worksheet is the capability to reorganize without redoing. To insert a row or column, point to and click on any cell in a column or a row. Click on Insert and click on Column to insert a column or click on Row to insert a row. The new row is inserted above the identified row and the new column is inserted to the left of the identified column.

To delete a row or column, click on any cell in the row or column and then select Edit from the menu bar and then Delete. The Delete dialog box, as shown in Figure 3.20, offers four options: Shift Cells Left, Shift Cells Up, Entire Row, or Entire Column.

Controlling Your View

Worksheets vary from small, simple one-screen displays to huge worksheets that use many rows and columns. To adjust your view of the worksheet, click on View to open the view menu. The Zoom option allows you to adjust your view from 200 percent to 25 percent. When

Figure 3.20   Delete dialog box.

lecturing in a large room, we use the 200 percent option so individuals in the back of the room can see. When trying to find something on a large worksheet we use 25 percent to display more cells on a single window.

Using Help

There is no way to remember the many options and exact syntax of every Excel function. You will soon learn the options and functions that you use consistently; however, you may need to use the Excel Help screens on the less familiar options and functions even after you become an Excel expert. Using the Help options eliminates many problems.

To use Help either press Alt+H or click on Help. Figure 3.21 illustrates the first Help menu. We prefer the first selection—Microsoft Excel Help. You should experiment with all the options to determine which one gives you the best results.

Figure 3.22 shows the results of a search for statistical functions by typing the first letters of the word statistical (stat). After selecting the About statistical analysis tools option, a complete list of statistical functions available in Excel xp is displayed.

We think that Microsoft makes a great product and that the Help feature has significantly improved over earlier versions of Excel. In addition to the Help options that are available in the program, Microsoft offers extensive help on the Internet by clicking on the Office on the Web option in the Help menu.

Figure 3.21 First Help menu.

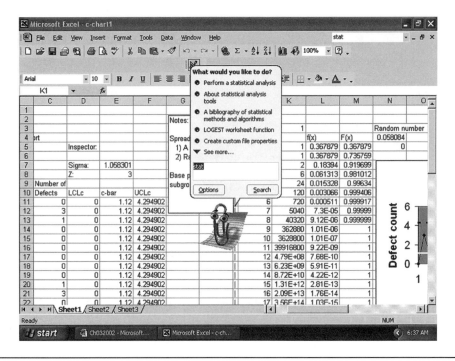

Figure 3.22   Searching Excel Help.

Summary

This chapter has presented the basic skills you should master to use Excel worksheets for SQC. The capabilities available in Excel provide the user with extensive capabilities to do everything from calculating the area under a normal distribution curve to formatting output with different size fonts for report headers and text. Excel has the capabilities needed to solve SQC problems easily and efficiently. Is Excel the best worksheet program for quality control analysis? The best worksheet program is the one you know how to use. With the aid of this text, we hope you will make Excel the best worksheet program for statistical quality control analysis.

4

Learning More about Excel

OUTLINE

Introduction

Chapter 3 introduced you to the most basic Excel functions that are required for Excel and for SQC. The first topics in chapter 4 cover some Excel functions that are routinely used to conduct statistical process control, such as checking spelling, sorting data, creating charts and graphs, and printing worksheets and graphs. Additional topics included in chapter 4 that are useful, but are not necessarily required for SQC, are creating text boxes, customized add-ins, importing data from other sources, and hypertext capabilities, which are used to create Web pages.

Checking Your Spelling

Checking the spelling in your worksheet can help ensure that your worksheets are accurate and may help you avoid embarrassment. Frequently worksheets that are created for statistical process control use terminology or abbreviations that are unique to an industry or business and are not found in a dictionary. These terms can be added to the Excel dictionary. To check the spelling in your worksheet:

1. Click on the <u>T</u>ools menu and click on <u>S</u>pelling or click on the Spelling button ![ABC check icon] in the standard toolbar.

2. If Excel xp finds a word that is not in the dictionary, it will be displayed as shown in Figure 4.1.

3. The following options are available:

    a. If your spelling is correct, click on the <u>I</u>gnore or <u>I</u>gnore All button.

    b. To change to one of the suggested options, highlight the correct option and click on the <u>C</u>hange or Change A<u>l</u>l button to change the word throughout the worksheet.

    c. If the word is correct as you typed it and you want to add the word to the dictionary, click on the <u>A</u>dd to Dictionary button.

If you want to check the spelling on a *range* of cells, select the *range* before you click on the Spelling button or select the Spelling option.

Figure 4.1 Spelling dialog box.

Sorting Data

Occasionally, SQC procedures require that worksheet data are sorted numerically, chronologically, or alphabetically. The sort function allows the user to sort a worksheet according to the contents of up to three types of information. Most SQC applications require that rows are sorted according to the contents of a column; however, Excel provides the capability to sort the columns of a data set as well.

There are two ways to sort data: (1) use the Sort option in the Data menu, or (2) use the Sort Ascending ⏏ or Sort Descending ⏏ buttons in the standard toolbar. In the example that follows, the worksheet contains the number of defects for various products at five locations. To sort the data first by the product number, then by location, and finally by the number of defects, follow these steps:

1. Click on any cell in the Product column that is the basis for the sort.

2. Click on the Data menu.

3. Click on Sort and the Sort dialog box is displayed with the column label *Product* in the first sort option (See Figure 4.2).

4. Check the Header Row option to be certain that Excel detects the column label.

5. Click on the arrow to the right of the first Then By edit area to display a list of the column labels.

6. Click on the column label *Plant*.

7. Click on the arrow to the right of the second Then By edit area to display a list of the column labels.

8. Click on the column label *No. of Defects.*

9. Then click on the OK button.

The result of the sort is shown in Figure 4.3.

Excel examines the database to determine if the worksheet contains a row header (a row that contains labels for each column). If Excel does not detect a header at the top of the column, the contents of the top cell will be included in the sort as if the cell contained data. When a header is detected, the option button Header Row will be darkened. If your worksheet contains headers that are not detected by Excel, you must click on the Header Row option button to maintain column or row labels.

Another option is to sort the same worksheet by the product ascending and by the number of defects descending. The result of this sort is shown in Figure 4.4.

Figure 4.2   Sort dialog box.

Figure 4.3 Worksheet sorted by product, plant, and number of defects.

Figure 4.4 Worksheet sorted by product ascending and number of defects descending.

To sort using the shortcut buttons, click on any cell in the column to be sorted and click on either the Sort Ascending icon [icon] or the Sort Descending icon [icon]. The worksheet is immediately sorted. You can undo a sort by selecting the Undo option in the <u>E</u>dit menu or by clicking on the Undo icon [icon] in the standard toolbar.

To rearrange columns of data, follow these steps:

1. From the <u>D</u>ata menu select the <u>S</u>ort option.

2. Click on the <u>O</u>ptions button in the Sort dialog box.

3. Click on the Sort Left to Right option button.

4. Click on the OK button to return to the Sort dialog box, where you should identify one or more fields for the sort. If the worksheet does not contain row labels, the top row number is displayed.

Creating Charts and Graphs

The Chart Wizard allows you to display charts or graphs on the worksheet along with the data or on separate sheets. Whenever changes are made to the data in the worksheet, the values in the chart or graph are updated. Creating a graph or chart using the Chart Wizard is easy and requires the following steps:

1. Select the *range* or *ranges* of data to be included in the chart.

2. Click the Chart Wizard button [icon].

3. Complete each of the four steps in the chart procedure.

4. Size the chart on the worksheet.

5. Edit text and axes in the charts.

Detailed instructions for each step follow.

Selecting the Graphing Range

To select the charting *range* for adjacent columns or rows, simply point to a corner cell and drag the mouse to highlight the *range* to be included in the chart. To select rows or columns that are not adjacent, hold the control (Ctrl) key as you drag the mouse to highlight each row or column. When the *range* is identified, click on the Chart Wizard icon in the standard toolbar.

Step 1 of 4—Choosing a Chart Type

The first step in the Chart Wizard process is to select the chart type. Excel xp has 14 standard and 20 custom chart types. The best way to determine which chart type is best for your data is to experiment with various types. The Chart Type dialog box is shown in Figure 4.5.

Step 2 of 4—Identifying Chart Source Data

Step 2 of the Chart Wizard process contains two dialog boxes—one dialog box to identify the Data Range and one dialog box to show the Series labels and the *range* for each series. The Data Range dialog box displays the *ranges* that were highlighted for inclusion in the chart. You may revise the *ranges* if the *range* shown is incorrect. The box also contains two option buttons that allow you to specify variables according to the rows or columns. The Data Range dialog box is shown in Figure 4.6.

The Series dialog box is shown in Figure 4.7. If the row or column labels were included in the identified range for the chart, the labels are displayed in the Series edit box. The box also displays the ranges for the series labels in the Name area, the *ranges* for the *x*- and *y*-axes, as well as a picture of the chart.

Figure 4.5 Chart Wizard step 1 of 4—Chart Type dialog box.

Figure 4.6   Chart Wizard step 2 of 4—Chart Source Data (Data Range) dialog box.

Figure 4.7   Chart Wizard step 2 of 4—Chart Source Data (Series) dialog box.

Step 3 of 4—Selecting Chart Options

Step 3 of the Chart Wizard process contains five dialog boxes: Titles, Axes, Gridlines, Legend, and Data Labels. Each of the five dialog boxes is displayed in Figures 4.8 through 4.12.

Each of the dialog boxes allows the user to choose how the values, labels, and chart titles are displayed, as described in Table 4.1.

Step 4 of 4—Choosing the Chart Location

Step 4 of the Chart Wizard process contains only one dialog box, shown in Figure 4.13, which allows you to specify if the chart is placed on a separate sheet or will be placed as an object in the worksheet. If you place the chart in a separate sheet, the edit area to the right of the As New Sheet option button allows you to enter the name of the sheet. If the chart is to be placed in a sheet in the workbook, the drop-down menu to the right of the As Object In button allows you to select the sheet in which the chart will be placed. Click on Finish to complete the chart.

To position the chart on the worksheet, click the left mouse button on the chart and drag the chart to the appropriate position on the worksheet. The size of the chart may be expanded or reduced by pointing to the boxes on the chart border and dragging the arrows.

Figure 4.8   Chart Wizard step 3 of 4—Chart Options (Titles).

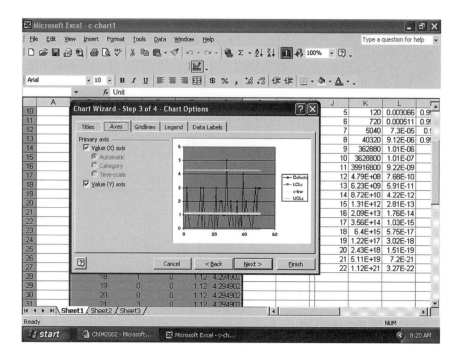

Figure 4.9   Chart Wizard step 3 of 4—Chart Options (Axes).

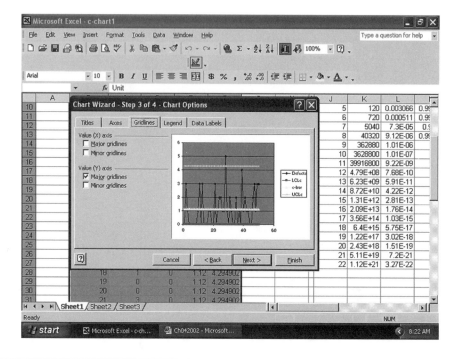

Figure 4.10   Chart Wizard step 3 of 4—Chart Options (Gridlines).

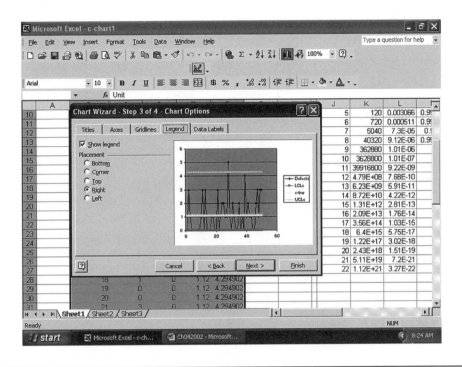

Figure 4.11   Chart Wizard step 3 of 4—Chart Options (Legend).

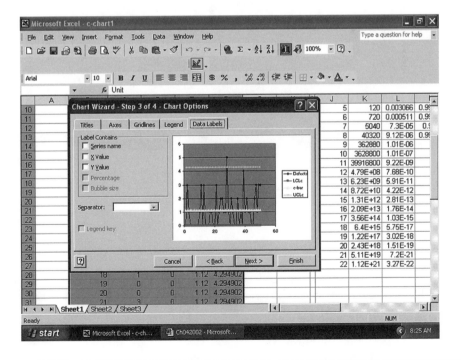

Figure 4.12   Chart Wizard step 3 of 4—Chart Options (Data Labels).

Table 4.1   Chart Options dialog boxes.

Dialog Box	Description
Titles	Type a chart title and type labels for the axes
Axes	Display values along the x-axis or the y-axis
Gridlines	Display gridlines for the x-axis or the y-axis
Legend	Display a legend on the chart area and place the legend in the chart area
Data Labels	Display labels for data values

Figure 4.13   Dialog box for choosing the chart location.

Formatting a Chart

Once the chart is placed, the elements of the chart may be revised or formatted to improve the readability or appearance of the chart. The elements of SQC charts that are commonly formatted are the legend, the chart title, the axes titles, the axes scales, and data series (or the appearance of the graph lines or bars).

There are two methods available to display the dialog boxes that offer options for editing the elements of a chart. To edit an element, you may:

1. Point to and left-click on the element. When the name of the element is displayed, right-click to display a submenu. Left-click on the option Formatting Element Name. A formatting dialog box with tabs is shown.

2. Point to and double-click on the element to display the formatting dialog box.

Formatting the Chart Title and Axis Titles

If you left-click on a chart title or an axis title and then right-click to display a menu, and left-click on Format Chart Title or Format Axis Title, the dialog box in Figure 4.14 appears. Or, you may double-click while pointing to the title. This dialog box contains three tabs:

1. *Patterns* allows the user to specify if the title will have a border, the style of the border, and the color and style of the area within the border.

2. *Font* allows the user to specify the type of font, the font style, font size, and special effects such as underline, bold, or italics.

3. *Alignment* allows the user to choose the horizontal and vertical placement, and rotate the orientation of the text.

Figure 4.14 Dialog box for editing chart titles.

Formatting the Axis Scale

Selection of an appropriate scale is important to the readability of a chart. If the values are too tightly clustered or sparsely scattered, the values in the chart may be difficult to comprehend. Occasionally the minimum and maximum scale values may be inappropriate. To adjust the minimum and maximum and the unit of measure in the scale, you may edit the scale.

If you left-click on the *x*- or *y*-axis and then right-click to display a menu, and left-click on Format Axis, the dialog box in Figure 4.15 appears. Or, you may double-click while pointing to an axis. This dialog box contains five tabs:

1. *Patterns* allows the user to specify the style of the line, color of the line and, if the line will have tick marks, the style of the tick marks.

2. *Scale* allows the user to specify the minimum value, maximum value, major and minor units, and the value at the origin.

3. *Font* allows the user to specify the type of font, the font style, font size, and special effects such as underline, bold, or italics.

4. *Number* offers a variety of categories for numbers such as currency, rational numbers, accounting, date, time, percentage, fractions, or custom formats.

5. *Alignment* allows the user to rotate the orientation of the scale labels.

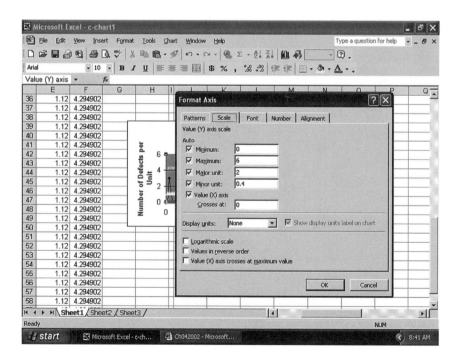

Figure 4.15   Dialog box for editing axis scales.

Formatting the Legend

The chart legend provides a description for each line or bar in the chart. Once you become familiar with SQC charts, you may decide that a legend is unnecessary, and you can delete the legend from the chart by clicking once while pointing to the legend and pressing the delete key. If you want to revise the legend, double-click on the legend or left-click on the legend; then right-click to display a menu, and left-click on F*o*rmat Legend to display the dialog box shown in Figure 4.16.

1. *Patterns* allows the user to specify if the legend will have a border, the style of the border, and the color and style of the area within the border.

2. *Font* allows the user to specify the type of font, the font style, font size, and special effects such as underline, bold, or italics.

3. *Placement* allows the user to specify the placement of the legend at the bottom, corner, top, right, or left.

Formatting the Appearance of Data Points and Lines

Most statistical control charts show an upper limit, lower limit, average, and observed data points. To improve the readability of the chart, it is customary to vary the line styles within the chart.

Figure 4.16   Format Legend dialog box.

Figure 4.17   Dialog box to Format Data Series.

If you left-click on the data line and then right-click to display a menu, and left-click on Format Data Series, the dialog box in Figure 4.17 appears. Or, you may double-click while pointing to the data line. This dialog box contains seven tabs, but only four are of interest in SQC:

1. *Patterns* allows the user to specify the style of the line, color of the line, and if the line will have tick marks, the style of the tick marks.

2. *Axis* allows the user to specify if the values are plotted on the primary or secondary axis.

3. *Data Labels* allows the user to specify if the data points values will be shown or if the data series label is shown on the chart.

4. *Series Order* allows the user to change the order of the series on the chart by moving a series up or down in the series order.

Figure 4.18 shows a *c* process control chart that was edited using these procedures.

Figure 4.18 Edited *c* process control chart.

Creating Text Boxes

To display text in any area of the worksheet, use a text box. A text box is a graphic image that can contain text of various fonts and sizes, patterns or special symbols, and borders. Text boxes can be moved, copied, and resized according to the user's perferences. To create a text box, follow these steps:

1. Click on the Drawing icon to start the Drawing menu if it is not on the screen.

2. Select the Text Box icon. The Text Box icon is just to the left of the Insert WordArt icon.

3. Draw a text box anyplace on the screen.

4. Type any text in the text box.

5. Right-click on the corner of the text box and left-click on Format Text Box.

6. Click on the Colors and Lines tab.

7. In the Line section, click on the Color: option and then click on the top selection No Line.

8. Left-click on the Alignment tab near the top of the screen.

9. Click on the Orientation of your choice and click on OK.

To change the size of a text box, click on the border of the box, and point to any of the circles on the border, as shown in Figure 4.19. When the box changes into an arrow, press the left mouse button and drag the

Figure 4.19   Text box.

arrow to move the border of the box. To reposition the text box in the worksheet, click on the border and press the left mouse button and drag the text box to the appropriate location. To edit the contents of the text box, double-click inside the border of the box, and use the arrow keys on the keyboard to move the cursor to the appropriate position.

Printing Worksheets and Graphs

Excel provides the options to print a portion of a worksheet, an entire worksheet, more than one worksheet in a workbook, or the entire workbook. Before printing the worksheet, you should set the print options using the Page Setup dialog boxes. After you specify the print options, it is a good idea to preview the worksheet to see how the printed pages will look before you print.

Page Setup Options

To set the print options, select the Page Setup option from the File menu. The Page Setup dialog box is shown. The Page Setup option contains four tabs: (1) Page, (2) Margins, (3) Header/Footer, and (4) Sheet. The

Figure 4.20   Page Setup (Page) dialog box.

Page dialog box is shown in Figure 4.20. This screen allows the user to set the orientation of the worksheet (either portrait or landscape), select a paper size, set the print quality, and determine the print scaling.

The second tab in the Page Setup dialog box is labeled *Margins*. This dialog box allows the user to set the margins for the worksheet, as well as the margins for the header and footer. The preview area displays how the margins affect the placement of the worksheet on the page. The *Margins* dialog box is shown in Figure 4.21.

The third Page Setup tab, shown in Figure 4.22, is for typing the text for the headers and footers. *Headers* are text or graphics that appear at the top of each printed worksheet page and *footers* are printed on the bottom of each page. To create a custom header or footer, click on the Custom Header or Custom Footer buttons. When the Custom Header button is selected the dialog box in Figure 4.23 displays. The Custom Footer dialog box offers the same options. This dialog box separates the header or footer into three areas—left, center, and right. The buttons on the dialog box allow the user to insert page numbers, print date, print time, workbook name, and sheet name. It is a good practice to include this information on each printout.

The fourth tab is the *Sheet* dialog box, shown in Figure 4.24. This dialog box allows the user to specify the print range and the *ranges* for the row or column titles. The user may also indicate if the cell borders should be

Figure 4.21   Page Setup (Margins) dialog box.

Figure 4.22   Page Setup (Headers/Footers) dialog box.

Figure 4.23   Custom Header dialog box.

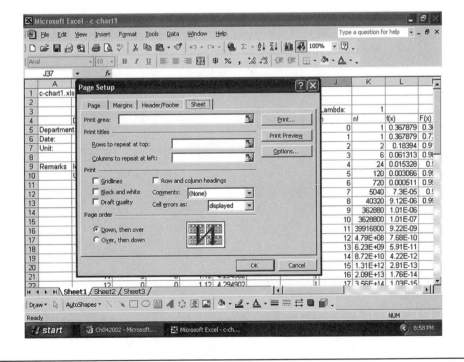

Figure 4.24   Page Setup (Sheet) dialog box.

printed. If the print range is too wide to fit the width of a single page, the user can set the order for the pages to print (down and then over or over and then down).

Manually-Set Page Breaks

Sometimes the page breaks occur on the printed copies in inappropriate places. Users can set page breaks manually by selecting Page Break from the Insert menu. To insert a vertical-only page break, click on the column letter to the right of where you want the page break. To insert a horizontal-only page break, click on the row number immediately below where you want the page break. To insert both vertical and horizontal page breaks, click in the cell to the right and below the breaks and then select Page Break from the Insert menu.

To remove a page break, click on a cell to the right of a vertical page break or below a horizontal page break. Then select Remove Page Break from the Insert menu. If Remove Page Break is not listed, there is no manual page break at the selected column or row.

Print Preview

After the print options are specified, we recommend that you preview the worksheet to view how your worksheet will be printed. Each of the Page Setup dialog boxes shown previously contains a Print Preview button. The standard toolbar also contains a Print Preview icon , or Print Preview may be selected from the File menu. A preview of a worksheet is shown in Figure 4.25. The options that were available in the Page Setup dialog boxes are also available in the Preview screen. When you are satisfied with the appearance of the worksheet, you are ready to print the worksheet.

Printing Worksheets

The preview screen contains a Print button. When you click on this button, the Print dialog box in Figure 4.26 displays. The Print dialog box is also activated by selecting the Print option from the File menu. The Print dialog box allows the user to select a printer, specify which pages should be printed, select the number of copies, and specify if the print area is a selected range, the active sheets, or an entire workbook.

1. Excel provides the options to print a portion of a worksheet, an entire worksheet, more than one sheet in a workbook, or the entire workbook:

   a. To print a portion of a worksheet, highlight the *range* of cells that is to be printed.

   b. To print an entire worksheet, open the workbook and activate the worksheet.

Figure 4.25   Print Preview.

Figure 4.26   Print dialog box.

c. To print more than one sheet in a workbook, click on the tab of the first sheet to be printed, and hold down the control (Ctrl) key while you click the tabs of the other sheets to be included.

d. To print the entire workbook, activate any worksheet in the workbook.

2. Activate the Print dialog box, and in the Print What area click on one of the options: Selection, Selected Sheets, or Entire Workbook.

3. Enter the number of copies if you want to print more than one.

4. Make a Print Range selection to indicate which pages will be printed.

5. Click OK to begin printing.

Worksheets can also be printed by clicking the Print button ▨ on the standard menu bar. The Print button does not display the Print dialog box, but sends the worksheet with the previously selected page setup options directly to the printer.

Customizing with Add-Ins

Microsoft Excel has a large collection of data analysis tools. Few individuals will need all the tools. If your Tools menu does not have Data Analysis as the last option, you must add in this feature by clicking on the Add-Ins. . . option to display the add-ins that are available. The Add-Ins dialog box is shown in Figure 4.27.

To add the Data Analysis option to the Tools menu, click on the Analysis ToolPak box to add this option. There are 19 options on the Data Analysis menu that offer numerous statistical procedures including descriptive statistics, ANOVA, t-tests, and regression analysis. Some of the Data Analysis functions are shown in Figure 4.28.

Importing Data from Other Sources

Computer files may be classified as:

1. American Standard Code for Information Interchange (ASCII) files

2. Binary files

An ASCII file uses a standard coding method that can be used by most programs. Many spreadsheet programs can read ASCII files, although getting data from a table stored as an ASCII file may be difficult; however, Excel xp makes it easy. Figure 4.29 illustrates opening a file. The same method is used no matter what type of file is being opened, with the exception that you must specify all files (*.*) in the Files of Type: area to find a file with a nonstandard extension.

Figure 4.27 Add-Ins dialog box.

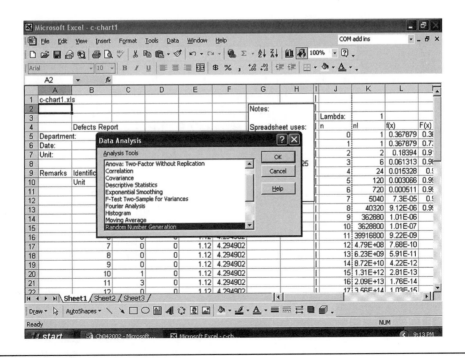

Figure 4.28 Data Analysis tools.

Figure 4.29   Open File dialog box.

Excel recognizes a file as an ASCII file. If the file includes a table, Excel gives you the option of dividing the portions of the table into fields so that numbers can be read into individual cells. Figure 4.30 illustrates a screen in which the user tells Excel where to locate the dividing lines to read the data into cells. Excel's capability of reading tables makes it the easiest program the authors have found for reading ASCII tables.

Most worksheet programs, including Excel, save data in binary files. These binary files can only be used by the program creating them unless another program is able to interpret (import) them. Usually, the latest version of a spreadsheet program can import files from earlier versions of spreadsheet programs. Excel is capable of importing data files that were saved in older worksheet programs.

After installing Excel, another worksheet program came out with a new version and a new file format. Excel could not read the new format. In most cases, there is no way an older worksheet program can read a new file type that is designed after the original worksheet program was released.

Excel allows you to export files into the binary version of other older worksheet programs. This is true of most programs coming onto the market now. Even if your version of the program cannot read a file created using the latest program, the new program can usually save the file as an earlier program format that your version of the program can use.

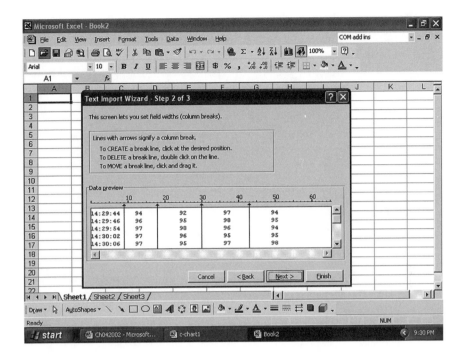

Figure 4.30   Selecting fields.

When moving from a new program to an old program you will sometimes lose material such as formatting, graphs, or other results because the older program cannot do what the new program can. We know of no solution to this problem. However, if you know that it will be necessary to use your worksheet in an earlier version of the software, you may decide to limit your use of special formatting techniques.

Importing Microsoft Access Data Files into Excel

Many companies use Microsoft Access database files to store information. The contents of Access tables can be exported as Excel files to create charts and graphs of the contents of the tables. To save an Access table as an Excel file, use the Export... option in the File menu and then select an Excel file type in the Save As Type drop-down list. After the Access table is exported as an Excel file, it can be opened in the Excel program.

Pasting Graphics, Text, and Tables between Programs

If there is anything that is magic about Microsoft Windows programs, it is the capability to cut, copy, and paste within and between all Microsoft programs. You can cut, copy, and paste text, tables, or graphics from other applications into Excel. For this text, we used the Print Screen key to copy a screen from Excel and then used the paste button to place the screen within the Microsoft Word document. You may also use the Print Screen capability to copy Excel graphs or tables to the Microsoft Photo Editor or into PowerPoint to prepare slides for a presentation.

Figure 4.31 illustrates a picture of one of the authors' four grandchildren copied from the Microsoft Photo Editor. The file was a *.BMP file. After giving the instruction to Edit–Copy the picture, Excel was opened and the Edit–Paste option was selected with the results shown.

Hypertext Capabilities

Hypertext is the language of the Internet. Homepages use hypertext to link and move between documents located on computers all over the world. Excel may be used to create hypertext pages as illustrated in Figure 4.32. The first step is to save the worksheet as a Web Page file using the Save As Web Page option in the File menu. When you select the Web Page option, the worksheet is saved as an *.html file that can be copied to a Web site.

Summary

Excel has more capabilities than one individual can ever use. Each version of Excel has improved over the last as the capabilities have grown. Excel allows users to check spelling, sort data, create text boxes, and create charts and graphs. Excel xp significantly improves the capability to utilize data from other programs and convert tables prepared in other programs to worksheets. Perhaps the most powerful feature of Excel is the Windows integrated environment that offers the capability to cut, copy, and paste material from one Windows program to another.

Figure 4.31   Photograph copied into a worksheet from Microsoft Photo Editor.

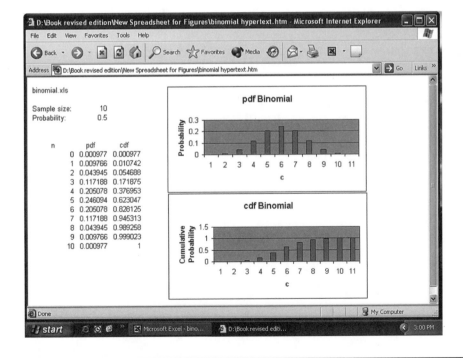

Figure 4.32   Hypertext page shown in Microsoft Internet Explorer.

5

Linking Excel and PowerPoint for Outstanding Presentations

OUTLINE

Introduction to Microsoft PowerPoint

Microsoft PowerPoint is software that helps users create attractive, easy-to-read visual aids for presentations that may be delivered using projectors connected to personal computers, the Internet, paper handouts, or transparencies on an overhead projector. The objective of any presentation is to provide a target audience with information for learning or decision making. A sales presentation is designed to influence the purchasing decision of your target audience; a management presentation is designed to influence managers' decisions; and a lecture on statistical quality control is designed to maximize understanding and learning. The visual aids for the presentation must be designed especially for the target audience using pictures, graphs, and words that effectively communicate the message.

PowerPoint is an integrated part of the Microsoft Office Suite. Text and graphics may be transferred into PowerPoint from Microsoft Office programs, including Excel, Word, Access, Photo Editor, and other Windows-based programs. Material may be edited either prior to transfer to PowerPoint or in PowerPoint. The most common way to transfer material into PowerPoint is to Copy and Paste, however, special dynamic links may be created from PowerPoint to Excel by using the Paste Special, the Paste link, or by using Hyperlink capabilities. When Excel worksheet cells and graphics are linked to PowerPoint, the user has the option of updating the information in the presentation to match revised information in the worksheet when the PowerPoint presentation is started.

Presentations are created using a series of pages. Each page in the presentation is called a *slide*. Like Excel, PowerPoint has many more features and tools than one can use in a single presentation. Even if the purpose of the presentation is to demonstrate the power of PowerPoint, it is unlikely that a presenter could use all the features in one presentation. This chapter covers only a few features that we believe help create effective presentations for quality control decisions.

PowerPoint helps you:

1. Provide attractive, colorful templates, which makes it easy to create visual aids.

2. Control the amount of material placed on each slide.

3. Animate the whole or parts of the presentation.

4. Coordinate the development of slides with other team members.

5. Facilitate editing of presentations.

6. Develop standard slide formats for a company or university.

Selecting the Design Template

PowerPoint has a number of design templates that may be selected for your presentation. A design template formats the various types of slide layouts to ensure a uniform look for all the slides in your presentation. To select a design template, click on the Format option in the Menu bar and then click on Slide Design. The design options are displayed as shown in Figure 5.1. Click on the design of your choice and then click on the arrow next to the design. Select the Apply to All Slides option.

To enter text in an area on the slide, click once in the area and then type the text as shown in Figure 5.2. To add a new slide to the presentation, click on Insert in the menu bar and then click on New Slide. Select the Slide Layout from the choices displayed on the left side of the screen by clicking once on the desired layout (shown in Figure 5.3). To enter text or graphics on the slide, simply click in the area where you want to type the text or insert the graphics. To change the font size or font type, select the text, click on Format, then Font, and select the appropriate size or font in the dialog box.

You can also create your own template by applying your own color scheme to your slides and inserting your own graphics. Then using the Save As option from the File menu, select Design Template from the drop-down menu in the Save As Type: dialog area shown in Figure 5.4. Name your template and click OK to save the template for future use.

Companies often create their own design templates. Figure 5.5 illustrates the use of a company's standard design template.

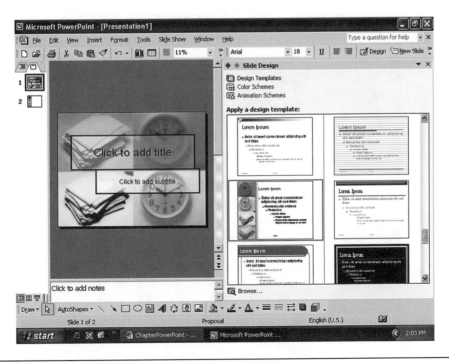

Figure 5.1   Selecting a design template for a presentation.

Figure 5.2   Entering text onto the presentation slide.

Figure 5.3   Selecting a layout for a new slide.

Figure 5.4   Saving a format as a design template.

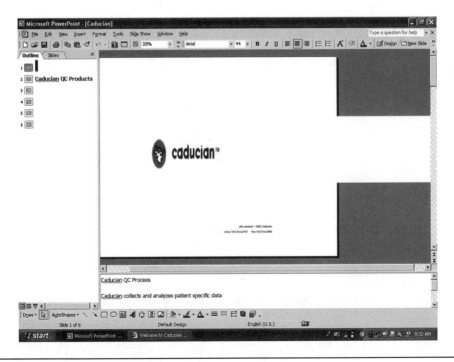

Figure 5.5   A company's design template.

Printed with permission of Kinn Moursund, President, Caducian, Inc. 2001.

Copying Graphics into a Presentation

The simplest way to move material from one Windows application to another is by blocking the material, clicking on the <u>C</u>opy icon , then moving into the application where the material is needed, such as PowerPoint, and clicking on the <u>P</u>aste icon . Figure 5.6 illustrates the opening slide for a presentation on the first edition of this book. The cover of the book was scanned and saved as a *.jpg file. The image was then inserted by using the steps below. Open the slide in the PowerPoint presentation where the picture is to be inserted, then:

1. Click on <u>I</u>nsert in the menu bar.

2. Click on <u>P</u>icture from the drop-down menu.

3. Click on the <u>F</u>rom File option.

4. Locate the picture in the appropriate directory and right-click on the picture.

5. Click on the <u>I</u>nsert button in the dialog box.

The title of the slide was added by clicking on the title area of the slide and then typing the text.

Figure 5.6   First edition cover inserted using a .jpg file.

Linking and Embedding Objects into a Presentation

PowerPoint allows users to embed or link objects such as charts, graphs, or a *range* of cells from a worksheet into a presentation. You may also embed or link an entire worksheet. When objects are *embedded*, the information becomes a part of the destination file and changes in the source file are not reflected in the destination file. When objects are *linked*, the user has the option of updating the object in the presentation to reflect the changes in the source file.

Embedded object: An object such as a chart, picture, text, *range* of cells, or a file that is created in a source application, such as Word, Excel, or Photo Editor and inserted into a destination file, for example a PowerPoint file. Changes made in the source file are *not* reflected in the destination file.

Linked object: Is an object such as a chart, picture, text, *range* of cells, or a file that was created in a source application, such as Word, Excel, or Photo Editor and inserted into a destination file, for example, a PowerPoint file. The linked object in the destination file may be updated whenever the information in the source file is updated.

Linking or Embedding an Excel Graph into a Presentation

To link an Excel graph to a PowerPoint presentation, follow these steps:

1. Create a graph in Excel.

2. Select the graph by pointing to the graph and clicking once with the right mouse key. The graph will be surrounded by a black border with boxes in each corner and on each side.

3. Click on the Copy icon .

4. Open or create a PowerPoint presentation.

5. Select the slide where the graph will be shown.

6. Click on the Edit option in the menu bar.

7. Click on the Paste Special option.

8. Select Paste or Paste Link in the Paste Special dialog box shown in Figure 5.7:

    a. Click on the Paste Link radio button to link the graph to the presentation (changes in the worksheet can be updated in the presentation).

    b. Click on the Paste radio button to embed the graph in the presentation (changes in the worksheet will *not* be updated in the presentation).

9. Click on the OK button.

Figure 5.7   Paste Special dialog box for linking and embedding objects.

A PowerPoint slide showing Excel graphs copied into a presentation is shown in Figure 5.8. The graph on the left side of the slide is linked to an Excel file, while the graph on the right side was cut and pasted into the slide using the Copy ▨ and Paste icons ▨. The linked graph is referred to as a *hot* graph because it can be updated from the original worksheet without recopying the graph.

The next time the presentation file is opened, the dialog box in Figure 5.9 displays, which gives the option of updating the chart based on changes in the worksheet.

Reconnecting or Breaking a Link

The link to the source file may be broken if the source file is deleted or moved to another folder. To reestablish a link, click on Edit in the menu bar, and then click on Link. The Link dialog box is shown in Figure 5.10. Using the options in the dialog box, you can open or change the source and change the type of updates from automatic to manual. You may also decide to break the link with the source file by clicking on the Break Link button. If you click on the Break Link option, an Undo Break Link option appears in the Edit menu, as shown in Figure 5.11. You must use the Undo Break Link option before you close the presentation, otherwise you must reestablish the link using the Link dialog box.

Figure 5.8 A PowerPoint slide with a linked Excel graph.

Figure 5.9 Linked object update option.

Figure 5.10 Links dialog box.

Figure 5.11 Undo Break Link option.

Linking or Embedding a Complete Excel Workbook into a Presentation

You can embed or link an entire Excel workbook into a PowerPoint presentation; however, only one worksheet may be displayed at a time. To embed or link the workbook, follow the steps below:

1. In the Excel workbook, click on any cell in the workbook.

2. Click on the Copy icon 📋.

3. Open the presentation file and select the slide where the link is to be placed.

4. Click on Edit in the menu bar.

5. Click on Paste Special.

6. In the Paste Special dialog box shown in Figure 5.12, click on the Paste radio button to embed the worksheet or click on Paste Link to link the worksheet.

7. Click on the Display as Icon click box. You also have the option of selecting another Icon which will be displayed on the slide.

8. Click on OK.

The result is shown in Figure 5.13.

Figure 5.12   Paste Special dialog box with Display As Icon option.

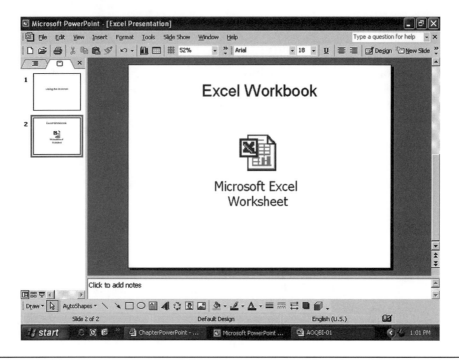

Figure 5.13   Excel workbook embedded in a PowerPoint Presentation.

To display the workbook, double click on the worksheet icon. One worksheet in the workbook displays. To display a different worksheet, click on the workbook tab at the bottom of the page. See the example in Figure 5.14.

Internet Graphics—Copyright Issues

Good presentations need graphics and there are many sources of graphics on the Internet, but there are legal limitations to using copyrighted material. If you copy material from the Internet, you must take great care that you are not violating copyright laws. Everything published on the Internet is copyrighted and, therefore, requires permission for use. We recommend that you never use any published work without the owner's permission.

Figure 5.15 illustrates a slide displaying part of a home page. One of the authors of this book is an officer of Biomedical Quality Control, the company that owns the Web site. He secured permission to use the graphic in this book. The screen was captured to the buffer using the Print Screen key and then saved to disk using a graphics editing program. The Insert Picture From File was used to paste the picture into a PowerPoint presentation.

Most of the time Web sites do not state the legal limitations for using the material on the site. If the conditions under which you can use the material are not stated, you must assume that usage will violate copyright

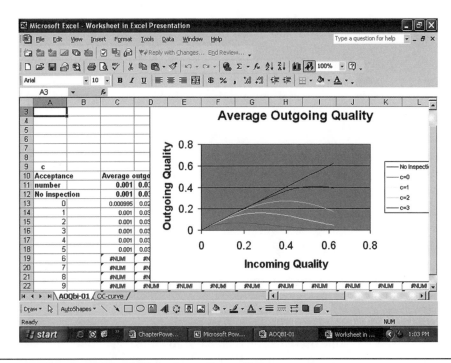

Figure 5.14 Excel workbook linked to a PowerPoint presentation.

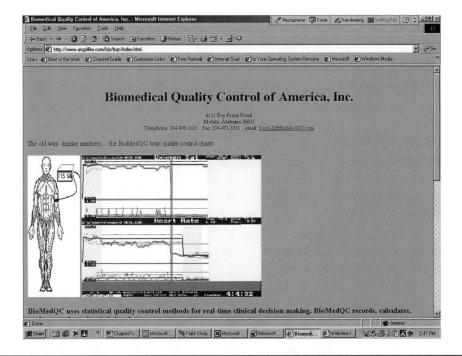

Figure 5.15 Internet screen capture.

Printed with permission of Steven M. Zimmerman, PhD, VP, Biomedical Quality Control of America.

laws. For more information we suggest that you check with your company's attorney or search the Internet for information on copyright law and intellectual property rights.

If you need illustrations from the Internet, we suggest you ask permission to use what you need. Sometimes you will be granted a limited license or you may be charged to use the information. Other sources of graphics are:

1. Creating your own using drawing or graphics software

2. Creating your own using digital photography

3. Asking friends or coworkers for assistance

Hyperlinks in Presentations

You can create links from PowerPoint to Excel, to Web sites, or to any other Windows file. Links allow you to display the file or Web site while you are making your presentation. Figure 5.16 illustrates a slide with three links. When the slide displays, simply click on a link to transfer to that file or Web site. Once the presentation is created, you must take care to ensure that files are not moved or renamed. We used the Microsoft home page as our example for the Internet link. We expect the Microsoft link will be available when you read this chapter.

Figure 5.16   Example links in a presentation.

To create a link, click on Insert in the menu bar and then click on Hyperlink; the dialog box shown in Figure 5.17 displays. Type the address of the Web site or the file to which you wish to link. The file extension determines what program is called when the file is selected. A file with the extension *.xls requires Microsoft Excel to open the file. A file with the extension *.doc requires Microsoft Word. We experimented with many other file types and could not find any that we could not link.

When you click on the link in the slide, Windows opens the linked file or Web site.

Animating Presentations

PowerPoint offers the capability to add special visual and sound effects to your presentation. Animation can be added to text on a slide, graphics, or in the transition from slide to slide using preset animation schemes or by designing your own custom animation.

Preset Animation Schemes

PowerPoint has several preset animation schemes that can be applied to single slides or to the entire presentation. To display the preset animation

Figure 5.17   Insert Hyperlink dialog box.

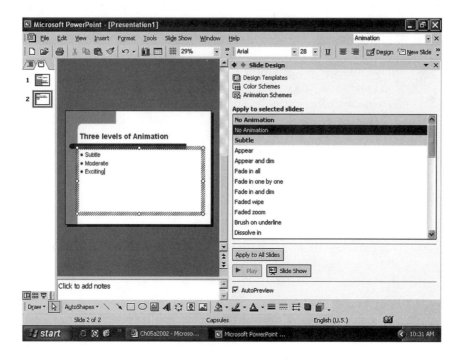

Figure 5.18   Animation schemes available in PowerPoint.

schemes shown in Figure 5.18, click on Slide Show in the menu bar and then click on Animation Schemes. Clicking on a scheme shows how it will affect the appearance of the information on the slide. For example, the Bounce option in the Exciting category bounces the title onto the screen and then scrolls each bullet onto the screen from the left side of the screen. You may apply the scheme to the entire presentation by clicking on the Apply to All Slides button or apply the scheme only to the selected slide by clicking on the scheme.

 Animate: To animate means to add special visual or sound effects to the text, graphics, or any object on a slide as a way of directing attention to important elements of a presentation or making a presentation more interesting.

Custom Animation

Custom animation allows the users to choose from a variety of animated effects. You may animate the entrance or the exit of text or graphics on the slide, or you may choose to place emphasis on text or objects. You can also set the timing between slides so that slides will transition according to a timed schedule. This allows the presenter to move freely around the room without worrying about returning to the computer to click the mouse to change to the next slide. To view the custom animation options, click on Slide Show and then click on Custom Animation. The Custom Animation dialog box is displayed in Figure 5.19 along with the Add Effect options.

To add a custom effect, select the area of the slide to be animated. For example, to animate the entrance of the slide title, click once in the title area. The title area will be surrounded by a box. If the Preview Option box is checked, as you click on the various options available in the Add Entrance Effect dialog box, the option is shown on your slide. See Figure 5.20. You may select the speed of the animation by selecting a speed from the Speed drop-down menu. You may change the motion path of the animation by choosing an option from the Motion Paths menu of options, which is shown in Figure 5.21.

As custom animation effects are added to the slide, numbers indicating the order of the animation events are displayed on the slide. A description of the animation is shown in the Custom Animation dialog box. See Figure 5.22.

Animation effects can also be added to graphs and pictures that are inserted or linked into the presentation. Figure 5.23 shows an Excel graph that was copied into a presentation and then animated to add interest to the presentation. We suggest that you experiment with the animation features that are available in PowerPoint to find the techniques that are most effective for your audience.

Figure 5.19   Custom Animation dialog box.

Figure 5.20   Add Entrance Effect options in PowerPoint.

Figure 5.21   Motion Paths options for custom animation.

Figure 5.22   List and description of animation applied to a slide.

Figure 5.23   Excel graph animated in a presentation.

Summary

Microsoft PowerPoint helps users create attractive, easy-to-read visual aids for presentations that may be delivered using projectors connected to personal computers, the Internet, paper handouts, or transparencies on an overhead projector. The visual aids for the presentation must be designed especially for the target audience using pictures, graphs, and words that effectively communicate the message.

PowerPoint helps quality specialists create effective presentations by providing attractive colorful templates, which make it easy to create visual aids; allowing the creator to animate the whole or part of the presentation; and integrating sound with the presentation.

In addition, text and graphics may be copied to or linked with PowerPoint from Microsoft programs, including Excel, Word, Access, Photo Editor, and other Windows-based programs. When the contents of other Windows-based programs are linked to PowerPoint, the user has the option of updating the information in the presentation to match revised information in the original source when the PowerPoint presentation is started.

This chapter has presented only a few features that we believe help create effective presentations for quality control decisions.

Exercises

5.1. Create a slide with a title and a copy of a graph from Excel.

5.2. Create a slide with a link to an Excel graph on half the slide and a copy of an Excel graph on the other side of the slide.

5.3. Create a slide with a hyperlink to a Web page.

5.4. Create a slide show selling a meeting of a club, church group, or school activity.

Part III

Fundamentals of Statistical Quality Control

6

Statistical Fundamentals Using Excel

KEY TERMS

Central tendency	Parameters
Cumulative distribution function	Probability density function
Distribution	Range
Frequency distribution	Standard deviation
Histogram	Statistics
Mean	Variance
Median	Variation
Mode	

OUTLINE

Statistical Fundamentals

Whenever sets of numerical data (measures) are collected, it is helpful to summarize the features of the data set. If the descriptive summary measures are computed from a sample of the population, the descriptive measures are called *statistics*. Descriptive statistics computed from a population are called *parameters*. Statistical quality control (SQC) is based on statistics. The SQC user does not have to be an expert in statistics; nevertheless, a fundamental understanding of statistics is required to interpret quality control charts. This chapter reviews selected statistical concepts that aid in understanding the principles of SQC. To enhance your understanding of what Excel can do for the SQC user, Excel is used to demonstrate the statistical concepts that are important for SQC.

The three most important properties that can be used to objectively describe data sets are: central tendency, variability or dispersion, and the shape of the distribution.

Parameters: Descriptive statistics computed from a population.

Statistics: Descriptive statistics computed from a sample.

Central Tendency

Most data sets display a tendency for the measurements to cluster around a particular value. *Central tendency* shows the value where most of the observations are concentrated. SQC primarily uses three measures of central tendency: the arithmetic mean (average), the median, and the mode.

Arithmetic Mean

The *arithmetic mean* is the sum of the values in a sample divided by the number of values in the sample. Often the objective of quality control is to calculate the mean of a sample (a statistic) to estimate if the value of the population mean (a parameter) has changed over time. The mean of a population may be referred to as mu (μ) or x-bar prime ($\overline{X}$)'. (Note: The use of prime generally refers to the population measure.)

To calculate the arithmetic sample mean using Excel, enter the following formula in a cell:

$$=\text{AVERAGE}(range)$$

where *range* specifies the cells that are to be included in the calculation. For example, =AVERAGE(B5:B35) will average the values from cell B5 through cell B35, or =AVERAGE(A9:C55) will average the values in all the cells in columns A, B and C, from row 9 through row 55.

Median

The *median* is the middle value in the sample, which has an equal number of values above and below. To compute the median manually, first arrange (sort) the measurement values in order, either ascending or descending. If the number of values in the set is an odd number, the value in the middle is the median. If the number of values is an even number, average the two middle values to obtain the median.

To calculate the median using Excel, enter the following formula in a cell:

$$=\text{MEDIAN}(range)$$

where *range* specifies the cells that are to be included in the calculation. When you use the Median function in Excel, the data do *not* have to be sorted.

Mode

The *mode* is the most frequently occurring value in the data set. The mode shows the value where most of the observations are concentrated; therefore, it indicates a value of central tendency. To calculate the mode manually, count the number of times each value appears in the data set (the frequency). The value that appears most often is the mode. Some distributions may have more than one mode. A distribution with two modes is called bimodal. A distribution with more than two modes is referred to as multimodal.

To calculate the mode using Excel, enter the following formula in a cell:

=MODE(*range*)

where *range* specifies the cells that are to be included in the calculation.

Central tendency: The value where most of the observations in a sample are concentrated.

Mean: The arithmetic mean is the sum of the values in a sample divided by the number of values in the sample.

Median: The median is the middle value in the sample, which has an equal number of values above and below.

Mode: The mode is the most frequently occurring value in the data set.

Variation

Variation is the second property that can objectively describe a data set. Variation is the amount of spread among the observation values. Figure 6.1 illustrates two samples with the same central tendency and different amounts of variation. The graph shows that *A* has less variation than *B*, therefore, we know the measurements in sample *A* cluster more tightly around the center of the distribution than the measurements in sample *B*. SQC primarily uses three measures of variation: the range, the variance, and the standard deviation.

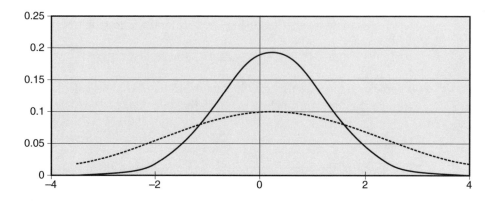

Figure 6.1   Two distributions with the same central tendency with different amounts of variation.

Range

A commonly used measure of sample dispersion is the range. The *statistical range* is the difference between the highest and the lowest value in the sample. The range is frequently used in SQC because of the ease with which it is manually calculated. The smallest value in the data set is subtracted from the largest value. Although the range provides a statistic that describes the width of dispersion, the range does not describe how the measurement values are distributed across the distribution or cluster around the center of the distribution. The variance and standard deviation offer better descriptions of the variability between the highest and lowest values of the sample.

To calculate the range in Excel, use the following formula:

$$= \text{max}(range) - \text{min}(range)$$

where *range* specifies the cell *range* for the sample. For example, =max(B5:F5) – min(B5:F5) instructs Excel to find the maximum value in the cells in row 5 from column B through column F and subtract from this value the minimum value in the same cell *range*. When this formula is copied to other rows, Excel adjusts the numbers to match the rows.

Variance

The *variance* describes how the values in the sample are dispersed about the sample mean. The variance is represented by the letter s^2. The variance is calculated by summing the squared differences between each observed value and the sample mean, and then dividing the sum by the number of observations minus one. The formula for calculating the variance follows. Since the variance is measured in squared units, interpretation of the variance may be difficult. Quality specialists usually prefer the standard deviation, which reports values in standard units.

$$s^2 = [(x_1 - \overline{X})^2 + (x_2 - \overline{X})^2 + \dots + (x_n - \overline{X})^2] / (n - 1)$$

To calculate the variance of the sample in Excel, use the following formula:

$$=\text{VAR}(range)$$

where *range* specifies the cell *range* for the sample. To calculate the variance of the population, use:

$$=\text{VARP}(range)$$

Most of the calculations for SQC and SPC use the variance of the sample.

Standard Deviation

The *standard deviation* of a sample is the square root of the variance. The sample standard deviation is represented by the letters *sd* or *s* (some SQC texts use σ). The formula for calculating the standard deviation is:

$$sd = \sqrt{\frac{\Sigma\left(X_i - \overline{X}\right)^2}{n-1}}$$

To calculate the standard deviation in Excel, use the following formula:

=STDEV(*range*)

where *range* specifies the cell *range* for the sample.

If one selects a dispersion measure from a statistical point of view, the sigma (standard deviation) control chart is preferred over the range control chart. Using Excel eliminates all the calculation considerations that historically favored range charts; therefore, many experts agree that theoretically the sigma chart (standard deviation chart) is the best choice for measuring dispersion in the data.

Variation: The dispersion among values in a data set.

Range (statistical):   The difference between the largest and smallest values in a data set.

Variance: A measure of a distribution's dispersion that is calculated by summing the squared differences between each observed value and the sample mean, and then dividing the sum by the number of observations minus one.

Standard deviation: A measure of a distribution's dispersion that is measured by the square root of the sum of the squared deviations from the mean for each value, divided by n – 1.

Shape of the Frequency Distribution

The third property that describes a data set is the *shape of the distribution*. A *distribution* is the pattern or shape in which the observation values are distributed. Statistical analysis is based on these patterns of numbers that are reproducible. A *frequency distribution* provides a picture of the central tendency and variation in a data set. The observations in a distribution can be measured with two types of numbers—integer (discrete) and real (continuous). *Integers* are whole numbers that report the number of defective items or the number of defects in a sample. *Real numbers* can take on any value within a given range. The only limit on the real values is due to the limitations of the measurement tools. For example, a measurement tool that has tenths of inches as the smallest unit of measure cannot measure to the precision of hundredths of an inch.

Distribution: The pattern or shape in which the observation values are distributed.

The first step in analyzing quality data is to construct a frequency distribution. A *frequency distribution* is a count of the number of times a particular value occurs in a sample or over several samples. The worksheet in Figure 6.2 shows the number of heartbeats per minute for a short-term newborn, measured by a vital sign monitor. The frequencies of the heart rate readings are shown in Figure 6.3 with a histogram, which shows the frequency distribution.

The histogram of the heart rate is not a symmetrical distribution. Control chart analysis suggests that there were periods of high heart rates mixed with periods of low heart rates. Because heart rate is not stable over time, it is better to use a control chart to study the variation in the process rather than a histogram.

As the examples demonstrate, some distributions are symmetrical or balanced and other distributions are skewed. If the mean and the median are equal, we can assume that the distribution is symmetrical. If the distribution is skewed to the left, the median is larger than the mean. When the distribution is skewed to the right, the mean is greater than the median.

	A	B	C	D	E	F	G	H	I	J	K	L	M	N	O	P	Q	R	S	T	U	V	W	X	
1	14B9B47.	BQC	7 14	1																		Max	194		
2																						Min	58		
3																								Bins	
4				Heart Rate																				58	
5																								59	
6	Time	Observations																						60	
7	9:47:51	135	135	132	132	133	133	134	134	135	136	137	138	138	138	139	140	140	141	141	141	F9		61	
8	9:48:02	141	141	141	141	140	139	137	136	136	136	134	129	129	129	129	129	124	119	115	111			62	
9	9:48:16	103	101	101	100	100	98	94	93	93	91	89	88	90	93	93	94	95	96	100	105			63	
10	9:48:40	124	126	129	131	134	136	137	138	137	137	139	142	143	145	144	144	146	148	149	150			64	
11	9:48:52	150	151	151	151	151	150	151	153	153	154	155	155	156	157	157	157	157	157	157	157			65	
12	9:49:03	154	154	154	153	152	152	151	151	151	151	150	150	149	149	148	148	148	148	148				66	
13	9:49:13	146	145	147	150	151	150	154	157	156	155	154	153	152	151	150	150	149	149	149	149			67	
14	9:49:26	147	147	146	146	145	145	145	145	144	145	145	146	145	145	145	146	146	145					68	
15	9:49:36	146	145	146	146	146	147	147	147	148	147	147	148	147	147	147	147	147	147	147	147			69	
16	9:49:46	146	146	146	146	146	146	146	146	146	146	146	145	145	145	145	145	145	145	145				70	
17	9:49:56	145	144	145	144	144	144	144	144	143	143	143	143	143	143	141	142	143						71	
18	9:50:07	142	141	142	142	142	143	143	143	144	144	144	144	144	144	145	145	145	145	145	146			72	
19	9:50:18	148	146	146	146	146	146	146	146	147	147	147	147	147	148	147	147	147	147	146				73	
20	9:50:28	147	147	146	146	146	146	145	144	144	145	144	144	144	145	146	148	150	150	149	148			74	
21	9:50:41	146	145	145	145	144	144	143	143	143	143	142	142	142	141	141	141	141	141	141				75	
22	9:50:51	141	141	141	141	141	141	142	141	142	142	142	142	142	142	142	141	141	142	142	142			76	
23	9:51:01	144	144	143	143	143	143	143	143	143	143	143	143	144	144	144	144	144	144	142	142			77	
24	9:51:12	143	144	143	143	143	142	142	145	146	150	150	151	151	151	150	150	150	148					78	
25	9:51:32	151	149	150	152	152	152	154	157	158	158	157	156	156	158	159	159	159	158	158	157	156		79	

Figure 6.2   Worksheet for short-term newborn heart rates.

Figure 6.3 Histogram of heart rates.

Recall that statistical analyses are based on the patterns of numbers (distributions) that are reproducible. Some of the most common distributions include:

Continuous distributions: Normal, uniform, exponential, f-distribution, Chi-square, student

Discrete distributions: Poisson, uniform, binomial, hypergeometric

The distributions listed in the first row are all continuous, while the distributions listed in the second row are all discrete. The analysis and application of each group of distributions use unique techniques; that is, all real distributions are analyzed using similar techniques and integer distributions are analyzed using different techniques. Because uniform distributions can have both real and integer data, the uniform distribution is in both lists.

Frequency distribution: The pattern formed by a group of values when the measurements are arranged according to the number of times each event (outcome) occurs.

Histogram: A bar graph showing the spread of values in a sample and the frequency of each value.

Probability Density Function (pdf)

The *probability density function* (pdf) is the distribution of relative frequencies that represents the probability of obtaining a particular value or outcome.[1] The probabilities are illustrated as the height of the curve for a given value of the independent variable *x*. For discrete data, the pdf simply graphs the relative frequencies of a distribution. When the data are distributed normally, the

---

[1]*Probability density function* (pdf) refers to the probability functions for both discrete and continuous distributions.

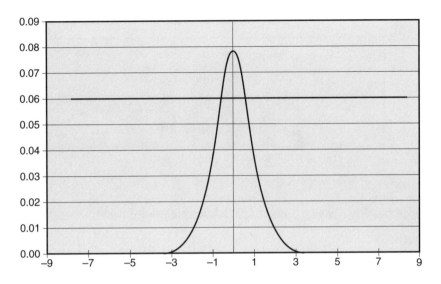

Figure 6.4 Graph of normal and uniform distributions probability density functions.

pdf is a bell-shaped curve; for the uniform distribution, it is a rectangle. Graphs of normal and uniform distributions are shown in Figure 6.4.

Cumulative Distribution Function (cdf)

When the relative frequencies of a distribution are added together, the result is a *cumulative distribution*. The probability density function and the cumulative distribution function for the binomial distribution are shown in Figures 6.5 and 6.6, respectively. The cdf is a function of the area underneath the pdf; therefore, the cdf is a never decreasing curve.

Probability density function (pdf):   Shows the probability that the value of any random variable will fall between any two points. Frequently shown with a histogram for discrete values and a curve for continuous values.

Cumulative distribution function (cdf):   Shows the cumulative probability of all events from negative infinity up to the point specified.

Using Excel to Understand Distributions

Quality specialists frequently use the uniform distribution, the normal distribution, the Poisson distribution, the binomial distribution, and the hypergeometric distribution. Excel worksheets aid in understanding what a distribution is and in learning how knowledge of particular distributions is utilized to generate random values that simulate a specific distribution.

The primary purpose of SQC is to facilitate decisions about the quality of ongoing processes or the quality of lots of product or material. Worksheets

Figure 6.5   Probability density function for a binomial distribution.

Figure 6.6   Cumulative distribution function for a binomial distribution.

offer the capability to generate fictitious quality measurements that match a particular distribution, thus creating a stable system of chance causes (environments). Then, the user can introduce an unstable system of chance causes and examine how these changes affect the control charts and lead the SQC specialist to realize that a change in the population distribution has occurred.

In real life, worksheets allow the user to enter real quality measurements, generate control charts, and determine if the frequency distribution has changed. Changes in the frequency distributions may be in the average, the variation, or the shape of the distribution. When a distribution changes, the change may be good, bad, or neutral relative to the production of quality output. If a change is good, the SQC user will want to identify the change and try to make it part of normal operations. If the change is bad, the SQC user will want to identify the change and try to keep it from happening in the future. If the change is neutral, the SQC user may ignore the change or identify it as a reference of an event that has no importance to quality.

Excel has many built-in capabilities for working with distributions. Table 6.1 lists some of the many Excel built-in worksheet (distribution) functions. Selected functions will be detailed later as needed to solve specific problems.

Table 6.1   Excel functions.

Function	*Distribution*
BINOMDIST (numbers, trials, probability, cumulative)	Binomial
CRITBINOM (trials, probability, alpha)	Binomial
HYPGEOMDIST (samples, number sample, population, number population)	Hypergeometric
NORMDIST (x, mean, standard deviation, True/False)	Normal
NORMSDIST (z)	Standardized normal
POISSON (x, mean, cumulative)	Poisson
ZTEST (array, x)$=1-$NORMDIST$((x-$mu$)/$ (sigma/root(n))	Normal

Standardized Normal Distribution

To demonstrate how Excel random number generators can generate random observations that fit particular distributions, a standardized normal distribution and a binomial distribution are generated and graphed in this chapter. The standardized normal distribution is a normal distribution with a mean equal to zero and a standard deviation equal to one.

Creating the Standardized Normal Worksheet

Entering Worksheet Text

To create the standardized normal worksheet, enter the following text and values in the appropriate cells by pointing to the cell and clicking once on the left mouse button. Next type the text in each cell and then press the Enter key.

Cell	**Label**
A1	norm.xls
A4	Low:
A5	High:
A6	Increment:
A8	z
B8	cdf
C8	pdf

To center the text in each column heading, highlight the range A8, B8, C8 by pointing to A8, pressing the left mouse button, and dragging the pointer across B8 to C8. When all the cells are highlighted, release the mouse button and complete these steps:

1. Click on Format.

2. Click on Cells.

3. Click on the Alignment tab.

4. Click on the Horizontal down arrow and select Center.

5. Click on OK.

Because formatting is a personal choice, we often leave the formatting selection to the reader. Another way to center the text is to highlight the range A8 through C8 and click once on the Center button on the toolbar.

Entering Worksheet Formulas and Values

To generate the values for *z*, the cdf, and the pdf, follow these steps:

1. In cell B4 type *–3.5* and press Enter (the –3.5 is the lowest value of the *z*-scale).

2. In cell B5 type *3.5* and press Enter (the 3.5 is the highest value of the *z*-scale).

3. In cell B6 type *0.05* and press Enter (the 0.05 is the counting increment for the *z*-scale).

4. In cell A9 type *+B4* and press Enter.

5. In cell A10 type *+$B$6+A9* and press Enter.

6. In cell B9 type *=normsdist(A9)* and press Enter.

7. Click on cell B9.

8. Click on Edit.

9. Click on Copy.

10. Click on B10 and press Enter.

11. In cell C9 type *0* and press Enter.

12. In cell C10 type *+B10–B9* and press Enter.

The first two rows of the worksheet formulas are complete. To copy the cell contents of A10, B10, and C10 into rows 11 through 149, follow these steps:

13. Highlight cells A10, B10, and C10 by holding down the left mouse key and dragging the mouse pointer over the cells.

14. Click on Edit.

15. Click on Copy.

16. Highlight the *range* A11:C149 and press Enter.

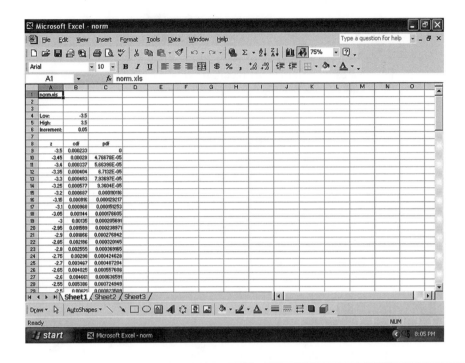

Figure 6.7 Worksheet of a standardized normal distribution.

The worksheet is complete. Examine the contents of the worksheet as shown in Figure 6.7. The z column shows the incremental values of the standard deviation from –3.5 to +3.5 in increments of 0.05. The =NORMSDIST(z) function calculates the cumulative probability (cdf) of each value of the standard deviation. The probability density function (pdf) is calculated from the cumulative distribution function (cdf) by successive subtraction. The probability density function is the difference between each of the values of the cumulative distribution function. The accuracy of the pdf depends upon using small increments in the value of z. It is for this reason that the increment 0.05 was chosen for this worksheet.

Save the worksheet in the subdirectory (folder) of your choice by clicking on File and then Save.

Creating the Probability Density Function Graph

To create the probability density function graph for the standardized normal distribution, follow these steps:

1. Highlight the graphing area A9:A149.

2. Depress and hold the control (Ctrl) key while you highlight the graphing area C9:C149.

3. Click on the Chart Wizard icon [icon].

4. In the Chart Wizard Step 1 of 4 select the XY (Scatter) and Chart subtype: Scatter with data points connected by smoothed lines without markers.

5. Click on Next>.

6. In step 2 of 4 click on Next>.

7. In step 3 of 4 name the chart *Normal Distribution*; name the *x*-axis Z, and name the *y*-axis *Probability*, and click on Finish.

8. When pressing the left mouse button changes the mouse pointer to a cross with four arrows, hold down the button and drag the graph into the desired position on the worksheet.

9. Click the legend box and press the Delete key; the results are shown in Figure 6.8.

Creating the Cumulative Distribution Function Graph

To create the cumulative distribution function graph for the standardized normal distribution, follow these steps:

1. Highlight the graphing area A9:B149.

2. Click on the Chart Wizard icon [icon].

3. In the Chart Wizard Step 1 of 4 select the XY (Scatter) and Chart subtype: Scatter with data points connected by smoothed lines without markers.

4. Click on Next>.

5. In step 2 of 4 click on Next>.

6. In step 3 of 4 name the chart *Cumulative Distribution Function*; name the *x*-axis Z, and name the *y*-axis *Probability*, and click on Finish.

7. When pressing the left mouse button changes the mouse pointer to a cross with four arrows, hold down the button and drag the graph into the desired position on the worksheet.

8. Click the legend box and press the Delete key; the results are shown in Figure 6.9.

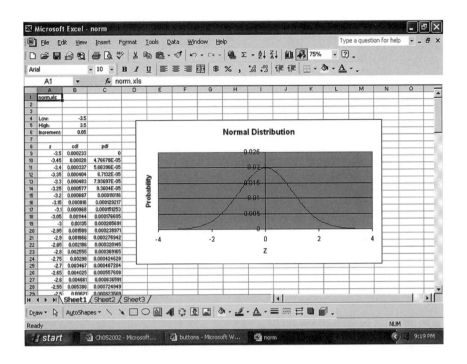

Figure 6.8   Normal probability density function.

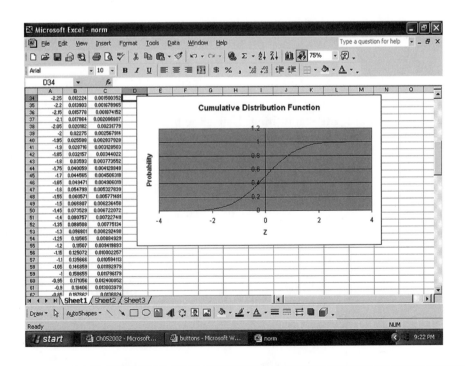

Figure 6.9   Cumulative distribution function for the standardized normal distribution.

Binomial Distribution

The *binomial distribution* (BINOMDIST) is a discrete distribution that is a function of sample size, probability, and the number of defective items or errors expected in the sample. The function BINOMDIST may be instructed to create either the probability density function or the cumulative function. When explaining the binomial distribution, we prefer to use the binomial formula[2]

$$\text{Prob}(x) = \begin{bmatrix} n \\ x \end{bmatrix} * p^x (1-p)^{n-x}$$

where:

n is the lot size

x is the sample size

p is the probability of the event of interest

The symbol
$$\begin{bmatrix} n \\ x \end{bmatrix} = \frac{n!}{x! * (n-x)!}$$

$$n! = n * (n-1) * (n-2)...1$$

$$0! = 1$$

The symbol

$$C_x^n$$

is often used in place of the symbol with the two vertical $\begin{bmatrix} n \\ x \end{bmatrix}$ bars. Both symbols mean the same thing. Using the binomial formula helps one understand what is required for the formulas in the Excel worksheet. In this chapter, we will use the Excel functions (random process generator) rather than generate the observation from the binomial formulas. Later chapters will generate observations using the binomial formula.

The function =BINOMDIST(number_s, trials, probability_s, cumulative) was used to calculate both the probability density function and cumulative function. *number_s* refers to the value of C in the binomial formula. C always varies from 0 to the number of trials (sample size). In this example, the probability (cell B4) is set at 0.5, because the binomial distribution is symmetrical when the probability is 0.5. Knowing how the distribution should look provides a check for your calculations. The results of binomial calculations may also be checked against binomial tables.

---

[2]The asterisk indicates multiplication, according to the mathematical symbols utilized in Excel.

Creating the Binomial Worksheet

Entering Worksheet Text

To create the binomial worksheet, enter the text and numbers into the appropriate cells.

Cell	Text	Description
A1	binomial.xls	Name of the worksheet
A3	Sample size:	Label
A4	Probability:	Label
B3	10	Number of observations in the sample
B4	0.5	Probability of obtaining a particular value
A7	*n*	Column label
B7	pdf	Column label for the probability density function
C7	cdf	Column label for the cumulative distribution function
A8	0	Zero representing no occurrences of the particular value

To number the rows of column A:

1. In cell A9 type *+1+A8* and press Enter (the value 1 should appear in cell A9).

2. Copy this formula into the *range* A10:A18 by pointing to the + on the bottom right corner of the A9 cell and dragging the + into cell A18. When you release the mouse button the rows should be numbered from 0 to 10.

To enter the functions for the probability density function and the cumulative distribution function, follow these steps:

1. Click on cell B8.

2. Click on the function key .

3. In the Or Select a Category: drop down list, click on STATISTICAL.

4. In the Select a Function dialog area, click on BINOMDIST and then click on OK.

5. The dialog box in Figure 6.10 appears.

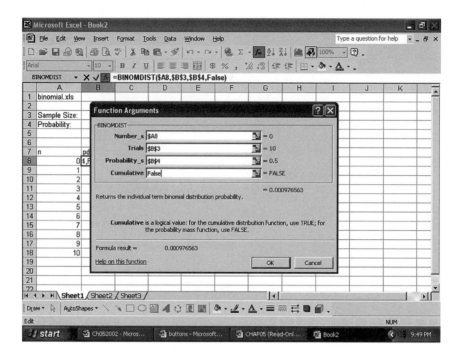

Figure 6.10   Binomial distribution (Function Arguments) window.

6. Enter the cell addresses that contain the appropriate information. For example, the number of occurrences is found in the A column in rows 8 through 18. The column address is fixed, but the row address is relative so that as the binomial function is copied into rows 8 through 18, the row addresses are adjusted.

   a. In the Number_s window type *$A8* and press the Tab key.

   b. In the Trials window type *$B$3* and press the Tab key.

   c. In the Probability_s window type *$B$4* and press the Tab key.

   d. In the Cumulative window type *False* and click on OK.

7. Copy the function in B8 into the *range* B9:B18 by pointing to the + on the bottom right corner of the cell, pressing the left mouse button, and dragging the + through cell B18.

To enter the values for the cumulative distribution function:

1. Click on cell C8.

2. Click on the function key 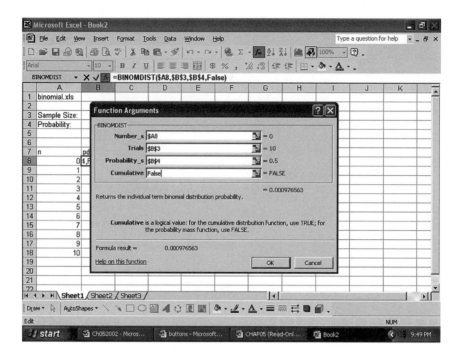.

3. In the Or Select a Category: drop down list, click on STATISTICAL.

4. In the Select a Function dialog area, click on BINOMDIST and then click on OK.

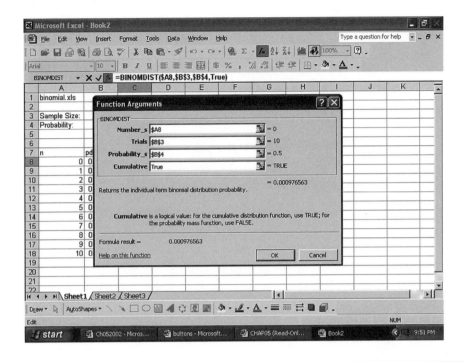

Figure 6.11 Binomial distribution options window.

5. The dialog box in Figure 6.11 appears.

6. Enter the cell addresses that contain the appropriate information:

   a. In the Number_s window type *$A8* and press the Tab key.

   b. In the Trials window type *$B$3* and press the Tab key.

   c. In the Probability_s window type *$B$4* and press the Tab key.

   d. In the Cumulative window type *True* and click on OK.

7. Copy the function in cell C8 into the *range* C9:C18.

Creating the Binomial pdf and cdf Graphs

To create the probability density function graph of the binomial distribution, follow these steps:

1. Highlight the graphing *range* B7:B18.

2. Click on the Chart Wizard button ![chart wizard icon].

3. In step 1 of 4 select the Column option with the chart subtype in the upper left corner (Clustered Column).

4. In Step 3 of 4 name the chart *pdf Binomial*; name the *x*-axis *c*; name the *y*-axis *Probability*, and click on Finish.

5. Adjust the placement of the graph.

6. Click on the legend and press Delete.

To create the cumulative distribution function graph of the binomial distribution, follow these steps:

1. Highlight the graphing *range* C7:C18.

2. Click on the Chart Wizard button 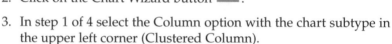.

3. In step 1 of 4 select the Column option with the chart subtype in the upper left corner (Clustered Column).

4. In step 3 of 4 name the chart *cdf Binomial*; name the *x*-axis *c*; name the *y*-axis *Probability*, and click on Finish.

5. Adjust the placement of the graph.

6. Click on the legend and press Delete; the result is shown in Figure 6.12.

Notice that the probability density function resembles the normal distribution and the cumulative distribution increases up to probabilities equal to one.

Figure 6.12 The probability density function and cumulative distribution function graphs for a binomial distribution.

Using Excel Functions

The task of covering all of Excel's statistical functions is overwhelming. There are many statistical functions that are useful to the quality control professional; only two were demonstrated in this chapter. You may search for a statistical function by clicking on the function icon ![icon] and then search for the one that you need. Figure 6.13 illustrates the screen after clicking on the function icon.

Usually, the brief explanation on the screen will give you the ability to use the function. Sometimes it may be necessary to experiment to make sure you understand the instructions. We recommend you always check to see if you are using a function correctly before you use it. In the case of statistical functions, the results may be checked by using published tables or by graphing the results.

One function that "fooled" us by returning unexpected results was =TDIST(x,deg_freedom,tails). The distribution only returns values for positive values of x. It always pays to spend a little time learning about a function the first time you use it.

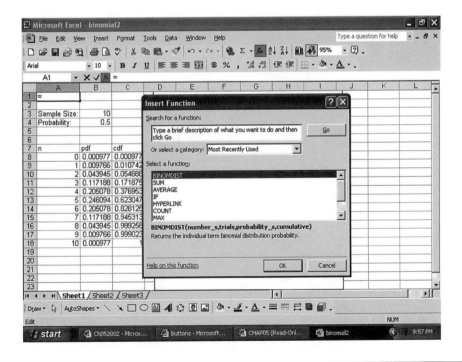

Figure 6.13   Excel function dialog box.

Summary

Statistics are computed measures based on a sample that summarize the characteristics of a data set. The three properties that objectively describe data sets are *central tendency, variation,* and the *shape of the distribution.* The sample arithmetic mean, the median, and the mode are the most common measures of central tendency. Variation of a data set is described using the statistical range, the variance, or the standard deviation.

The shape of the distribution can be described by examining the frequency distribution of the values in the data set. A *distribution* is a pattern of observation values that are reproducible. Distributions may be symmetrical or skewed. When the mean and the median are equal, the distribution is usually symmetrical.

The *probability density function* is a distribution of relative frequencies that indicates the probability of obtaining a particular value or outcome in the data set. The *cumulative distribution function* is the sum of the relative frequencies of the probability density function; consequently, the cdf is a function of the area under the probability density function.

Quality specialists often use the following distributions: uniform, Poisson, binomial, hypergeometric, and normal. Excel worksheets can generate random observation values that replicate each of the distributions. Then the SQC student can change the data and observe how the changes affect control charts. In real life, SQC specialists can enter quality measurements, generate control charts, and examine the frequency distribution to identify appropriate distribution. As additional data are collected, these new observations can be compared to the observations in the base period to determine if the quality of the output has changed. The standardized normal and the binomial distributions were demonstrated in this chapter.

7

Talking Statistical Quality Control

Introduction

Statistical quality control (SQC) includes the activities involved in ensuring that products and services satisfy customer needs. Quality is the composite characteristics of a product or service, which includes aspects of engineering, manufacturing, design, and service. The level of quality determines the degree to which a product or service meets the expectations of customers. The analytical methods of statistical quality control may be divided into two groups: acceptance sampling and statistical process control. In addition, measurements that are taken may be identified as *attributions* (characteristics) or *variables* (continuous or real numbers).

Specifications

A *specification* describes the characteristics of a product or service that are represented by measurements, such as the length of a machine bolt, the weight of an airplane wing, a premature infant's oxygen saturation, and the time lapsing between placing and receiving a fast-food order. Specifications are often limits developed for a product, service, or components of a product to define whether the product or service meets minimum standards. Creating a set of specifications assumes that one can measure the specification and that the organization has the capability to produce products and services to meet the specifications. Spreadsheet (worksheet) programs may be created to analyze the capability of a process and to compare the results to upper and lower specification limits.

Inspection

Inspection is the act of comparing material, products, and performance against the established specification standards and limits. Without inspection and the ability to measure product and service characteristics, quality control would not exist. Inspections may examine every item produced in a lot (100 percent inspection) or examine items selected from a production process (process control) or a product lot (sampling). Inspection results may be recorded manually on an inspection sheet or by automated computer software. Spreadsheet programs are used to help maintain inspection records, calculate statistics, and generate process control charts, which assist the quality specialist in making decisions.

Inspection: Act of comparing material, products, and performance against the established specification standards and limits.

Specifications: Characteristics of a product or service that are represented by measurements that define whether the product or service meets minimum standards.

Acceptance Sampling

Acceptance sampling assumes that the product is produced at a location, collected into a lot, and shipped to the user. The producer or the user may take a sample from the lot to determine if the lot will be accepted, rejected, or processed in a special manner. The decision to accept or reject the lot is based on the number of defective (nonconforming) items found in the sample. When acceptance sampling is applied to a series of lots, the quality specialist knows the specified risk of accepting lots of a given quality based on the operating characteristic curve (Figure 7.1). The operating characteristic curve plots the probability of acceptance given incoming levels of quality, for a specific acceptable quality level (AQL). The

Figure 7.1　An operating characteristic curve.

maximum number of defective units that can be found in a sample before the lot is rejected is the *acceptance number*.

The original work in developing sets of sampling plans was performed by Dodge and Romig at Bell Telephone Laboratories. During World War II, a set of sampling plans developed by the military was known as Mil-Std-105. Mil-Std-105 was revised by the American, British, Canada Standard (ABC-Std-105). Currently, the most influential standards are the ANSI/ASQC standards and the ISO standards.

The operating characteristic curve shows the probability of acceptance for various levels of incoming quality. In other words, given a particular level of incoming quality (horizontal axis), the probability of accepting a bad lot is the probability of acceptance on the vertical axis. Two points on the operating characteristic curve are of interest to the quality specialist. The first point is the acceptable quality level (AQL) versus the probability of acceptance, and the second is the lot tolerance percent defective (LTPD) versus the probability of acceptance. The producer's risk of rejecting good product is one minus the probability of acceptance at the AQL. The consumer's risk is the probability of acceptance of accepting bad product (at the LTPD level). The Dodge-Romig sampling plans are indexed on the LTPD while the ABC-Std-105 are indexed on the AQL.

A simple single attribute sampling plan consists of taking a sample of *n* items from a lot of *N* items and accepting the lot if the number of bad products in the sample is equal to or less than the acceptance number. All measurements are performed on the sample, but the decision is made regarding whether to accept or reject the lot.

If the size of the lot N is large relative to the sample size n, then the binomial distribution is used as the foundation for decision making. If the size of the lot N is small relative to the sample size n, then the hypergeometric distribution is used. Functions for both the binomial and hypergeometric distributions are available in Excel.

Acceptance sampling may also be performed using variable (continuous) measures. A sample of parts is selected and measured. If the average measurement of the sample is beyond a selected limit, the lot is rejected. These sampling plans using continuous measures are somewhat more complicated than attribute acceptance sampling.

Statistical Process Control

While acceptance sampling is a method to assist with decision making regarding acceptance or rejection of a lot, statistical process control is a method of managing processes that produce goods or services. It is a powerful management-by-exception decision-making technique. *Statistical process control* is the method for analyzing data collected from an ongoing process and using the analytical results to make decisions about the process.

The $\overline{X}$ and range control chart pair is frequently used for variable data when small subgroup sizes are used. A *subgroup* is a series of observations that are collected at approximately the same time. A commonly used subgroup size is five. The subgroup average $\overline{X}$ is used to measure the central tendency of the process while the **range** or the standard deviation may be used to measure the variation in the process. Since the **range** is the difference between the highest and lowest values in the subgroup, as the subgroup size increases, the **range** is a less precise measure of variation. In the early years of process control, the **range** was often used because it was easy to observe the **range** of a subgroup (the highest and lowest values) without computers. As computers have enhanced quality specialists' capabilities to calculate statistics, experts recommend the use of the standard deviation to measure variation in the data instead of the **range**. Standard deviations are used in sigma control charts.

The steps for creating an $\overline{X}$ and **range** control chart pair are:

1. Collect data for a base period (often 20 to 25 subgroups of size n).

2. Calculate the average ($\overline{X}$) and the **range** for each subgroup in the base period.

3. Calculate the average of the averages ($\overline{\overline{X}}$) and the average of the **ranges** ($\overline{r}$).

4. Calculate the upper and lower control limits for the averages and the **ranges**.

5. Collect more data representing 20 to 25 additional subgroups, and compare the subgroup measurements to the base period limits.

When a subgroup average $\overline{X}$ or **range** is beyond a control limit, it is assumed that the process has changed and management action is required. When the subgroup average $\overline{X}$ and the **range** are inside the control limits, then it is assumed that no changes have taken place and no management action is required. Like all decision-making processes, it is possible to have a subgroup statistic fall outside the control limits by chance alone and to look for a cause when there is none, or to have a subgroup statistic inside the control limits when a change has occurred and to miss an event. Normal practice assumes that setting the control limits at three standard deviations (sigma limits) from the average balances the two types of errors. Figure 7.2 illustrates an $\overline{X}$ and **range** control chart pair for controlled random numbers with control limits calculated for the first 20 subgroups and then again for the second 20 subgroups. There is a small difference between the first set of control limits and the second set of control limits, due to chance causes.

Recall that *specifications* are the characteristics of the product that define if the product or service meets minimum requirements. The upper and lower control limits of the control charts are calculated from the base period data and may be revised as observations are collected. Consequently, a process may be in control while producing many defective parts

Figure 7.2 $\overline{X}$ and the **range** of the subgroups.

(parts that do not meet specifications). On the other hand, a process may be producing products beyond the control limits and still not producing defective parts because the parts meet the product specifications. A procedure known as a *process capability study* (see chapter 14) is used to relate the control limits and the specification limits.

Sometimes it is necessary to search for the standard system of chance causes using only one set of data. Each subgroup beyond the control limits is analyzed and the quality control professional makes a decision on whether it should be included in the data set. Usually, points are not removed without cause. Sometimes when documentation is poor, all points beyond the control limits are removed and the remaining points are used as the foundation for calculating the standard system of chance causes. It is critical to document your work carefully if this approach is used.

Control charts using attribute measurements include p, np, u, and c charts, which are powerful decision-making tools. Figure 7.3 illustrates a p chart with variable control limits. These charts require larger sample sizes than continuous variable control charts such as $\overline{X}$ and **range** control charts. Attribute charts, however, depend on a definition of an event to count as an error or defect. The definition is an external specification limit. Only the variable charts use a set of control limits based on the numeric behavior of prior data and need no external specification(s).

Figure 7.3   *p* chart for variable sample size.

Summary

Statistical quality control (SQC) ensures that the level of quality of products and services satisfies the customer needs. *Quality* is composed of the characteristics of a product or service that are measured against predetermined specifications using inspection techniques. Quality control specialists create worksheets to analyze the capability of a process and to compare the results to upper and lower specification limits.

The analytical methods of statistical quality control may be divided into two groups: acceptance sampling and statistical process control. In addition, measurements of specifications may be identified as *attributes* (characteristics) or *variables* (continuous or real numbers).

When inspection sampling is utilized, a sample is taken at random from a product lot. Each sample item is inspected for defects. If the number of defective items in the sample exceeds the acceptance level, the lot is rejected; otherwise the lot is accepted. Quality specialists use operating characteristics to determine the probability of accepting a lot that does not meet minimum specifications at various acceptance levels. The sampling plan is developed to balance the risks of the producer against the risks of the consumer.

Process control is an ongoing activity that tries to control the performance of a process within a given set of limits. Such control requires the ability to measure the characteristics of a process, product, or service. When statistical process control is utilized, data are collected and analyzed from an ongoing process and decisions are made regarding whether the variation in the process is due to random error or outside causes.

The subgroup average measures the central tendency of the process while the range or standard deviation measures variation in the process. If the subgroup statistics extend beyond the control limit, it is assumed that the process has changed and management action is required. When the subgroup statistics are inside the control limits, then it is assumed that no changes have taken place and no management action is required. Like all decision-making processes, it is possible to have a subgroup statistic fall outside the control limits by chance alone and to look for a cause when there is none, or to have a subgroup statistic inside the control limits when a change has occurred and to miss an event. Normal practice is to set the control limits at three standard deviations from the average. Setting such wide control limits reduces the probability of having subgroup points beyond the limits by chance alone. Excel worksheets are ideal tools to help quality control specialists record inspection records, analyze the inspection data, and generate control charts.

8

Distributions

Prior Knowledge

From previous chapters, you should know how to open a new worksheet, enter text, enter formulas, and cut, copy, and paste the contents of one cell or a *range* of cells to another place in the worksheet. You should also understand the concept of *distributions*.

Introduction

Recall from chapter 6 that statistical analysis is based on patterns of numbers that are reproducible within limits. These patterns are called *distributions*. This chapter introduces four distributions routinely used in SQC: uniform, normal, exponential, and Poisson distributions. Spreadsheet programs help us understand what a distribution is, allow us to view the relationships among the values within a distribution, and help us learn how distributions can be used to produce randomly generated values that fit a specific distribution. The graphing capabilities in Excel allow us to view the theoretical shape and size of a distribution.

Chapter 5 introduced the continuous (normal type) and discrete (binomial type) distributions. We learned that by using selected Excel functions, we can calculate the area and/or height of both continuous and discrete distributions. In addition to calculating the probabilities of specific values of a distribution, it is useful to have the ability to generate random numbers that fit a given distribution. Being able to generate any given distribution using random numbers provides a tool for testing control charts. A *process generator* creates random numbers that replicate a specific distribution. This capability offers the opportunity to control the generated values representing inspection measurements, and then study the effects of changes on the output. In other words, you can study how changes in the distribution parameters affect control charts. These exercises can increase your confidence in understanding and using control charts.

Probability

There are two approaches to probability: the classical approach and the relative frequency approach. *Classical probability theory* assumes knowledge of the underlying process. The classical approach to probability starts with the concept of a fair coin tossed a number of times. The expected outcomes are that half of the time the *heads* side of the coin will face up when the coin comes to rest and the other half of the time the *tails* side will face up. The only possible outcomes in the activity of tossing the coin are assumed to be the heads or the tails side of the coin facing up. The outcome of the coin standing on edge is assumed never to occur even though it does occasionally.

The *relative frequency approach* to probability involves replicating an experiment (activity) a large number of times, counting the number of occurrences of an event of interest, and evaluating the results. The activity could be tossing a coin and counting the number of times *heads* occurs. No assumption is made about the types of outcomes that may occur. For example, if the coin stands on its edge, it is defined as a unique outcome and is counted as an event.

A stable system is a system that is working in an environment in which only normal random variation is present. When the data generated by a *stable system* are examined, they usually take the form of a given distribution.

Figure 8.1 Poisson distribution for rolling a pair of fair dice.

According to the classical theory of statistics, the numbers generated from rolling an honest pair of dice should behave as shown in Figure 8.1. The reason for the expected results is that there is one way to roll a 2, two ways to roll a 3 . . . six ways to roll a 7 . . . and one way to roll a 12.

On the other hand, an *unstable system of chance causes* is a system in which some additional source of variation is present. The purpose of creating worksheets that contain observation values that fit a particular distribution is to see how control charts behave when additional variance in the measurements is introduced.

Classical probability: Statistical analysis based on knowledge of the process.

Process generator: A computer procedure that uses a random number generator to produce numerical values that fit a specific distribution.

Relative frequency: Shows the probability of an outcome given all possible outcomes.

Stable system: A system working in an environment in which only normal random variation is present.

Unstable system of chance causes: A system working in an environment in which some source of variation, in addition to normal random variation, is present.

Uniform Distribution

A *process generator* is a set of instructions that generates random values for a specific process or distribution. Excel has a function called *RAND* that generates values between 0 and 1 that conform to a uniform distribution.

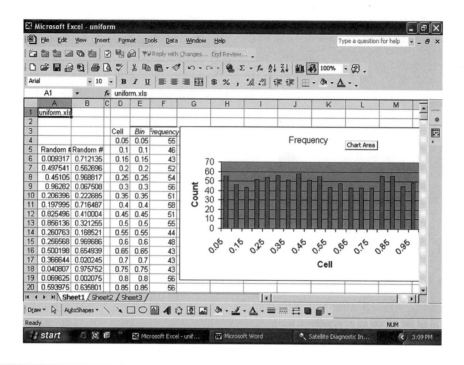

Figure 8.2   Random numbers histogram for a uniform distribution.

Excel xp uses the continuous uniform distribution as the basis for developing other distributions. Figure 8.2 illustrates a histogram of the results of generating 1000 random numbers. Regardless of the number of times the experiment is replicated, the probability that a value occurs in any given cell is the same. These results approximate a *uniform distribution*. A uniform distribution assumes that the probability of obtaining a number falling between two numbers is the same as that of obtaining any other number in that range.

The uniform distribution may be either continuous or discrete. A *continuous distribution* is a collection of values that can take on any value in the range, for example, 1.22, 1.222, 1.2222, and so on. A *discrete distribution* is a collection of numbers that can take on only selected values in the range, for example, only whole numbers such as 1, 2, or 3, not 1.2 or 3.66.

An example of a process resulting in a uniform distribution is rolling one honest die with the numbers 1, 2, 3, 4, 5, and 6 on each side of the die. The probability of rolling 1 is the same as that of rolling any other number. In addition to the visual tests provided by histograms, one may test the operation of the random number generator using statistical tests.

To randomly generate values that represent a uniform distribution, follow these steps:

1. In cell A1 type *uniform.xls*

2. In cell A6 type *=rand()*

3. Copy the contents of A6 into the *range* A6:B505.

4. Enter the cell numbers (the categories for the frequencies) in column D by typing *0.05* in D4 and press Enter.

5. In D5 type *+D4+0.05* and press Enter.

6. Copy this formula into the *range* D6:D22.

7. Click on the <u>T</u>ools menu.

8. Click on <u>D</u>ata Analysis.

9. Click on Histogram and then OK to display the histogram dialog box:

    a. Type the <u>I</u>nput Range as *A6:B505*

    b. Type the <u>B</u>in Range as *D4:D22*

    c. Type the <u>O</u>utput Range as *E3*

10. Click on OK.

11. Using the Chart Wizard ▨ , chart the values in columns E and F as a column chart to create the frequency chart.

The frequency chart in Figure 8.2 shows the results of the number of times each value rounded to the nearest hundredth of a point is contained in the data set. If you press F9 to change the values in the data set, you will get approximately the same results.

Central Limit Theorem

The *central limit theorem* provides the foundation for quality control analysis. The central limit theorem states that the sum or average of a number of values will approach a normal distribution as the number of observations in the sample increases. In other words, regardless of the shape of a population's distribution, the distribution of the subgroups' means will tend toward a normal distribution as the subgroup size increases.

The worksheet *CLT.xls*, shown in Figure 8.3, illustrates the central limit theorem. This example uses random numbers representing 200 subgroups, each with five observations. Each row contains observations for the subgroups. To create this worksheet, follow these steps:

Enter the text in the appropriate cells:

Cell	Text
A3	1
B3	2
C3	3
D3	4
E3	5
F3	Average
G2	Rounded
G3	Average
H2	Categories

The random numbers may be generated in one of two ways:

1. Use the =RAND() equation.

2. Use the random number process generator.

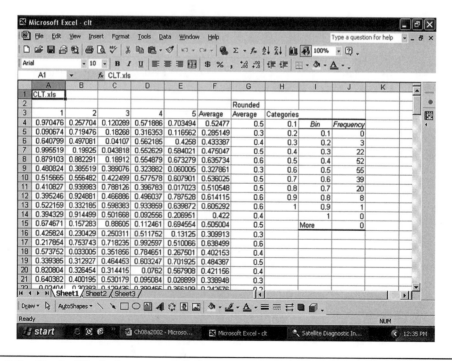

Figure 8.3   Central limit theorem worksheet.

To use the =RAND() equation, type this equation into A4 and copy the formula into the *range* A4:E203.

To use the random number process generator:

1. Click on the Tools menu.

2. Select Data Analysis.

3. Scroll to the Random Number Generation option and click on OK.

4. Enter the following values in the dialog box:

    a. Number of Variables—enter *5*

    b. Number of Random Numbers—enter *200*

    c. Select the Uniform Distribution option.

    d. Set the parameters between *0* and *1*

    e. Input the Output Range as *A4:E203*

    f. Click on OK.

The random variables are generated.
To calculate the average of each subgroup:

5. In F4 type =*AVERAGE(A4:E4)* and press Enter.

6. Copy this formula into the *range* F5:F203.

7. To place the rounded values in column F into column G, in G4 type =*ROUND(F4,1)* and press ENTER.

8. Copy this formula into *range* G5:G203.

Enter the values for the frequency calculation:

9. In cell H4 type *0.1* and press Enter.

10. In cell H5 type +*H4+0.1* and press Enter.

11. Copy this formula into the *range* H6:H13.

Calculate the frequencies:

12. Click on I4.

13. Click on the Tools menu.

14. Click on Data Analysis.

15. Select Histogram and click on OK.

14. Enter the Input Range as *G4:G203*

15. Enter the Bin Range as *H4:H13*

16. Enter the Output Range as *I4*

17. Click OK.

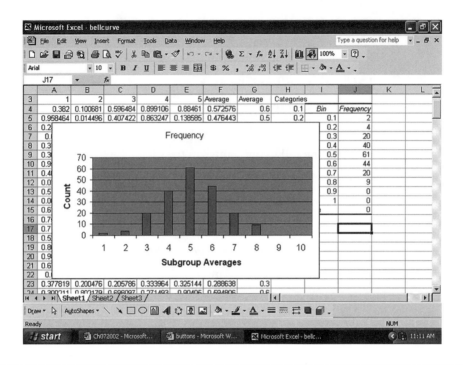

Figure 8.4 Bar graph of the subgroup averages of a uniform distribution.

The frequencies of each value are calculated. The values are shown in column I and the frequencies are listed in column J. The values in column J can be charted using the Chart Wizard and by selecting the column type chart, as shown in Figure 8.4. This graph does not look like a uniform distribution, but resembles the bell-shaped curve of a normal distribution. As more subgroups are included in the graph, and as more observations are added to each subgroup, the results will look more like a bell curve. This exercise illustrates the operation of the central limit theorem.

Normal Distribution

Using the central limit theorem, we can create a simple process generator for a normal distribution by adding two or more random numbers. Simulation theory proves that 12 random numbers are needed. The steps are:

1. Generate the sum of 12 random numbers.

2. Subtract 6 from the sum ($0.5 \times 12 = 6$ to set the mean at zero).

3. Multiply the results by the desired standard deviation.

4. Add the desired mean to the results.

The formula is:

$$=(rand()+rand()+rand()+rand()+rand()+rand()+rand()$$
$$+rand()+rand()+rand()+rand()+rand()-6)*sd+mean$$

where *sd* is the cell (address) where the value of the standard deviation is stored and *mean* is the cell (address) where the value of the mean is stored. Before we multiply by the standard deviation and add the mean, the process generates a standardized normal distribution. A Z transformation converts the mean of the normal distribution to zero and the standard deviation to one. Multiplying by the standard deviation and adding the mean is a *reverse* Z transformation; that is, a standard normal distribution with a mean of zero and a standard deviation of one is transferred into a normal distribution with any specified mean and any specified standard deviation. The reverse transformation is accomplished with the following steps. The sum of 12 random numbers with an expected value of 0.5 is 6 ($0.5 \times 12 = 6$). Six (6) is subtracted from the sum so that the average value is zero. The standard deviation is set to one. All of these steps may be performed in a single worksheet cell.

The objective is to create a worksheet that generates observations containing random numbers that approximate a normal distribution, and to visually compare the observed distribution with the expected distribution. Three graphic alternatives are available.

You can graph:

1. The frequency of observed values as a percentage against the probability density function for a given distribution

2. The frequency of observed values as a count against the probability density function multiplied by the total number of expected observations

3. The cumulative frequency of observed values as a percentage against the cumulative distribution function for a given distribution

From a statistical point of view, continuous distributions are best compared using a cumulative distribution function graph, while discrete distributions are best compared using the probability density function. However, for a normal distribution, we prefer to use the second option, comparing the observed frequency count versus the expected count (the bell-shaped curve). Figure 8.5 illustrates the worksheet for this analysis and the graphical results. The procedures for creating a worksheet for the normal distribution follow.

Type the text or numbers into the cells as indicated in Table 8.1. After typing the content in each cell, press Enter, the Tab key, or an arrow key.

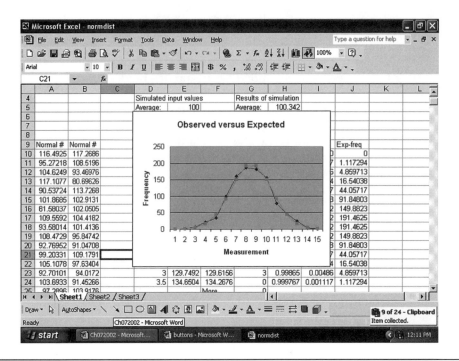

Figure 8.5   Graph of observed frequency counts versus expected frequencies for a normal distribution.

Entering Worksheet Formulas

Enter the following formulas into the appropriate cells.

1. In cell A10 type

   =(rand()+rand()+rand()+rand()+rand()+rand()+rand()
   +rand()+rand()+rand()+rand()+rand()–6)*$E$6+$E$5

   and press Enter.

2. Click on A10 and click on the Copy icon 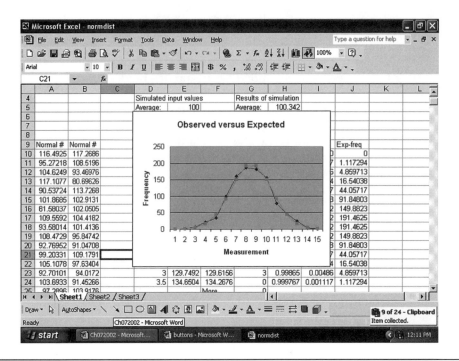.

3. Select the range A10:B509 and press Enter (the random numbers are generated).

4. In cell E7 type =COUNT(A10:B509) and press Enter.

5. In cell H5 type =AVERAGE(A10:B509) and press Enter.

6. In cell H6 type =STDEV(A10:B509) and press Enter.

7. In cell D10 type –3.50 and press Enter.

8. In cell D11 type +D10+0.5 and press Enter.

9. Copy the formula into the *range* D12:D24.

10. In cell E10 type =*D10*$H$6+$H$5* and press Enter.

11. Copy the formula in E10 into the *range* E11:E24.

To create a histogram, use the <u>D</u>ata Analysis option in the <u>T</u>ools menu:

12. Click on <u>T</u>ools.

13. Click on <u>D</u>ata Analysis.

14. Click on Histogram, and then click on OK:

    a. Type in the <u>I</u>nput Range as *A10:B509*

    b. Type in the <u>B</u>in Range as *E10:E24*

    c. Type in the <u>O</u>utput range as *F9* and click on OK.

Table 8.1   Text for normal distribution worksheet.

Cell	Text Input	Notes
A1	Normdist.xls	Worksheet name
D4	Simulated input values	Label
D5	Average:	
D6	Std. Dev.:	
D7	Count	
E5	100	Average value
E6	10	Standard deviation value
G4	Result of simulation	Label
G5	Average:	
G6	Std. Dev.:	
F8	Observed results	
H8	Expected results	
A9	Normal #	
B9	Normal #	
D9	Cells	
E9	Reverse Z	
H9	cdf	
I9	pdf	
J9	Exp-freq	

To calculate the expected results, use the function NORMSDIST:

15. Click in cell H10 and click on the Function icon .

16. Select Statistical from the Or Select a Category drop down list.

17. Use the scroll bar to locate the function NORMSDIST in the Select a Function area.

18. For the *z* value, type *D10* and click OK.

19. Copy the function in H10 into the *range* H11:H24.

20. In cell I10 type *0* and press Enter.

21. In cell I11 type *=H11-H10* and press Enter.

22. Copy the formula in cell I11 into *range* I12:I24.

23. In cell J10 type *=I10*$E$7* and press Enter.

24. Copy the formula in J10 into *range* J11:J24.

All the values are now entered in the worksheet.

To compare the frequency of observed values as a count against the probability density function, create the graph with these procedures:

1. Highlight the *range* G10:G24.

2. Depress the control (Ctrl) key and highlight the *range* J10:J24.

3. Click on the Chart Wizard icon .

4. Select a Line Chart type, with markers displayed at each value, connected by smoothed lines.

5. Complete all four steps of the chart generation process.

6. When the chart is displayed on the worksheet, double click on the Frequency Series line.

7. Select the Patterns dialog box, and in the Line option click on None.

In this example, there were 1000 randomly generated normal numbers. The symbols in Figure 8.5 represent the count of the observations in selected cells. The bell-shaped curve is the expected result for a normal distribution. As you can see, some of the symbols are above the line, others below the line, and the rest are almost exactly on the line. Visually, it appears that the random number generator has generated values that fit the normal distribution, with a mean of 100 and a standard deviation equal to 10.

Exponential Distribution

The *exponential distribution* is a continuous distribution that has only positive numbers. The formula for the cumulative distribution function of the exponential distribution is

$$F(t) = 1 - e^{-t/\lambda}$$

Where lambda (λ) is the mean of the distribution and t is time. The exponential distribution may be used for many applications that require a continuous distribution that does not produce negative numbers. The length of time between customer arrivals is often assumed to follow an exponential distribution. Service time, such as length of time that the customer service representative spends with each customer, or the length of time required for the mechanic to service an automobile, are other examples.

To generate values that represent an exponential function, use the Excel function EXPONDIST. To begin the worksheet, type the text in Table 8.2 in the worksheet.

To generate 500 random numbers that fit the exponential distribution, follow these steps:

1. In cell A7 type =$B$3*LN(RAND()) and press Enter.

2. Copy the formula in A7 into the *range* A8:A506.

3. In cell B7 type =0.50 and press Enter.

4. In cell B8 type =B7+0.50 and press Enter.

5. Copy the formula in B8 into the *range* B9:B29.

6. Click on the Tools menu.

7. Click on the Data Analysis option.

8. Click on Histogram and click on OK; in the dialog box enter the following values:

    a. In the Input Range type *A7:A509*

    b. In the Bin Range type *B7:B29*

    c. Click on the Output range box and type *C6* and click on OK.

To graph the distribution, highlight the range D7:D29. Click on the Chart Wizard ▥ and select a line type chart, with smooth lines and no markers. The worksheet and the graph of the exponential function are shown in Figure 8.6.

Table 8.2 Exponential distribution worksheet text.

Cell	Text
A1	Expon.xls
A3	Average:
B3	–2 (negative number)
C2	Minimum
C3	Maximum
C4	Increment
D2	.001
D3	11.2
D4	0.50
A6	Numbers
B6	Bins

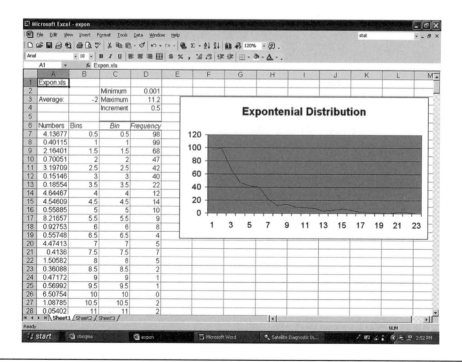

Figure 8.6 Exponential distribution worksheet and graph.

Poisson Distribution

The *Poisson distribution* is a discrete distribution of nonnegative values that range from zero to infinity. The formula for the Poisson distribution is

$$P(x \leq n) = \lambda^n * e^{-\lambda} / n!$$

The Poisson distribution is important for measuring customer service. For example, the number of customers that arrive within a specific time frame or the number of times a specific item will be requested in a retail store are both examples of events that often conform to a Poisson distribution. When quality specialists measure the number of defects in an item, the Poisson distribution is also useful for generating control charts. When the probability of an event is small, the Poisson distribution can be used to approximate a binomial distribution. (The binomial distribution was presented in chapter 5.) When the average of a Poisson distribution is large, the distribution is symmetrical, and according to the central limit theorem, resembles a normal distribution.

Values that simulate a Poisson distribution can be generated using Excel's random number generator, by following these steps:

1. In cell A1 type *Poisson.xls* and press Enter.

2. In cell B2 type *Simulated Values* and press Enter.

3. In cell G2 type *Cell Values* and press Enter.

4. Click on cell A3.

5. Click on Tools in the menu bar.

6. Click on Data Analysis.

7. Click on Random Number Generation and then click on OK.

8. Enter the following information in the dialog box:

   a. In the Number of Variables, type *5*

   b. In the Number of Random Numbers, type *1000*

   c. Select the Poisson Distribution.

   d. In Lambda, type *6*

   e. In the Output range, type *A3*

   The random values are generated for the range A3:E1002.

9. In cell G3 type *0* and press Enter.

10. In cell G4 type *=G3+1* and press Enter.

11. Copy the formula in G4 into the *range* G5:G23.

12. To compute the histogram of the frequency of each value:

    a. Click in cell H3.

    b. Click on Tools.

    c. Click on Data Analysis.

    d. Select Histogram in the dialog box and click on OK.

    e. Enter the following cell addresses:

       • In Input Range enter *A3:E1002*

       • In Bin Range enter *G3:G23*

       • In the Output Range enter *H3* and click on OK.

The Poisson worksheet is displayed in Figure 8.7. The frequency of the simulated observations is shown in the Frequency column. A column graph of the Poisson distribution is shown in Figure 8.8.

Summary

The *classical approach* to statistical probability is based on knowledge of the underlying pattern of observations in a process. The *relative frequency approach* to statistical analysis is based on data collection, counting, and analysis. A *distribution* is the pattern of a set of numbers that is reproducible. A *stable system of chance causes* is a system in which only normal random variation is present. When other sources of variation are present, the system becomes *unstable*.

Measurements taken in the conduct of statistical quality control include the uniform, normal, exponential, and Poisson distributions. The normal and exponential distributions are continuous distributions. A *continuous distribution* is a collection of numbers that may take on any value in a range. The *Poisson distribution* is based on discrete measurements, which are integer values in a range. A *statistical range* is the difference between the highest and lowest values that may occur. The uniform distribution may be either continuous or discrete. The *uniform distribution* is a distribution that describes a process in which the outcome is equally likely to fall at any point between two values. The uniform distribution is important because it provides the basis for creating process generators for other distributions. A *process generator* is a computer program that generates random numbers that fit a certain distribution.

The central limit theorem states that, regardless of the shape of the distribution of a population, the distribution averages of a subgroup of size *n* will become normally distributed as the subgroup size increases or as the number of subgroups increases. The normal distribution has a bell-shaped curve and no limits on the high and low values in the distribution.

Figure 8.7   Poisson worksheet.

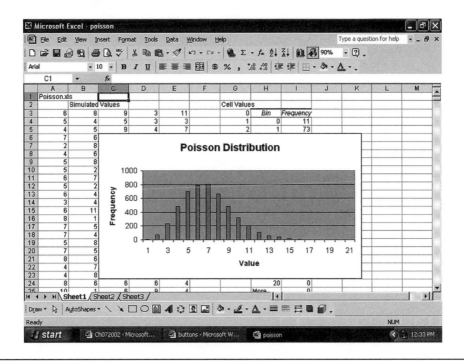

Figure 8.8   Frequency chart of the Poisson distribution.

Excel xp provides the tools to observe the frequency distribution in a data set. A *frequency distribution* is the pattern formed by a set of values when the measurements are arranged according to the number of times each value occurs. A frequency distribution may be graphed using a *histogram*, which is a bar chart showing the frequency of each value and how the values are distributed across the distribution. Generating charts and graphs of observations is the foundation of statistical quality control.

9

Selected Functions and Data Analysis Tools

Introduction

Excel's extensive sets of functions and add-in tools were beyond the dreams of spreadsheet users just a few years ago. Excel xp has so many capabilities that sometimes we have difficulty locating a specific capability. Functions are programmed instructions that manipulate numbers or text. There are two places to find special capabilities: (1) the Function

icon ![icon] and (2) in the <u>T</u>ools menu with the Add-<u>I</u>ns or <u>D</u>ata Analysis options. Whenever you want to execute an Excel function, you must enter values and cell addresses, or select function options to provide the information necessary to complete the function. The Data Analysis tools are also functions that complete statistical, financial, engineering, and other types of analyses.

There is no way to review all of the capabilities available in Excel xp in one text; however, learning to use one function is similar to learning any other function. This chapter covers capabilities that are not used in other chapters, but are likely to be of interest to readers. The following functions and data analysis tools were selected for review:

> **Functions**
> CHIDIST
> CORREL
> COUNTBLANK
> TREND and Trendlines
>
> **Data analysis tools**
> Rank and Percentile
> Regression
> Single-factor ANOVA

Excel xp Functions

Chi-square Function

The *Chi-square distribution* (CHIDIST) is used for testing how well a data set conforms to a Chi-square distribution. One application of the Chi-square test is to compare the number of defective parts with the expected number of defective parts to determine if the proportion of the observed number is significantly different from the proportion of the number expected. The test statistic is based on the ratio of the proportion of expected values to the proportion of observed values and the degrees of freedom. In this example, the test statistic is calculated by squaring the difference between the number of defective parts and the expected number of defective parts, and dividing by the expected frequency in each subgroup and summing over all subgroups.

Chi-square distribution: The distribution of variances when the population is normally distributed. The Chi-square distribution is used to conduct goodness-of-fit tests to determine how well a sample distribution conforms to a theoretical Chi-square distribution.

Since the Chi-square distribution is a function of the ratio of two squared values, negative values cannot exist in this distribution because a squared number must be positive. The parameter of a Chi-square distribution is the *degrees of freedom*. The variance is equal to two times the mean. Many Chi-square tables are *right-tail tables*, which provide the Chi-square value for a given probability only in the right tail; Table 9.1 is an example of a Chi-square table. The column labels show the selected probabilities of obtaining the value of a ratio by chance, and the degrees of freedom are shown in the row labels. The Excel function CHIDIST(χ^2, *df*) yields the cumulative values to the right of the χ^2 value entered. This result does not lend itself to producing a standard Chi-square table as illustrated in Table 9.1, which shows the probability density function. The Excel function may create a cumulative density function or a graph of the probability density function. To generate the values to graph the Chi-square distribution, follow these steps:

1. In cell A2 type *Chi-square Distribution*

2. In cell C3 type *Degrees of Freedom*

3. In cell A5 type *0* and press Enter.

4. In cell B4 type *5*

5. In cell C4 type *+B4+5* and press Enter.

6. Copy the contents of C4 into the *range* D4:E4.

7. In cell A6 type *+A5+1* and press Enter.

8. Copy the contents of A6 into the *range* A7:A17.

9. In cell B5 type *=+CHIDIST($A5,B$4)–CHIDIST($A6,B$4)* and press Enter.

10. Copy this formula into the *range* B5:E17.

To graph the probability density function:

11. Highlight the *range* B4:E17.

12. Click on the Chart Wizard icon ▦.

13. Select the chart type Line with smooth lines without markers.

14. Complete the four steps of the chart generation process described in chapter 4.

Table 9.1   Classic Chi-square table.

Critical Values of Chi-Square

| DF | Right-Tail Area | | | |
	1.10	**0.05**	**0.02**	**0.01**
1	2.706	3.841	5.412	6.635
2	4.605	5.991	7.824	9.210
3	6.251	7.815	9.837	11.345
4	7.779	9.488	11.668	13.277
5	9.236	11.070	13.388	15.086
6	10.645	12.592	15.033	16.812

Figure 9.1 illustrates an Excel worksheet for creating the probability density function of the Chi-square distribution and graphs of the distribution for 5, 10, 15, and 20 degrees of freedom. Notice that as the degrees of freedom increase, the distribution becomes wider and flatter. Examine the formula in cell B5 [=+CHIDIST($A5,B$4)–CHIDIST($A6,B$4)]. It illustrates how the Excel function CHIDIST(χ^2, *df*) works. We recommend you experiment with any and all Excel functions before using them to make sure you understand what must be entered into the formula and what is produced by the formula.

Correlation Function (CORREL)

The correlation function (CORREL) calculates the *correlation coefficient* between two sets of numbers. At times it is important to measure the relationship between two sets of observations or between two variables. The Excel instructions use the statistical term of *array*, rather than the worksheet term *range*. To calculate a correlation:

1. Open any worksheet that contains the values.

2. Click on an empty cell.

3. Click on the Function button.

4. Click on "Statistical" in the Or Select a Category drop down list.

5. Click on CORREL in the Select a Function area and click on OK.

6. In the CORREL dialog box, enter the *range* for the values in the first array area and then enter the *range* for the values in the second array area. See Figure 9.2.

7. Click on OK.

The correlation coefficient displays in the cell, as shown in Figure 9.3.

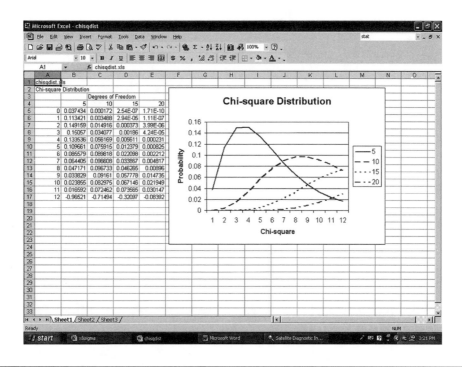

Figure 9.1 Chi-square probability function.

Figure 9.2 CORREL dialog box.

Figure 9.3 Results of the Correlation function.

Correlation coefficient: A value between –1.0 and +1.0 that shows the degree of linear association between two variables.

COUNTBLANK Function

Sometimes it is important to know something about the values or strings in a *range* of cells, such as the number of observations that are missing or blank in a data set. The COUNTBLANK function counts the number of empty cells in a *range* (Figure 9.4). The COUNTBLANK function is typical of the string-handling functions available in Excel.

To execute the COUNTBLANK function:

1. Open a new worksheet or the worksheet *trend.xls*

2. In cell A3 type *1*

3. In cell A4 type *+A3+1*

4. Copy this formula into the *range* A5:A17.

5. In cell B3 type *=rand()*100*

6. Copy this formula into the *range* B3:F17.

7. Click on B3 and press the Delete key.

8. Click on C6 and press the Delete key.

9. Click on D8 and press the Delete key.

10. Click on the Function icon .

11. In the Or Select a Category drop down list, select Statistical.

12. Click on COUNTBLANK in the Select a Function area.

13. Type the *range* B3:F17 in the Range area.

14. Click on OK.

The number of missing cells is calculated and is shown in cell H2 in Figure 9.4.

TREND Function and Trendlines

The TREND function produces values that represent a straight trendline fitted to a data set. The values are calculated using the least squares method. If the data are changed, the TREND function calculates new values. The trend values may be graphed along with the other series using the Chart Wizard. The TREND function does not display the value of the slope or intercept.

	A	B	C	D	E	F	G	H	I	J	K	L
1	trend.xls											
2								3				
3	1	94.15881	54.83217	27.91242	48.96207	77.59255	24.99829					
4	2	57.60761	85.48366	56.12339	8.990142	13.32212	27.44798					
5	3		57.64736	75.85873	29.67525	61.72804	29.89768					
6	4	52.18359	16.15767	5.570286	26.91214	25.24522	32.34737					
7	5	54.43665	43.50093	43.77729	57.92449	97.52387	34.79706					
8	6	3.019625		76.86803	42.0203	2.493098	37.24676					
9	7	5.844077	15.81677	57.66105	10.26411	25.00319	39.69645					
10	8	77.43412	1.578938		27.88567	86.3086	42.14614					
11	9	57.92311	84.01076	90.78519	22.50156	8.954508	44.59584					
12	10	63.36059	85.48164	36.30515	74.02887	58.69295	47.04553					
13	11	44.62904	22.89463	69.31	14.59567	65.16926	49.49523					
14	12	48.43416	92.97236	2.7053	89.88124	44.8185	51.94492					
15	13	83.5827	86.79583	43.02767	95.84222	87.6097	54.39461					
16	14	35.9654	37.36448	77.65036	25.34887	72.43278	56.84431					
17	15	83.42176	6.245668	59.83466	57.35955	49.30552	59.294					
18												
19												
20												
21												
22												

Figure 9.4 COUNTBLANK function.

Trendline: A line that predicts new values based on previous values.

To calculate the trend values, follow these steps:

1. Open the worksheet *trend.xls* containing the data set.

2. Click on G1.

3. Click on the Function icon .

4. From the Or Select a Category drop down list, select Statistical.

5. In the Select a Function list scroll down to TREND.

The TREND dialog box requires four pieces of information. See Figure 9.5.

TREND(*y*-range, *x*-range, *x*-new range, TRUE)

6. Enter the appropriate values in the dialog box. (Note: Be careful to enter absolute addresses for the *y* values and the *x* values and a relative address for the new *x* value.)

   a. Type the *y*-range as *$E$3:$E$17*

   b. Type the *x*-range as *$A$3:$A$17*

   c. Type *x*-new range as *A1*

   d. Type *True* in the Const dialog area, which means to calculate a line with a calculated intercept value; *False* means to calculate a line going through the origin.

7. Click on OK.

8. Copy the TREND function into the appropriate *range*, in this example G3:G17.

The existing and new *x* and *y* values can be graphed using the graphing procedures described in chapter 4. It is also possible to use the Trendline option in the Chart Wizard shown in Figure 9.6 to fit a line to a graph.

In Figure 9.7, we added a straight line (series 1) to a graph of the data in column E. First, create a line graph of column E. (Specific procedures are detailed in chapter 4.) When the graph is displayed in the worksheet, point to the Series line, and click the right mouse button. When the Edit menu is displayed, select Add Trendline and then choose the type of trendline and click on OK. The Add Trendline procedure produces a line that is similar to the TREND function.

Figure 9.5 TREND function dialog box.

Figure 9.6 Add trendline to a series menu option.

Figure 9.7   A series with a trendline added.

Data Analysis Tools

Another place to look for functions is in the <u>T</u>ools menu in the <u>D</u>ata Analysis option. If the <u>D</u>ata Analysis option is not displayed near the bottom of the <u>T</u>ools menu, you must add it to the menu by selecting Add-<u>I</u>ns. When the Add-Ins dialog box is displayed, click on the Analysis ToolPak option and click on OK.

When you select the type of analysis and input the data ranges and function parameters, the data analysis tools complete complex statistical, engineering, financial, and other analyses. Each of these analysis tools is based on a macro—a series of programmed instructions. When the analysis is completed, the output is often in the form of an output table. Before you attempt to use these functions, you should understand the purpose and correct usage of the analysis.

Figure 9.8 illustrates the <u>D</u>ata Analysis dialog box. Approximately half of the available selections are shown in this figure. Three <u>D</u>ata Analysis functions are presented in this chapter: Rank and Percentile; Regression; and single-factor ANOVA.

Figure 9.8 Data analysis functions.

Rank and Percentile

Sorting and ranking defects, complaints, errors, or other types of observations is a common activity in SQC. The Data Analysis—Rank and Percentile Analysis tool is easy to use and understand. This tool produces a table of each value in the data set sorted in order, along with the frequency and percentage of each value. The data shown in Figure 9.9 is a small collection of grades from an exam in column B and the Rank and Percentile dialog box.

The inputs required to generate the output table are:

1. Input Range—the range of cells that contain the values to be analyzed.

2. Grouped By—option buttons to indicate if the data are arranged in columns or rows.

3. Labels in First Row/Labels in First Column—the check-box allows the user to indicate if the first row or first column contains a label for the data. If the input range has no labels, click to clear the check-box.

4. Output Options—include three options:

   a. Output Range area—allows the user to place the output table in the current worksheet and specify the location of the table by identifying the top left cell of the output table

   b. New Worksheet Ply—allows the user to insert a new worksheet in the workbook, with the output table positioned in cell A1

   c. New Workbook—allows the user to create a new workbook with the output

After specifying the location for the results, the calculations show the place of each grade by rank and percentile, as shown in Figure 9.10. The highest grade is 76, which is in the 100th percentile because all other grades were lower than 76.

Regression Analysis

The *regression analysis* option fits a line through the observations using the least squares method and provides all the statistics relative to fitting a line to a set of data points. This option accommodates 16 independent variables and one dependent variable. Regression is often used to measure how the dependent variable is affected by the independent variables. In other words,

Figure 9.9   Rank and Percentile dialog box.

Figure 9.10   Rank and Percentile output table.

regression may be used to predict the value of the dependent variable (for example, number of defects or the level of customer satisfaction) if we have previously established the impact of the independent variables on the dependent variable.

The regression output includes some ANOVA type analysis, correlation output, as well as the slope and intercept. In Figure 9.11 the *Trend 2* worksheet is displayed with the regression results. The intercept is located in cell E17 and the slope is located in cell E18. These values may be used to calculate a trendline. The procedure produces detail numbers and analysis, and in some ways, produces a result similar to the TREND() function reviewed earlier in this chapter. Unlike TREND(), regression must be rerun each time the data are changed.

Figure 9.12 illustrates the screen after the selections Tools, Data Analysis, and Regression have been selected. The following options are available:

1. Input Y Range—enter the range for the *y*-values (dependent variables). The creators of Excel seem to always select the *y*-values and then the *x*-values. We have found that a number of first-time users consistently enter the *x*-values first. When we first started to use Excel we made this error a number of times.

2. Input X Range—enter the range for the *x*-values (independent values).

Figure 9.11   Regression results.

Figure 9.12   Regression dialog box.

3. Labels—specify if the input ranges contain labels.

4. Confidence Level—specify another confidence level in addition to the default 95 percent confidence level.

5. Constant Is Zero—click on if the regression line is to pass through the origin of the *x*–*y* graph.

6. Output Options—includes eight options:

   a. Output Range area—allows the user to place the output table in the current worksheet and specify the location of the table by identifying the top left cell of the output table

   b. New Worksheet Ply—allows the user to insert a new worksheet in the workbook, with the output table positioned in cell A1

   c. New Workbook—allows the user to create a new workbook with the output

   d. Residuals—prints the residuals in the output table

   e. Standardized Residuals—prints the standardized residuals in the output table

   f. Residual Plots—prints a chart for each independent variable against the residuals

   g. Line Fit Plots—prints a chart of predicted values compared to the observed values

   h. Normal Probability Plots—prints a chart of the normal probabilities

Single-Factor ANOVA

Analysis of variance (ANOVA) is one of the most popular techniques for analyzing differences among factors or groups. The simplest of the ANOVA procedures is *single factor*. If you are interested in the mathematics, you will find that the derivation of process control chart analysis and ANOVA are the same. Process control charts are a graphical procedure for performing one-way ANOVA, with the factor being *time*.

Figure 9.13 illustrates the results of a single-factor ANOVA. The data along with the headings are in the area indicated by a border. The results are shown to the right of the data. The Excel documentation contains instructions on how to perform ANOVA, but you will need to read a text on ANOVA to understand what the output means. The output created by Excel xp is consistent with the format used in statistics textbooks and the output in the field.

Regression analysis: A statistical technique for investigating and describing the relationships among variables.

Figure 9.13   Single-Factor ANOVA.

Analysis of variance: A statistical technique for estimating the relationships among the variables when the independent variables are categorical.

Summary

Excel includes an extensive set of functions and analysis tools that may be of value as you develop skill in conducting SQC. In our experience, there are more tools than we can ever use. Four functions and three analysis tools were reviewed in this chapter. Although none of these tools are required to solve the statistical quality control problems in this book, we hope that you will learn to use these and other Excel tools in your quality analyses.

Part IV
Statistical Process Control

10

$\overline{X}$ and Range Control Charts

KEY TERMS	
Attribute data	Type II error
Cell-range	UCL_r
LCL_r	$UCL_{\overline{x}}$
$LCL_{\overline{x}}$	Variable data
R	$\overline{X}$ and range control charts
Range	$\overline{X}$
Type I error	$\overline{\overline{X}}$

OUTLINE

Graphing the $\overline{X}$ Control Chart

Graphing the Range Control Chart

Formatting Text

Tools and Spelling

Template

Expanding the $\overline{X}$ and Range Control Charts

    Copying Sheet 1 to Sheet 2

    Recording Base Period Control Chart Parameters

    Copying Parameter Values into Columns

    Calculating the Subgroup Averages and Ranges

    Editing the Control Graphs

Creating a Comparison Graph

    Creating Worksheet 3

        Numbering the Columns

        Entering the Rows

        Entering Control Parameters from Sheet 1

        Entering Control Parameters from Sheet 2

    Graphing the $\overline{X}$ and Range Control Charts for Worksheet 3

Using $\overline{X}$ and Range Control Charts

    No Change in Variation, Two-Sigma Increase in the Mean

    No Change in the Mean, One-Sigma Increase in the Variation

Real Life

Summary

Exercises

Prior Knowledge

From earlier chapters, you should know how to open and save files, how to cut and copy a *range* of cells from part of a worksheet to another, and how to use the function =RAND().

What Is Statistical Process Control?

The essence of *statistical process control* (SPC) is to regulate processes to ensure that quality standards are met. A *process* is an ongoing activity such as driving a car, operating an oil refinery, or manufacturing paper. Every process has variation, which may be stable or unstable. When the process is stable, only normal (random) variation is present. Although a process is stable, the process may not be centered where it is needed or a process may have more variation than is desired. Usually, one set of actions centers a distribution, while a completely different set of actions controls the variation in a distribution.

An unstable process experiences normal random variation in addition to variation caused by outside forces, for example, a driver who has consumed a large amount of alcohol and is trying to steer the automobile straight down the road. The outside force is the alcohol. Similarly, a paper machine's process that is affected by lost hydraulic pressure is experiencing the effects of an outside force.

SPC is a method for collecting and analyzing data from an ongoing process in order to make decisions about the process. Any numbers (measurements) generated from the process may be used in SPC. You may recall from chapter 2 that the numbers used to measure a process may be *variables* (continuous measurements) or *attributes* (counts of occurrences). When process output can be measured as variable data, the most informative charts are the *central tendency chart* ($\overline{X}$ chart) and a *matched variation control chart* (range or sigma chart). Variable measures are obtained using devices such as micrometers, scales, and rules, and they should be precise. Measurements are precise when the measurement unit is accurate enough to allow the SPC professional to identify underlying variation in the process. Rounded or truncated numbers can reduce the value of control charts. Examples of individual variable measurements are the weight of a manufactured part, the length of the part, the diameter of a hole, or the length of a shaft.

Why Use $\overline{X}$ and Range Control Charts?

Quality control professionals who do not have extensive knowledge of statistics, but who are familiar with their processes, can use $\overline{X}$ and *range* charts to analyze and control these processes to ensure that satisfactory goods and services are produced. These charts are most effective when they are used together as a matched pair. Each chart individually shows only a portion of information concerning the process. The $\overline{X}$ (average) *control chart* shows how the process average (central tendency) changes. The *range* (R) *control chart* shows when the variation of a process has changed. It is important to control both the process central tendency (average) and variation (range). Different actions are needed to control the process central tendency and variation.

$\overline{X}$ **and R charts:**   A pair of control charts for controlling the central tendency and variation of a process using the range.

Variable data: Data representing a quality characteristic that is measured.

> **Attribute data:** Measurements of the characteristics of items (components or products) that are classified as either meeting or not meeting specifications (accept or reject; go or not go.
>
> **Type I error:** Numbers indicate a change when there is none and time and money are wasted looking for the change.
>
> **Type II error:** Numbers do not indicate a change when one has occurred and we miss an opportunity to improve the process.

Creating $\overline{X}$ and Range Worksheets

The creation of $\overline{X}$ and R control charts begins with the manual collection of data on a form similar to that shown in Figure 10.1, or electronically in a computer file that makes it easy to create output on a form similar to the form in Figure 10.1. The form may be revised according to the data collection sampling scheme and the preferences of the users, however, all $\overline{X}$ and R process control charts will be similar.

$\overline{X}$ and R charts require that data are divided into subgroups. The data within each subgroup are collected closely enough in time to maintain a low probability that within the subgroup there is a change in the process mean or variation. Often data collection time between subgroups is lengthened to increase the probability that changes in the process mean or variation will occur between subgroups.

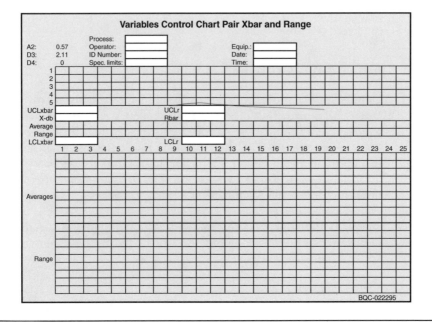

Figure 10.1 Manual data collection form.

We have used subgroup sizes from two to 20 observations. The example presented in this chapter uses a subgroup of five because five is the most commonly used (manual) subgroup size; however, subgroup size is irrelevant when using a worksheet program. A worksheet program can use a variety of subgroup sizes with ease.

In order to identify when a change has occurred in a process, the QC professional must establish the parameters of the process by selecting a base period. Often, the first 25 subgroups of data collected are used as the base period. Statistical process control analyses focus on identifying how recent measurements differ from the limits calculated using the base period measurements.

Base period data should be as free from external effects as possible. The base period is often a sample of convenience that includes the first 20 to 40 subgroups collected; however, the number of subgroups depends on the data collection costs and the costs of missing a change. For example, if the cost of missing a change is life or death and data collection costs are low, then sampling rates of one subgroup every ten seconds or faster can be justified. Fast collection rates often lead to autocorrelated data that require special control chart procedures that are beyond the scope of this book. A usual situation is to collect a subgroup of five observations once per hour, or if inspection costs are high, a subgroup of five observations once per day. We often work with data that are collected once per week or once per month, however, for data rates this slow we use individual observation charts for central tendency and a moving range chart for variation. In some situations, we work with data that are collected once or twice per year using custom design cumulative control charts.

Often, the base period data are based on measurements that are readily available or easy to collect rather than on systematic data collection procedures. In addition to comparing current data to a prior base period, current data may be compared to other similar processes or data from a previous cycle such as last year's data.

The steps required to create X̄ and range charts are:

1. Identify the appropriate measures by identifying the purpose of the measurements.

2. Specify the subgroup size n.

3. Select a base period.

4. Collect and analyze data (from the base period) to establish the parameters that define base conditions. This analysis includes identifying and eliminating external causes for variation in the base period data.

5. Collect additional data, looking for indicators of change, taking action when change occurs, or making changes in the process before changes are observed and studying subsequent data to determine if the action effectively improved the process.

$\overline{X}$ and Range Chart Formulas

The mathematical formulas for process control calculations look complex, but are simple when stated in computer spreadsheet terms (Excel), as listed in Table 10.1. In these instructions and formulas, the word *range* applies to two specific concepts with different meanings—a *range of cells* (worksheet *range*) and a *range of values* (statistical **range**). We format the spreadsheet *range* in italic and the statistical **range** in bold for clarification.

The *range* of cells is a block of cells that is defined by the cell in the upper left position and the cell in the lower right position. The statistical **range** is the difference between the highest and lowest values in a subgroup or in a sample. This **range** is a measure of variation.

The values of A_2, D_3, and D_4 are a function of the subgroup size. In general, as the subgroup size gets larger, the values of A_2 will be smaller and the values of D_3 and D_4 will be larger. A table of values for these variables is found in the appendix.

The process charts' control limits divide the subgroup statistics into three groups:

1. Subgroup averages or **ranges** that are higher than (above) the upper control limit

2. Subgroup averages or **ranges** that are lower than (below) the lower control limit

3. Subgroup averages or **ranges** that are within the control limits

---

range (cell):   A cell *range* is defined by a cell in the upper left position and a cell in the lower right position. All the cells between are in the cell *range*.

range (statistical):   The difference between the largest and smallest values in a data set; a measure of variation.

$\overline{X}$**:**   The subgroup average; a measure of central tendency.

$\overline{\overline{X}}$**:**   The average of subgroup averages.

$\overline{R}$**:**   The average of the subgroup **ranges**, a measure of dispersion.

UCL$_{\overline{x}}$:   Upper control limit $\overline{X}$.

LCL$_{\overline{x}}$:   Lower control limit $\overline{X}$.

UCL$_r$:   Upper control limit **range**.

LCL$_r$:   Lower control limit **range**.

Usually a manual data collection form for control chart data suggests the appropriate layout for the Excel worksheet. Figure 10.1 illustrates a manual data collection form. As illustrated in Figure 10.2, Excel includes many desktop publishing capabilities that allow you to design an Excel worksheet to match the manual form. Minor changes were made in the worksheet in Figure 10.2 to make graphing easier. For large data sets (that

Table 10.1   Formulas.

	Mathematical	Computer
1. Calculate subgroup average	$\overline{x} = \Sigma x_i / n$	=average(cell-range)
2. Calculate subgroup **range**	$r = \max(n) - \min(n)$	=max(cell-range)-min(cell-range)
3. Calculate average of averages	$\overline{\overline{X}} = \Sigma \overline{x} / k$	=average(cell-range)
4. Calculate average of **ranges**	$\overline{R} = \Sigma r / k$	=average(cell-range)
5. Calculate control limits for average control chart	$UCL_{\overline{x}} = \overline{\overline{X}} + A_2 * \overline{R}$ $LCL_{\overline{x}} = \overline{\overline{X}} - A_2 * \overline{R}$	
6. Calculate the control limits for the range control chart	$UCL_r = D_4 * \overline{R}$ $LCL_r = D_3 * \overline{R}$	

Figure 10.2   Excel worksheet.

do not fit on a page) you may find it easier to create your worksheet vertically, but if the data set is small (fits on a page), a horizontal layout is often used. The horizontal Excel worksheet layout is illustrated in Figure 10.2.

Because subgroups of five are common in industry, the manual data collection form uses five observations per subgroup. The data within each subgroup are collected at approximately the same time. Many quality control professionals consider it good practice to skip some observations between subgroups. With the exception of autocorrelated data (*autocorrelated* data occurs when an observation is a function of the prior observation, as well as random change), collect the observations within a subgroup as closely as possible. You may or may not skip data between subgroups depending on the nature of the decision-making process and the cost of data collection.

Almost all tasks in Excel can be accomplished in a variety of ways. Explaining all possible options is beyond the limitations of this text and would likely result in total confusion. There is no one correct way to use Excel to create a worksheet; the method presented in this text is simply one way.

Entering Worksheet Text

In earlier chapters you learned that an Excel worksheet cell is usually labeled by its column–row position. Often we place the name of our worksheet in cell A1 to make it easy to find a worksheet computer file when looking at a hard copy. We typed *xbar-2.xls* (and pressed Enter) in cell A1.

Excel has the capability of using row–column cell location procedures. For advanced mathematical tasks the row–column location method is useful. We do not use the row–column location method in this book.

The upper left position of our SPC spreadsheet starts in cell B6 because of the formatting required in this exercise. Since text is easy to enter and move, we recommend you start by entering text. To enter text in a particular cell, place the mouse pointer within the cell and press (click) the left mouse button. The border around the cell will be highlighted. Type the text and press the Enter key. Table 10.2 contains a list of the cells and the text you should type into each cell.

If you make an error in a cell, make that cell the active cell and press function key F2 (function keys are found on the top of most computer keyboards) to go into the Edit mode. Left-click on Ｖiew and Ｚoom to change the screen magnification. When laying out our worksheet, we like to use the 75 percent or 50 percent view; when working with formulas we like to use the 100 percent magnification; when giving a lecture we use the 200 percent magnification so the individuals in the back of the room can see what we are doing.

Numbering Rows and Columns

The next step is to enter the row and column labels that identify the subgroups and the observations within each subgroup. Use the following Excel commands to number the rows and columns.

Table 10.2　Worksheet text.

Cell	Text	Notes
B6	A2	Name of a factor needed to create X-bar and range process control charts
B7	D4	Name of a factor needed to create X-bar and range process control charts
B8	D3	Name of a factor needed to create X-bar and range process control charts
B9	Xdbar:	Identification for the average of the averages
B10	Rbar:	Identification for the average of the standard deviation
F7	Process:	Title
F8	Operator:	Title
F9	ID Number:	Title
F10	Spec. limits:	Title
M6	Variables Control chart pair X-bar and range	Title
P8	Equipment:	Title
P9	Date:	Title
P10	Time:	Title
B17	UCLxbar	Title—upper control limit X-bar calculations
B18	Average	Title—subgroup average; we often use the X-bar label
B19	Xbarbar	Title—average of the averages
B20	LCLxbar	Title—lower control limit X-bar calculations
B21	UCLr	Title—upper control limit of the range
B22	Range	Title—subgroup range
B23	Rbar	Title—average of the subgroup ranges
B24	LCLr	Title—lower control limit of the range
B30	Averages	Label for the X-bar control chart
B38	Range	Label for the range control chart

To number the columns:

1. Point to and click on cell D11.

2. Type *1* and press Enter.

3. Point to and click on cell E11.

4. Type *=1+*

5. Point to and click on cell D11 and press Enter (the number 2 should appear in cell E11).

6. Point to and click on cell E11.

7. Point to and click on the Edit menu selection.

8. Point to and click on Copy (cell E11 will be identified by a flashing dashed box).

9. Point to cell F11 and hold down the left mouse key as you drag the pointer across the cells in row 11 until you have highlighted all the cells from F11 to AB11.

10. With the cells in *range* F11:AB11 highlighted, release the mouse button and press Enter.

These last steps should copy the formula from E11 to all the cells in the range. The numbers from 1 through 25 should appear in row 11.

To number the rows:

1. Point to and click on cell C12.

2. Type *1* and press Enter.

3. Cell C13 is highlighted, so type *=1+*

4. Point to and click on cell C12 and press Enter (the number 2 should appear in cell C13).

5. Point to and click on cell C13.

6. Point to and click on the Edit menu selection.

7. Point to and click on Copy (Cell C13 will be identified by a flashing dashed box).

8. Point to cell C14 and hold down the left mouse key as you drag the pointer across the *range* C14 through C16.

9. Release the left mouse key and press Enter (the formula from cell C13 should be copied into the *range* C14:C16).

Entering Observation Data

The worksheet in this example has room for 25 subgroups with five observations in each subgroup. Each column contains the observations from one subgroup. You may enter your own data or follow these instructions to enter random numbers into the chart.

Generating Random Numbers for Observations

This random number formula was explained in chapter 8.

1. Point to and click on cell D2.

2. Type *Average:* and press Enter (the label Average: will appear in cell D2 and cell D3 will be highlighted).

3. Type *Std dev:* and press Enter (the label Std dev: will appear in cell D3 and cell D4 will be highlighted).

4. Point to and click on cell G2.

5. Type *100* and press Enter (the number 100 will appear in cell G2 and cell G3 will be highlighted).

6. Type *10* and press Enter (the number 10 will appear in cell G3 and cell G4 will be highlighted). The values 100 and 10 will be used to generate random numbers for the subgroup data.

7. Point to and click on cell D12.

8. Type *=(rand()+rand()+rand()+rand()+rand()+rand()+rand()+rand() +rand()+rand()+rand()+rand()–6)*$G$3+$G$2* and press Enter. (Rand() is typed 12 times. A number between 70 and 130 will appear in cell D12 more than 99 percent of the time). Note that the dollar signs ($) mean that cells G3 and G2 will be used in all formulas after a copy. Cells identified with dollar signs use absolute addresses, while cells identified without dollar signs use relative addresses.

9. Point and click on cell D12.

10. Point to and click on <u>E</u>dit menu selection.

11. Point to and click on <u>C</u>opy (the cell is highlighted with a dashed line).

12. Point to and press the left mouse button as you drag the mouse to highlight the cells in the *range* from D12 through AB16.

13. Release the mouse button and press Enter (random numbers should appear in each cell).

The function RAND() produces a number between 000 and .999 with an average value of 0.5. Based on this average value of 0.5, the sum of 12 random numbers is 6. Subtracting 6 from the sum centers the distribution mean at zero, with a standard deviation of one. Multiplying by 10 (the value in G3) and adding 100 is a reverse Z (normal distribution) transformation. The result is a distribution with a mean of approximately 100 and a standard deviation of 10. The regular Z transformation allows us to use a normal distribution table based on the standard normal distribution (mean zero and standard deviation one). The reverse Z transformation allows us to use a normal random number generator with a mean of zero and standard deviation of one to generate any normal distribution.

Entering Factors

Control limit calculations require a selection of factors depending on the combination of charts used. The $\overline{X}$ and range chart combination requires three factors: A2, D3, and D4. An explanation of these factors is found in the appendix.

1. Point to and click on cell D6.

2. Type *0.58* and press Enter (the value 0.58 will appear in cell D6 and cell D7 will be highlighted).

3. Type *2.11* in cell D7 and press Enter (the value 2.11 will appear in cell D7 and cell D8 will be highlighted).

4. Type *0* and press Enter (the value 0 will appear in cell D8).

Entering Formulas

The mathematical formulas to calculate the subgroup averages, ranges, and control limits are entered into the cells directly below each subgroup. Each formula will be entered for the first subgroup and then the formulas will be copied to the other subgroups.

The dollar signs are used to identify an absolute address rather than a relative address. An absolute address does not change when a formula is copied. A relative address changes as a formula is copied. Excel is not case sensitive—you may type the formulas using lower- or uppercase letters. Excel will change the letter to uppercase when the formula is accepted.

1. Point to and click on cell D9.

2. Type *=average(D12:AB16)* and press Enter (the value in cell D9 is the average of all the data and the average of the subgroup averages).

3. Point and click on cell D10.

4. Type *=average(D22:AB22)* and press Enter. Because there are no values in the worksheet range specified, you will see the error message #DIV/0!, meaning division by zero. This error will disappear when data are entered into the range.

5. Point and click on cell D17.

6. Type *=$D$9+$D$6*$D$10* and press Enter (this is the formula that calculates the upper control limit for the average control chart). You will again see the error message #DIV/0! because cell D10 has the error and D10 is used in the formula.

7. Cell D18 is highlighted.

8. Type *=average(D12:D16)* and press Enter (this formula calculates the average for the observations found in the range of cells from D12 through D16).

9. Cell D19 is highlighted.

10. Type *+$D$9* and press Enter (this formula writes the average of all subgroups to cell D19).

11. Cell D20 is highlighted.

12. Type *=$D$9-$D$6*$D$10* and press Enter (this formula calculates the lower control limit for the average range chart). Again we see the #DIV/0! error message.

13. Cell D21 is highlighted.

14. Type *=$D$7*$D$10* and press Enter (this formula calculates the upper control limit for the range process control chart). Again we see the #DIV/0! error message.

15. Cell D22 is highlighted.

16. Type *=max(D12:D16)–min(D12:D16)* and press Enter (this formula calculates the range of the first subgroup. When this formula is copied to other columns, Excel will adjust the letters to match the column). All the #DIV/0! error messages will disappear when this value is entered.

17. Cell D23 is highlighted.

18. Type *=$D$10* and press Enter (this formula enters the value of the average range of all the subgroups in cell D23).

19. Cell D24 is highlighted.

20. Type *0* and press Enter (the correct formula in D24 should be D_3*R, however because D_3 is always zero for subgroups of six or less, you can enter zero rather than the formula).

To copy the formulas to the appropriate cells, follow these instructions:

1. Point to cell D17 and hold the left mouse button while you drag the pointer to highlight the *range* D17:D24.

2. Release the mouse button.

3. Point to and click on Edit and then click on Copy.

4. Point to cell E17 and hold the left mouse button while you drag the pointer to highlight the *range* E17:AB24.

5. Release the mouse button and press Enter. (Your calculations are complete as displayed in Figure 10.3.)

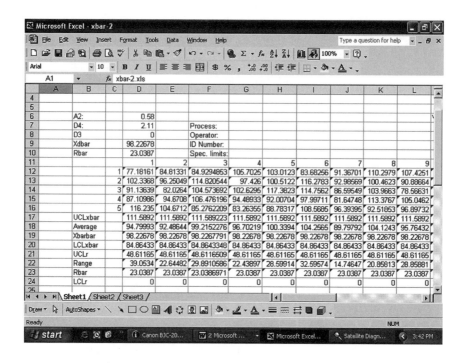

Figure 10.3 $\overline{X}$ and range control worksheet.

It is not unusual to make an error such as leaving out the dollar signs. If you do, you will get strange results, such as #DIV/0! or some other error message, or some very large or very small numbers. Do not panic when you see such errors—they are easy to correct and are simply part of the process of creating worksheets.

Graphing the $\overline{X}$ Control Chart

To create the $\overline{X}$ control chart, follow the steps below:

1. Point to cell D11 and hold down the left mouse button while you drag the pointer across row 11 to define the *range* D11:AB11 (these cells define the x-axis).

2. Release the mouse button.

3. Hold the Control key down as you point to cell D17; continue to hold the Control key down along with the left mouse button while you drag the pointer to define the *range* D17:AB20.

4. Release the Control key and the left mouse button.

Figure 10.4   Chart Wizard Step 1 of 4—Chart Type.

5. Point and left-click on the Chart Wizard icon . Your screen should look similar to the illustration in Figure 10.4.

6. Click on the XY(Scatter) selection and select the bottom left chart option (Scatter with data points connected by lines). Figure 10.5 illustrates the option. This option provides the best match to manual practice.

7. Click on <u>N</u>ext>. Figure 10.6 illustrates the results.

8. It is good practice to name all the lines on a chart. Click on the Series tab and click on *Series 1* in the <u>S</u>eries dialog area and then click in the <u>N</u>ame: edit box and type *UCLxbar*.

9. Click on *Series2*, and then click in the <u>N</u>ame: edit box and type *Xbar*.

10. Click on Series3, and then click in the <u>N</u>ame: edit box and type *Xbarbar*.

11. Click on *Series4*, and then click in the <u>N</u>ame: edit box and type *LCLxbar* (Figure 10.7 shows the Series screen).

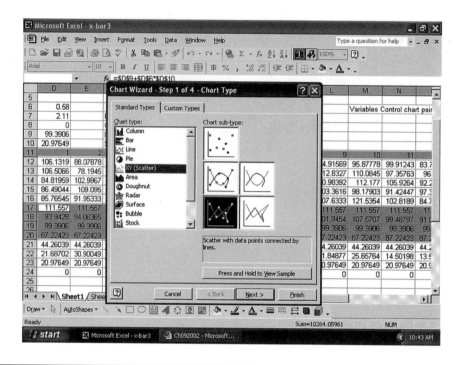

Figure 10.5   Chart Wizard Step 1 of 4—XY (Scatter Chart) Type selected.

Figure 10.6   Chart Wizard Step 2 of 4—identify Data Range.

Figure 10.7   Chart Wizard Step 2 of 4—identify Name Series.

12. Click on <u>N</u>ext >. (Excel identifies this screen as Chart Wizard Step 3 of 4—Chart Options. There are five tabs: Titles, Axes, Gridlines, Legend, and Data Labels.)

13. With the Titles menu showing, enter *Xbar Control Chart* as the Chart title, enter *Subgroup Number* as the Value (X) axis, and enter *Subgroup Average* as the Value (Y) axis. We selected to use the default setting for the other tabs so no additional work is needed.

14. Click on <u>N</u>ext >.

15. Our control chart design requires that we place the chart as an objective within sheet 1 of our worksheet. This is the default selection in Chart Wizard Step 4 of 4—Chart Location. Click on <u>F</u>inish.

Figure 10.8 illustrates the results of the graphing steps. The next step is to size and locate the graph. Sizing is not a simple exercise. For this task it is necessary to use the <u>V</u>iew and <u>Z</u>oom capability and select a variety of zoom levels. In addition:

1. Double-left-click on the numbers on the Y scale and change the Value (Y) axis scale to a minimum of 70 (all other scaling aspects were left on Auto).

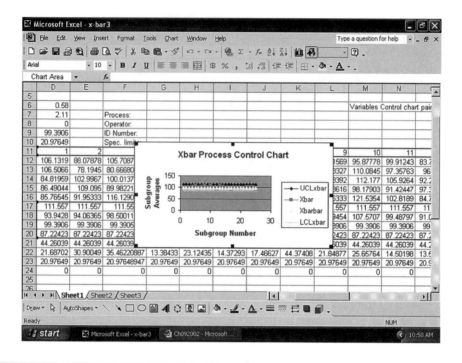

Figure 10.8   The $\overline{X}$ control chart.

2. Double-left-click on the numbers on the *x*-axis and change the Value (X) axis scale to a minimum of 1 and a maximum of 25 (all other scaling aspects are left on Auto).

3. Double-left-click on the UCLxbar line and change the <u>S</u>tyle to a dashed line and specify N<u>o</u>ne for the Marker (all other selections remain on Automatic).

4. Double-left-click on the Xbarbar line and change the <u>W</u>eight to double width, the <u>C</u>olor to black, and the Marker to N<u>o</u>ne.

5. Double-left-click on the LCLxbar line and change the <u>S</u>tyle to match the UCLxbar line and specify N<u>o</u>ne for the Marker (all other selections remain on Automatic).

6. Enlarge the chart by pointing to the square in any corner of the chart and dragging the square out.

It takes a number of cycles to align and arrange chart elements to your satisfaction. If you have trouble formatting the special features of the graph, refer to the instructions in chapter 4 on "Formatting Charts and Graphs." Figure 10.9 illustrates the result.

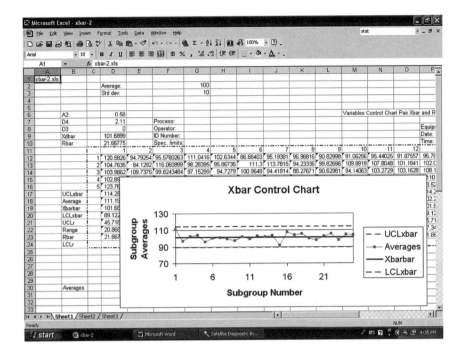

Figure 10.9   Results of chart formatting.

Graphing the Range Control Chart

The range chart is similar to the $\overline{X}$ chart. The graphing *ranges* are:

D11:AB11 for the *x*-axis

D21:AB24 for the control limits

Position the chart within the *range* D34:AB41. Creation of the range chart is left as an exercise. The line color and type are adjusted similarly to those in the X control chart except for the lower control limit. Common practice is to make the lower control limit a solid line when its value is zero. Figure 10.10 illustrates the results.

Formatting Text

The text in the individual cells, groups of cells, rows, or columns may be changed to various fonts, styles, and sizes. To format text in a cell, place the cell pointer at the cell by pointing the mouse and clicking. Cell M6 contains the text *Variables Control chart pair $\overline{X}$ and range*. Move the cell pointer to cell M6 and click. Click on Format and then click once on Cells. Figure 10.11 illustrates the Format Cells dialog box with six tab options. The tabs are Number, Alignment, Font, Border, Patterns, and Protection. Point to and click on Font.

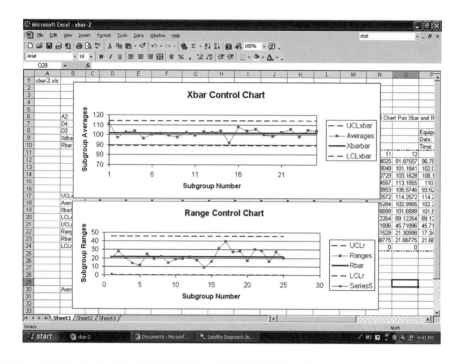

Figure 10.10 $\overline{X}$ and range control charts.

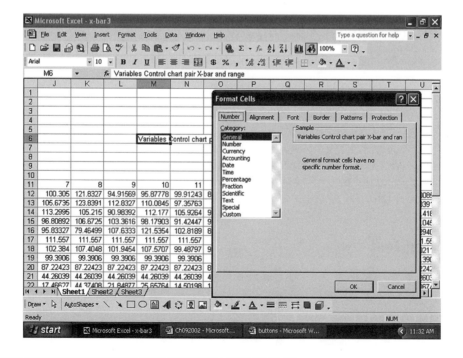

Figure 10.11 Format Cells dialog box.

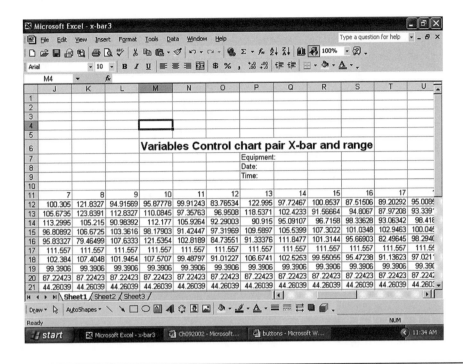

Figure 10.12 Formatted text.

Figure 10.12 illustrates the screen after the Font tab was clicked, *Bold* was selected for Font Style, and 16 was selected for *Size*. A click on OK completes the text format.

Another useful formatting procedure allows you to place a border around any given *range* of cells. We recommend you experiment with this capability on a new spreadsheet before adding borders to an existing worksheet. The steps for adding a border are:

1. Define a *range* (C11:AB24) by holding down the left mouse key and dragging it from the cell in the upper left position to the cell in the lower right position.

2. Click on Format.

3. Click on Cells. . .

4. Click on the tab marked Border.

5. Select the Border preset Outline.

6. Click on the Style of line preferred.

7. Click on each of the four border buttons: top, bottom, left, and right.

8. Click on OK.

The results are shown in Figure 10.13.

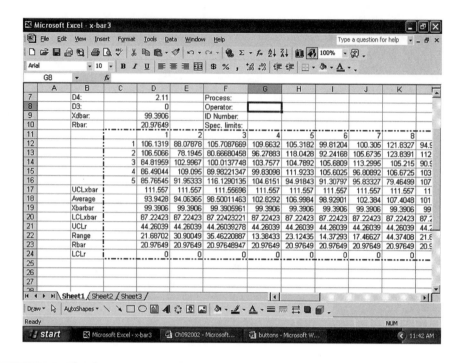

Figure 10.13   Cells with a border.

Tools and Spelling

Worksheet spelling may be checked by clicking on Tools and then clicking on Spelling. Excel checks the spelling of each word against its dictionary. When a word is found in the worksheet that does not match a word in the dictionary, Excel displays the word with a list of suggested words that may be the correct replacement for the misspelled word. Words such as X-bar will be highlighted as misspelled because these labels are not words contained in the dictionary.

Template

Template xbar-2.xls is the basic worksheet that contains the $\overline{X}$ and range control charts developed in this chapter. This chart is limited to 25 subgroups, each with five observations; however, the worksheet can be expanded easily.

Expanding the $\overline{X}$ and Range Control Charts

Changes in averages and standard deviations of randomly generated data allow one to study how changes in a process affect control charts. The objective is to see how control charts change when modifications are made in the process average or in the process variation. The procedure is outlined in the four steps below and detailed in the following section.

1. Add a second worksheet (sheet 2) behind the first worksheet for 25 additional subgroups.

2. Graph data from worksheet 2 against the process limits (base conditions) established using the subgroups one through 25.

3. Create the $\overline{X}$ and R control charts of all the subgroups one through 50 using a third worksheet behind the first and second worksheets.

4. Change the random number generation base on worksheet 2 by changing the values to reflect a different average or standard deviation.

Copying Sheet 1 to Sheet 2

To copy the worksheet from sheet 1 to sheet 2, follow these steps. (Note: change from sheet 1 to sheet 2 by clicking on the tab near the bottom of the screen.)

1. On sheet 1 define the *range* B2:AB16 by pointing to cell B2 and holding the left mouse button down as you drag the pointer through cell AB16.

2. Release the mouse button.

3. Click on Edit.

4. Click on Copy (a dashed line will blink around the selected range).

5. Click on the sheet 2 tab near the bottom of the screen.

6. Point to and click on cell B2.

7. Click on Edit.

8. Click on Paste (the cells from sheet 1 are duplicated onto sheet 2).

Copy the labels for rows 17 through 24 with these steps:

1. On sheet 1 define the *range* B17:B24.

2. Click on Edit.

3. Click on Copy.

4. Click on the sheet 2 tab near the bottom of the screen.

5. Point to and click on cell B17.

6. Click on <u>E</u>dit.

7. Click on <u>P</u>aste (the labels are copied into the cells).

You may change the view or change the size of the columns to see more of the worksheet at one time. To change the column width, the steps are:

1. Point to cell A1 and hold the left button to define the *range* A1:AB1.

2. Release the mouse button.

3. Click on F<u>o</u>rmat.

4. Click on <u>C</u>olumn.

5. Click on <u>W</u>idth.

6. Type 4 for <u>C</u>olumn width.

7. Click on OK.

Renumber the subgroups in sheet 2 by clicking on D11, typing *26,* and pressing Enter. The subgroups are numbered from 26 through 50.

Recording Base Period Control Chart Parameters

The fundamental idea behind control charts is to collect data for a base period and then compare later observations with the base period. The base period data are recorded in sheet 1. The control chart parameters for the base period must be transferred from sheet 1 to sheet 2 to establish the control limits. The following parameters must be copied to sheet 2:

- Upper and lower control limits for the average process chart (UCLxbar and LCLxbar, rows 17 and 20)

- Average of the averages of all subgroups ($\overline{\overline{X}}$) in sheet 1 (xbarbar in row 19)

- Upper and lower control limits for the range control chart (UCLr and LCLr, rows 21 and 24)

- Average range of all the subgroups in sheet 1 (Rbar, row 23).

The subgroup averages (row 18) and the subgroup ranges (row 22) for sheet 2 will not be transferred from sheet 1, but will be calculated from the random numbers generated in sheet 2.

Follow these steps below to record the control chart parameters in sheet 2:

1. In sheet 2 point to and click on cell D17.

2. Type a plus sign (+) in cell D17.

3. Click on the Sheet 1 tab.

4. In sheet 1 point to and click on cell D17.

5. Press Enter.

6. The screen should return to sheet 2.

7. Point to and click on cell D17.

8. Click on Edit.

9. Click on Copy (a dashed line will blink around cell D17).

10. Point to cell D19; hold the left mouse button and drag to highlight the *range* D19:D21.

11. Release the mouse button.

12. Press Enter (the values from worksheet 1 will be placed in these cells).

13. Point to and click on cell D21.

14. Click on Edit.

15. Click on Copy.

16. Point to cell D23; hold the left mouse button and drag to highlight the *range* D23:D24.

17. Release the mouse button and press Enter.

Copying Parameter Values into Columns

1. Click on cell E17 on sheet 2.

2. Type a plus sign (+).

3. Click on cell D17 in sheet 2 and press Enter.

4. Point to cell E17.

5. Click on Edit and Copy.

6. Point to cell F17; hold the left mouse button and drag to highlight the *range* F17:AB17.

7. Release the mouse button and press Enter.

8. Click on cell E17.

9. Click on Edit and Copy.

10. Point to cell E19; hold the left mouse button and drag to highlight the *range* E19:AB21.

11. Release the mouse button and press Enter.

12. Click on cell E17.

13. Click on Edit and Copy.

14. Point to cell E23; hold the left mouse button and drag to highlight the *range* E23:AB24.

15. Release the mouse button and press Enter.

Calculating the Subgroup Averages and Ranges

To calculate the averages and ranges for the subgroups in sheet 2, enter and copy the following formulas:

1. In cell D18 type =*average(D12:D16)*

2. Copy this formula into the *range* E18:AB18.

3. In cell D22 type =*max(D12:D16)-min(D12:D16)*

4. Copy this formula into the *range* D18:AB22.

Editing the Control Graphs

Follow the steps used in sheet 1 to create the graphs for sheet 2. The *ranges* for graphing the $\overline{X}$ control chart are D11:AB11 and D17:AB20. The *ranges* for graphing the range control chart are D11:AB11 and D21:AB24.

Creating a Comparison Graph

To create one chart that shows the averages and ranges for all 50 sub-groups, a third sheet is added to the worksheet. The third sheet will use only the results in rows 17 through 24 from sheets 1 and 2.

Creating Worksheet 3

Since this spreadsheet is quite wide, adjusting the view and reducing the column width assists the user.

Numbering the Columns

1. Click on sheet 3.

2. Define the *range* by pointing to the top of columns A through BD and holding down the left mouse key as you drag the pointer through column BD.

3. Release the mouse key.

4. Click on Format.

5. Click on Column.

6. Click on Width and type 3 to increase the range of columns displayed and click on OK.

7. Point to cell D11 and click.

8. Type a plus sign (+).

9. Click on sheet 1.

10. Point to and click on cell D11.

11. Press Enter.

12. The screen returns to sheet 3.

13. Point to and click on cell D11 in sheet 3.

14. Click on Edit and Copy.

15. Point to cell E11 and hold the left mouse button as you drag the pointer to highlight the *range* E11:AB11.

16. Press Enter (the numbers 1 through 25 should appear in the columns from D through AB).

17. To add the numbers 26 through 50, click on cell AC11 and type =1+

18. Click on cell AB11 and press Enter.

19. Click on cell AC11.

20. Click on Edit and Copy.

21. Click on cell AD11 and hold the left mouse button as you drag the pointer to highlight the *range* AD11:BA11, then press Enter.

The columns in row 11 should be numbered from one to 50 beginning in column D.

Entering the Rows

Because the third worksheet will not contain the values in rows 12 through 16, the values from rows 17 through 24 will be copied to rows 12 through 19 in sheet 3.

1. Point to and click on cell B12 in sheet 3.

2. Type a plus sign (+).

3. Click on the sheet 1 tab.

4. Point to and click on cell B17 in sheet 1.

5. Press Enter.

6. The screen returns to sheet 3; the label UCLxbar should be in cell B12 on sheet 3.

7. Point to and click on cell B12.

8. Click on Edit and Copy.

9. Point to cell B13 and hold down the left mouse button as you drag the pointer down the column through B19 to highlight the *range* B13:B19.

10. Release the mouse button.

11. Press Enter (all the row labels should appear).

Entering Control Parameters from Sheet 1

Begin by copying the data from sheet 1:

1. On sheet 3 point to and click on cell D12.

2. Type a plus sign (+).

3. Click on the sheet 1 tab.

4. Point to and click on cell D17 in sheet 1 and press Enter. If you see the characters ##, the column is not wide enough to display the number. The column width can be adjusted.

5. Point to cell D12.

6. Click on Edit and Copy.

7. Click on cell D12 and then drag the mouse to define the *range* D12:AB19.

8. Release the mouse and press Enter.

Entering Control Parameters from Sheet 2

The control parameters from sheet 2 must be copied to the *range* AC12:BA19.

1. In sheet 3 click on cell AC12.

2. Type a plus sign (+).

3. Click on the sheet 2 tab.

4. Click on cell D17 and press Enter.

5. In sheet 3 click on cell AD12.

6. Type a plus sign (+).

7. Click on cell AC12 in sheet 3 and press ENTER.

8. Copy the contents of AD12 into the *range* AE12:BA12.

Repeat the same sequence of steps using the relative cells to enter the parameters from sheet 2 into sheet 3 for rows 14, 15, 16, 18, and 19, skipping row 13, which contains the sample averages, and row 17, which contains the sample **ranges**. The contents of these rows will be entered next. Table 10.3 shows which rows in sheet 3 correspond to rows in sheets 2 and 3.

To enter the averages and **ranges** for subgroups 26 through 50, follow these steps:

1. Click on cell AC13 and type a plus sign (+).

2. Click on the sheet 2 tab.

3. Click on D18 in sheet 2 and press Enter.

4. Click on AC13.

5. Click on Edit and Copy.

6. Hold the left mouse button down and drag to define the *range* AD13:BA13.

7. Press Enter.

8. Click on cell AC17 and type a plus sign (+).

9. Click on the sheet 2 tab.

10. Click on D22 in sheet 2 and press Enter.

11. Click on AC17.

12. Click on <u>E</u>dit and <u>C</u>opy.

13. Hold the left mouse button down and drag to define the *range* AD17:BA17.

14. Press Enter.

Each of the subgroup averages and ranges for subgroups 26 through 50 from sheet 2 are now copied to sheet 3.

Graphing the $\overline{X}$ and Range Control Charts for Worksheet 3

The procedures for creating the $\overline{X}$ and Range process charts are the same as the procedures described in the sections Graphing the $\overline{X}$ Control Charts and Graphing the Range Control Charts. The only difference is the identification of the *ranges* in sheet 3.

The graphing *ranges* for the $\overline{X}$ process chart are:

D11:BA11 for the *x*-axis

D12:BA15 for the control limits and subgroup averages.

Locate the graph in the *range* D20:BA26. The graphing *ranges* for the range process chart are:

D11:BA11 for the *x*-axis

D16:BA19 for the control limits and subgroup ranges

Table 10.3 Corresponding rows in sheets 1, 2 and 3.

Parameter	Sheets 1 and 2 Rows	Sheet 3 Rows
UCLxbar	17	12
Average	18	13
Xbarbar	19	14
LCLxbar	20	15
UCLr	21	16
Range	22	17
Rbar	23	18
LCLr	24	19

Locate the graph in the *range* D27:BA32. Figure 10.14 illustrates the results. Note: from now on in this chapter we will use the instruction Copy to mean left click, Edit, Copy, and then press Enter when the To range has been identified. We will also use these shortcut instructions:

Shortcut Instruction	Meaning
Copy by dragging	Point to the box on the bottom right-hand corner of the cell, press the left mouse button, and drag the contents of the original cell to adjacent cells
Copy cell contents	Activate the cell by pointing and clicking the left mouse button; click on the Copy icon; click on the target cell or highlight the target cells, and press Enter

On sheet 2 in cell G2 is the average for the second 25 subgroups and in cell G3 is the standard deviation for the second 25 subgroups. You may experiment with the values in these cells to see what effect changing these values has on the control charts. Each time you change the numbers, press F9, and all the subgroup values are recalculated. We discuss the significance of these changes in the remaining sections in this chapter.

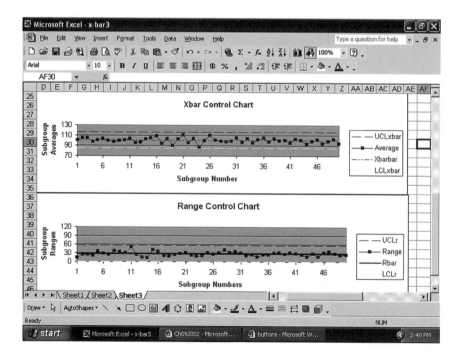

Figure 10.14   Results.

Using $\overline{X}$ and Range Control Charts

The new control chart template provides a tool to examine control chart behavior as a function of changes in the process average and process **range** (variation). We know that individually and/or together the average and variation of a distribution can cycle, jump, shift, trend, and go in and out of autocorrelation. Numbers alone do not always lead to the correct decision. There are two types of errors that may be made when analyzing numbers; they are:

Type I error: numbers indicate a change when there is none and time and money are wasted looking for the change

Type II error: numbers do not indicate a change when a change has occurred and an opportunity to improve the process is missed

There is a balance between type I and type II errors. All actions to reduce the type I error result in an increase in type II errors. In order to reasonably balance the cost of searching for the cause of an error when none exists and failure to search for a cause that is present, Shewhart recommended the use of three sigma limits above and below the mean.[1] Another critical mistake occurs when one measures the wrong parameter. Usually, the selection of a parameter as a measure of some quality characteristic is a matter of using the best professional judgment available.

The procedure for using the worksheet to study the two types of errors is:

1. Use sheet 1 for the base period; that is, to define the standard for average ($\overline{X}$) and **range** (variation) to define the upper and lower limits.

2. Introduce a shift in the average and/or standard deviation in sheet 2.

3. Examine the results in sheet 3.

Sheet 2 could be rewritten to add cycles, jumps, trends, and changes in autocorrelation. Because an examination of shifting the average and variation results in over nine conditions (Table 10.4) when the order of magnitude of the change is considered, this chapter presents only two cases:

1. No change in variation and a two-sigma increase in the mean.

2. No change in the average and a one-sigma increase in the variation.

Consideration of different combinations of changes at different levels, cycles, jumps, trends, and autocorrelation is left for future exercises.

No Change in Variation, Two-Sigma Increase in the Mean

In sheet 1, the average was set at 100 and the standard deviation was set at 10. In sheet 2, one can change the average of the subgroups by two sigma by resetting the average to 120 and keeping the standard deviation

1. Shewart, Walter A. *Statistical Methods from the Viewpoint of Quality Control.* (W. Edwards Deming, Editor), Washington, D.C.: The Department of Agriculture, 1939.

Table 10.4 Nine change options.

	No Change	Up	Down
Variation	x		
Average	x		
Variation	x		
Average		x	←
Variation	x		
Average			x
Variation		x	
Average	x		←
Variation		x	
Average		x	
Variation		x	
Average			x
Variation			x
Average	x		
Variation			x
Average		x	
Variation			x
Average			x

at 10. After logging into sheet 3, press F9 several times (F9 recalculates all the random number entries) and examine the behavior of the control chart when the average is increased by two sigma for the second set of 25 subgroups. Figure 10.15 illustrates a typical result of a two-sigma shift in the mean. Most of the subgroup averages are beyond the upper control limit, but not all. A small percentage of the runs resulted in only a few subgroup averages above the upper control limit, while only an occasional run resulted in all the subgroup averages beyond the upper control limit.

No Change in the Mean, One-Sigma Increase in the Variation

The average and standard deviation values in sheet 1 remain at 100 and 10 respectively. The average in sheet 2 should be changed back to 100 and the standard deviation should be changed to 20. Figure 10.16 illustrates a typical result of the one-sigma shift in the standard deviation. The average chart shows swings both above the upper control limit and below the lower control limit, while the **range** chart shows a number of subgroup **ranges** above the upper control limit.

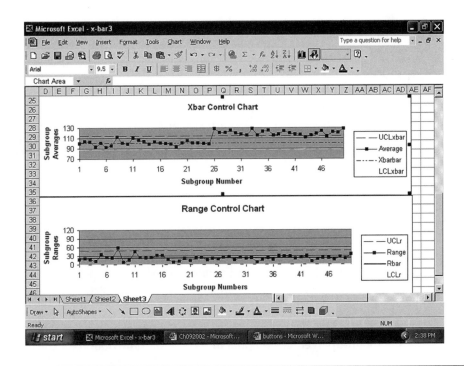

Figure 10.15   Two-sigma shift in the mean, no change in variation.

Figure 10.16   No change in the mean, one-sigma increase in the variation.

Real Life

The $\overline{X}$ and range control chart pair may be used to control all types of processes, from manufacturing processes, to infection rates in an ICU, to ecological processes. The results obtained when using control charts depend on the relationship between the *natural limits* of the process (NTL) and the *specification limits* (SL). Most authors refer to the natural limits of a process as the *upper natural tolerance limit* (UNTL) and the *lower natural tolerance limit* (LNTL). There are three possible relationships between the natural tolerance limits of a process and the specification limits:

1. Natural tolerance limits may be extremely wide relative to the specification limits.

2. Natural tolerance limits may be narrower than the specification limits.

3. Natural tolerance limits may be equal to the specification limits.

Natural tolerance limits and specification limits refer to individual pieces or observations, while *control limits* refer to the average and **range** of subgroups. If the data are normally distributed, then the standard deviation for subgroup averages is equal to the standard deviation for the individual observations divided by the square root of the subgroup size, that is:

$$\sigma_{\overline{X}} = \sigma' / \sqrt{n}$$

where

$\sigma_{\overline{X}}$ is the standard deviation of the subgroup averages

σ' is the standard deviation of the individual observations

n is the subgroup size

Figure 10.17 illustrates the relationship between distribution of subgroup averages ($\overline{X}$) and the distribution of individuals, X_i. The distribution of $\overline{X}$ is smaller than the distribution of X_is because there is only one subgroup for n (subgroup size) X_is. The extreme points on the distribution of $\overline{X}$s are not as extreme as on the distribution of X_is because the extreme points are averaged with normal data.

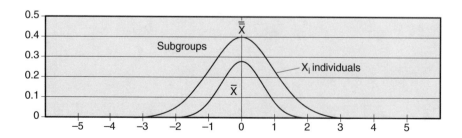

Figure 10.17 $\overline{X}$ versus X_is distribution.

An objective of Japanese management has been to reduce the amount of variation in their manufacturing processes so that the probability of a defect is extremely small; that is, to make the natural tolerance limits narrow relative to the specification limits. Figure 10.18 illustrates the conditions where the natural tolerance limits are narrow relative to the specification limits.

It is common to find wide specification limits with small natural tolerance limits in applications such as die wear, single-point tool wear, and skin temperatures, among others.

Figure 10.19 illustrates a control chart pair for the dimension of a hole produced from a punch-press operation. The hole size decreases and the amount of variation increases as the tool wears. The downward step control

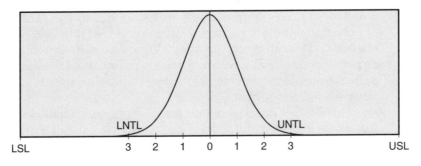

Figure 10.18 Natural tolerance limits narrow compared to specification limits (SP-NLT).

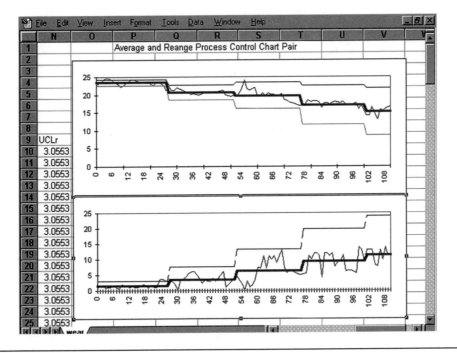

Figure 10.19 Tool wear control charts.

limits are a result of recalculating the control limits periodically. Graphed in this manner, the downward trend of the averages and the upward trend of the variation are easy to see. The trends are allowed to occur because the upper and lower specification limits are wide compared to the natural tolerance limits of the distribution. What action should be taken to reverse these trends? The answer to this question is an engineering, managerial, or medical issue, not a statistical issue. Numbers can only illustrate how the process is behaving. Effective control of the process requires knowledge and an understanding of the process that extends beyond the numbers.

Summary

$\bar{X}$ and range process control charts are tools for controlling almost any type of process. Control charts start with data collected during a base period to establish an overall mean and **range**. The calculations are simple and may be performed manually, with a calculator, or by using a worksheet program such as Excel. Excel provides formatting control that greatly exceeds many other worksheet programs.

A worksheet program allows the user to create a model or a template that can be reused many times. This chapter presented the procedures for creating a control chart template for $\bar{X}$ and range control charts. After the model was created it was expanded to analyze potential changes in the average and variation of a process. Two types of changes were analyzed:

1. No change in variation, two-sigma increase in the mean

2. No change in the mean, one-sigma increase in the variation

The real-life example demonstrates how process control charts can help quality control professionals analyze a process's behavior. Using these charts, one is able to see how the dimension of a quality characteristic changes during the life of a tool.

Exercises

10.1   Edit the example worksheet *xbar-2.xls* such that the control chart runs down the page rather than across the page.

10.2   Experiment with the mean and standard deviation used to simulate the data in *xbar-2.xls*. For the first 25 observations, use a mean of 100 and standard deviation of 10, then in the next 25 observations change the average to 105, 110, 115, 120, 125, 130, and 135. At each new value of the mean, run the system 10 times, count the number of subgroups that occur after the change, and before there is an outlier (individually on the $\bar{X}$ and range charts) at each level. Record the results; use Excel to graph the value of the *new* mean versus the average number of subgroups before an outlier occurs on each control chart separately.

10.3 Replicate problem 10.2, except this time hold the average constant at 100 and vary the standard deviation from: 10, 15, 20, 25, 30, 35, and 40. Replicate the experiment 10 times at each level and calculate the average number of subgroups before an outlier occurs on the $\overline{X}$ and the range charts. Graph the new standard deviation versus the average number of subgroups before an outlier occurs on each control chart separately.

10.4 Given the data in the following table, in Excel create an $\overline{X}$ and range control chart pair. Identify outliers, if any.

Subgroup	Data				
1	66	57	56	52	60
2	43	44	64	56	56
3	54	61	57	64	48
4	56	65	70	44	54
5	54	50	57	58	68
6	56	57	47	54	58
7	52	60	61	54	44
8	54	64	58	59	52
9	62	56	73	47	51
10	61	53	58	59	44
11	61	56	67	62	65
12	62	63	69	51	50
13	43	57	58	61	58
14	53	62	54	66	58
15	66	70	61	63	49
16	44	46	57	42	50
17	60	57	67	69	65
18	21	50	54	77	53
19	54	44	49	64	53
20	45	55	48	53	50
21	57	54	52	54	61
22	57	59	56	50	71
23	21	23	33	46	49
24	51	61	57	56	52
25	59	48	44	49	52

10.5   In a textbook on statistical process control, find a sample problem illustrating $\overline{X}$ and range charts. Enter that text's data into an Excel worksheet and compare the charts from that text with your result.[2]

---

2. Possible texts include: Grant, Eugene L. *Statistical Quality Control.* New York: McGraw-Hill, 1988; or Wheeler, Donald J. *Advanced Topics in Statistical Process Control, the Power of Shewhart's Charts.* Knoxville, TN:SPC Press, 1995. For a list of texts refer to the reference section.

11

$\overline{X}$ and Sigma Control Charts

KEY TERMS

$LCL_{\bar{s}}$	Type II error
$LCL_{\bar{X}}$	$UCL_{\bar{s}}$
Range	$UCL_{\bar{X}}$
$\overline{S}$	Variable data
Sigma	$\overline{X}$
Standard deviation	$\overline{X}$ and sigma control charts
Type I error	$\overline{\overline{X}}$

OUTLINE

Prior Knowledge

From previous chapters, you should know how to open and save worksheets, and copy the contents of a *range* of cells into other cells.

Why Use $\overline{X}$ and Sigma Control Charts?

A key to controlling a process is the ability to measure or count a variable that is relevant to process performance. *Variable data* represent quality characteristics that are measured with devices such as rulers, scales, or micrometers; they are best studied using a matched pair of control charts—one for central tendency (averages) and the other for variation (dispersion). Chapter 9 presented the use of $\overline{X}$ and range charts to analyze and control processes. $\overline{X}$ and sigma (standard deviation) charts are similar to $\overline{X}$ and range charts. Both sets of charts are used with the same type of data, but each pair provides a different view of the data. The $\overline{X}$ chart indicates changes in the process average (central tendency) compared to the average during the base period. Generally, the $\overline{X}$ control chart is the control chart of choice for central tendency; however, in rare applications, one could also measure central tendency using the mode or the median. The *sigma chart* indicates changes in process variation by showing how the variation in the subgroups compares to the variation of data collected during a base period. To measure process variation, a number of alternatives are available such as range, standard deviation, absolute serial difference, and serial difference. The selection of a variation measure often depends on the needs and capabilities of the end user rather than on statistical considerations.

The **range** is calculated by subtracting the smallest value in the subgroup from the largest value, while sigma is calculated from *all* the values in the subgroup. If the data generation rate is slow such that the subgroup size is five or less, the range and sigma charts yield approximately the same results. If the data generation rate is fast, such that the subgroup size is greater than five, $\overline{X}$ and sigma control charts are preferred because all of the subgroup values are utilized; consequently, no information is lost. The range chart is often selected when the calculations must be completed manually. The arguments for using the range chart include: 1) ease of (manual) calculations; 2) historical use with satisfactory results; and 3) range charts are easier to explain and understand than sigma charts.

Sigma (standard deviation) is often referred to by the Greek symbol for sigma (σ) or by the letters *sd*, and expresses the amount of dispersion (variation) among observations in a subgroup. A large value for sigma indicates wide dispersion among the observations, and small values indicate relatively little variation among the observations.

If one selects a dispersion measure from a statistical point of view, the sigma (standard deviation) control chart is preferred over the range control chart, because the calculation of the standard deviation uses all the data points collected, not just the highest and lowest values. Using Excel eliminates all the calculation considerations that historically favored range charts; therefore, many experts agree that, theoretically, the sigma chart is the best choice for measuring dispersion in the data.

$\overline{X}$ and sigma charts help identify process changes in a timely manner. Most often increases in variation (standard deviations) are viewed as bad. If sigma increases, the reason for the increase must be investigated and eliminated from standard operating conditions. On the other hand, decreases in sigma are usually viewed positively. If sigma is reduced, then the reason for the reduction should be identified and incorporated into standard operating procedures.

$\overline{X}$ **and sigma control charts:** A pair of control charts for controlling the central tendency and variation of a process using the standard deviation.

Sigma: The standard deviation of a subgroup.

Variable data: Data representing a quality characteristic that is measured.

Creating $\overline{X}$ and Sigma Control Worksheets

Often, the goal is to create a worksheet similar to the manual form used to collect process information. In chapter 10, such a form was presented for the $\overline{X}$ and range charts. Since the format and layout of the $\overline{X}$ and sigma charts are identical to the $\overline{X}$ and range charts, one can simply change the formulas in the worksheet from chapter 10; however, when the number of observations in a subgroup is greater than five, a worksheet that runs down a page is easier to use. Therefore, this chapter demonstrates how to create a vertical worksheet for the $\overline{X}$ and sigma charts.

When creating an $\overline{X}$ and sigma chart for a process, one can create an Excel worksheet by:

1. Entering worksheet text and column headings

2. Entering the formulas for appropriate calculations

3. Entering the process observations for each subgroup

In order to demonstrate the creation of worksheets and the charting of data, it is necessary to either manually enter or generate fictitious data using a random number generation procedure. The random number generator is used in the following example.

The steps required to create $\overline{X}$ and sigma charts are identical to the steps used to create $\overline{X}$ and range charts in chapter 10:

1. Identify appropriate measures by identifying the purpose of the measurements.

2. Specify a subgroup size n.

3. Select a base period.

4. Collect and analyze data (from the base period) to establish parameters that define base conditions. This analysis includes identifying and eliminating external causes for variation in the base period data.

5. Collect additional data, looking for indicators of change and taking action when change occurs; or making changes to the process and studying data behavior to determine if the change was effective (this trial approach for improving processes is often overlooked).

Statistical process control (SPC) focuses on comparing current data to base period data (in some applications the *base period* is the period during which all the initial data were collected). In order to identify when a change occurs in a process, the QC professional must establish the parameters of the process by selecting a base period. Data collected during an initial base period are the data that establish the parameters. Base period data should be as free from external effects as possible. The base period frequently is the first 25 subgroups of data collected; however, the number of subgroups included in the base period depends on data collection costs and the costs of missing a change. In general, the base period data are a function of data availability and ease of data collection. In addition to comparing current data to the base period data, current data may be compared to other similar processes or data from previous periods (that is, a previous cycle).

$\overline{X}$ and Sigma Chart Formulas

The mathematical statements of the control chart calculations look complex, but are simple when stated in computer worksheet terms (Excel) as listed in Table 11.1. The formulas use the concept of a *range* of cells. The

Table 11.1　Formulas.

	Mathematical	Computer
1. Calculate average for each subgroup	$\bar{x} = \sum x_i / n$	=average(cell *range*)
2. Calculate sigma, the standard deviation for each subgroup	$\sigma = \sqrt{\dfrac{\sum_{(x_i - \overline{X})}^{2}}{(n-1)}}$	=stdev(cell *range*)

(Note: STDEV(cell *range*) returns the standard deviation of a sample, i.e. divide by $n - 1$, while STDEVP(cell *range*) returns the standard deviation of a population, i.e. divide by n. This application uses the $n - 1$ sample formula for calculating subgroup standard deviations.)

	Mathematical	Computer
3. Calculate the average of the subgroup averages	$\overline{\overline{X}} = \sum \bar{x} / k$	=average(*range*)
4. Calculate the average of the standard deviations	$\overline{S} = \sum s / k$	=average(*range*)
5. Calculate control limits for the average process control chart	$UCL_{\overline{x}} = \overline{\overline{X}} + A_3 * \overline{S}$	
	$LCL_{\overline{x}} = \overline{\overline{X}} - A_3 * \overline{S}$	
6. Calculate the control limits for the sigma process control chart	$UCL_S = B_4 * \overline{S}$	
	$LCL_S = B_3 * \overline{S}$	

range of cells is a block of cells defined by the cell in the upper left position and the cell in the lower right position.

The values of A_3, B_3, and B_4 are a function of subgroup size. In general, as size increases, the values of A_3, B_3, and B_4 decrease. A table of values for A_3, B_3, and B_4 is found in Table A.2 in the appendix. The process chart's control limits divide the subgroup statistics into three groups: 1) subgroups (averages and/or sigmas) that are different on the high side; 2) subgroups (averages and/or sigmas) that are different on the low side; and 3) subgroups (averages and/or sigmas) that are numerically the same.

range (cell):　A cell *range* is defined by the cell in the upper left position and the cell in the lower right position. All the cells between are in the cell *range*.

Standard deviation:　A measure of a distribution's dispersion that is measured by the square root of the sum of the squared deviations from the mean for each value, divided by $n - 1$.

$\overline{X}$:　The subgroup average; a measure of central tendency.

$\overline{\overline{X}}$:　The average of subgroup averages.

$\overline{S}$:　The average of subgroup standard deviations.

$UCL_{\overline{x}}$:　Upper control limit of the subgroup average.

LCL$_{\bar{x}}$:   Lower control limit of the subgroup average.

UCL$_s$:   Upper control limit of subgroup standard deviations.

LCL$_s$:   Lower control limit of subgroup standard deviations.

Entering Worksheet Text

Figure 11.1 illustrates the top of the $\bar{X}$ and sigma control worksheet (*x&sigma.xls*). All entries are simple text. To enter text or numbers, use the mouse pointer and click on the left button to make the selected cell active and then type in the text and press the Enter key. For example, pointing and left clicking on cell A1 makes it the active cell. Type *x&sigma.xls* and press Enter to place the text in the cell. It is a good practice to enter the name of the worksheet file in cell A1 to make it easy to find and identify worksheet files with hardcopy output.

In addition to the column headings shown in Figure 11.1, Table 11.2 lists the material that could not be displayed using the default column width and screen view. Left-click on the right scroll arrow on the bottom of the worksheet to change the view and then use the mouse pointer to left-click to select the active cell and type the appropriate text in each cell. If the text in a cell needs to be edited, locate the cell pointer with your mouse, left-click to make it the active cell, and then press function key F2 to begin

Figure 11.1   Top of worksheet.

the edit mode or double-click on the cell. In the edit mode you may insert, delete, and overtype any character. Pressing the Insert key toggles the system between the overtype mode and the insert mode.

Generating Sample Data

This example will use analysis based on 36 subgroups, which are identified by the consecutive numbers in column B. To enter the identification numbers for each subgroup, point with the mouse to cell B10 and left-click to make it the active cell, type the value *1*, and press Enter. The active cell is now B11. Type *+1+*, then left-click on cell B10 and press Enter. The value 2 will appear in B11 and the active cell is now B12. Left-click on B11 and left-

click on Copy icon . Define the *range* B12:B45 and press Enter; the numbers 3 through 36 appear in rows 12 to 45.

This worksheet design requires sample data observations to be entered in the worksheet *range* C10:G45; that is, the data start in column C row 10 and continue to column G row 45, which is the end of the data set. We prefer to use a normal random process generator to create sample data for worksheet design and development. Using the normal process generator ensures that the data are approximately normally distributed. To generate normally distributed data, one must enter the average and standard deviations desired for the sample. In the cell *range* P1:Q3 (outside the *range* of cells that will contain the data), enter the simulation values as shown in Table 11.3. Text is entered in cells P1, P2, and P3, while the values for the average and standard deviations are keyed in cells Q2 and Q3.

Table 11.2 Additional column heads.

Cell	Text	Cell	Text
J9	LCLxbar	M9	LCLs
K9	Xbarbar	N9	Sbar
L9	UCLxbar	O9	UCLs

Table 11.3 Simulation values.

	Columns	
	P	Q
Rows		
1	Simulation Values:	
2	Average:	100
3	Std Dev:	10

In cell C10, enter the normal process generator formula:

=(rand()+rand()+rand()+rand()+rand()+rand()+rand()
+rand()+rand()+rand()+rand()+rand()−6)*$Q$3+$Q$2

that is, 12 uniform random numbers [rand()] minus 6, and that quantity multiplied by the standard deviation (the value in cell Q3) and added to the average (the value in cell Q2). This formula is based on the central limit theorem, which states that no matter how the parent population is distributed (in this case *uniform*), the distribution of the (12) sums is normal. Subtracting 6 centers the distribution around zero with a standard deviation of one (the standard normal). Multiplying by the standard deviation plus the mean is a reverse Z transformation to give the observation data the mean and standard deviation specified in cells Q2 and Q3, respectively.

Make cell C10 the active cell. Click on the Copy icon ⧉. To complete the generation of data, point to cell C10 and left-click on Edit and Copy, then hold down the left mouse button to define the *range* C10:G45 and press Enter. Random numbers should appear in each cell in the *range* from C10 through G45. The generation of sample data is now complete.

Entering Formulas

Recall that six formulas are required to generate the $\overline{X}$ and sigma charts. Each formula must be entered into the appropriate worksheet cells.

1. Subgroup average: make cell H10 the active cell, by typing

=average(

then use the left mouse button to define the *range* C10:G10, and press Enter. The *range* C10:G10 will appear in the formula as *=average(C10:G10)*. This formula calculates the average for each subgroup. The formula must be copied into the *range* H11:H45.

Left-click on H10 and left-click on the Copy icon ⧉, then highlight the *range* H11:H45 and press ENTER. The average for each subgroup is calculated.

2. Subgroup standard deviation: Make cell I10 the active cell by typing

=stdev(

Use the left mouse button to define the *range* C10:G10, and press Enter. This formula calculates the standard deviation for the first subgroup. This formula must be copied into the *range* I11:I45. Left-click on I10 and left-click on the Copy icon ⧉. Then, highlight the *range* I11:I45 and press Enter. The standard deviation for each subgroup is calculated.

3. Average of the subgroup averages: Make cell K10 active by left-clicking and typing

=average(

Move the mouse pointer to H10 and hold the left key down and drag to define the *range* H10:H45, and press Enter. The average of all the subgroup averages is calculated. Do not copy this formula into the *range* K11:K45, all the values for columns J through O will be completed later using one step after all the formulas are entered.

4. Average of the subgroup standard deviations: Make cell N10 active by left-clicking and typing

=average(

Move the mouse pointer to I10 and hold the left key down to define the *range* I10:I45, and press Enter. Do not copy this formula into the *range* K11:K45, all the values for columns J through O will be completed later using one step after all the formulas are entered.

The instructions for entering the following formulas allow the user to enter the formula without typing in the cells or ranges; however, if the user finds it difficult to follow these procedures the formulas may be typed in the appropriate cells.

5. Control limits for the average control chart: To calculate the lower control limit for the average control chart, move the mouse pointer to cell J10. To enter the formula without typing the formula follow these steps:

    a. Click on J10 and type +

    b. Click on K10 and type –

    c. Click on E3 and type *

    d. Click on N10, and press Enter

The formula *+K10–E3*N10* should appear in cell J10.

To calculate the upper control limit for the average control chart, move the cell pointer to cell L10. To enter the formula without typing, follow these steps:

    a. Click on L10 and type +

    b. Click on K10 and type +

    c. Click on E3 and type *

    d. Click on N10, and press Enter

The formula: *+K10+E3*N10* should appear in cell L10.

6. Control limits for the sigma control chart: To calculate the lower limit for the sigma control chart, move the cell pointer to cell M10. To enter the formula without typing, follow these steps:

    a. Click on M10 and type +

    b. Click on E4 and type *

    c. Click on N10, and press Enter

The formula +E4*N10 should appear in cell M10. Because the value in cell E4 is zero, the value in cell M10 is zero.

To calculate the upper control limit for the sigma control chart, move the cell pointer to cell O10. To enter the formula without typing, follow these steps:

    a. Click on O10 and type +

    b. Click on E5 and type *

    c. Click on N10, and press Enter

The formula +E5*N10 should appear in cell O10.

To copy the values in the *range* J10:O10 to the range J11:O45, activate cell J11, type +, then click on J10, and press Enter. The value from cell J10

appears in cell J11. Click on cell J11 and click on the <u>C</u>opy icon . Hold down the left mouse button and drag to define the *range* J11:O45, and press Enter. The worksheet calculations are complete.

Worksheet calculations are simple and easy. We recommend that you review what you have done until you understand each step. Figure 11.2 displays the worksheet *range* E1:O24. The actual values in your worksheet will probably be different because the observation values were generated with the random number generator.

Creating the $\overline{X}$ Control Chart

Point to cell B9 and hold the left mouse button down and drag to define the

range B9:B45, left-click on the Up arrow ▲ on the right side of the screen until cell H9 is showing, then press and hold the Control key down along with the left mouse button and drag to define the *range* H9:H45. Left-click

on the Up arrow ▲ on the right side of the screen until cell J9 is showing. Hold the Control key down and define the *range* J9:L45.

To create the $\overline{X}$ control chart, follow these steps:

1. Click on the Chart Wizard icon ▦ .

2. Select the XY (Scatter) type graph, then select the option in the bottom left corner (Scatter with data points connected by lines), and click on <u>N</u>ext>.

	E	F	G	H	I	J	K	L	M	N	O	P
8				Subgroup	Subgroup							
9				Average	Std-dev	LCLxbar	Xbarbar	UCLxbar	LCLs	Sbar	UCLs	
10	83.16319	110.0786	114.4275	99.77276	12.5988	85.56395	98.65148	111.739	0	9.152121	18.85337	
11	81.42317	107.6699	88.29121	90.66724	11.03483	85.56395	98.65148	111.739	0	9.152121	18.85337	
12	97.36715	103.1771	94.20266	100.5244	7.039987	85.56395	98.65148	111.739	0	9.152121	18.85337	
13	94.32335	90.35935	104.9145	95.11081	5.713316	85.56395	98.65148	111.739	0	9.152121	18.85337	
14	95.69621	99.63189	107.137	99.15396	4.881966	85.56395	98.65148	111.739	0	9.152121	18.85337	
15	105.4773	101.3883	102.3689	101.5494	8.206821	85.56395	98.65148	111.739	0	9.152121	18.85337	
16	86.44182	85.82228	114.4919	95.69844	14.63221	85.56395	98.65148	111.739	0	9.152121	18.85337	
17	116.4319	103.5424	90.5409	98.95672	11.13566	85.56395	98.65148	111.739	0	9.152121	18.85337	
18	95.97833	97.96333	96.0805	95.38553	1.980046	85.56395	98.65148	111.739	0	9.152121	18.85337	
19	108.993	102.893	100.5896	101.24	5.695621	85.56395	98.65148	111.739	0	9.152121	18.85337	
20	95.00271	98.73854	102.0182	99.50474	9.219694	85.56395	98.65148	111.739	0	9.152121	18.85337	
21	107.5556	100.6214	94.33679	96.65159	7.409389	85.56395	98.65148	111.739	0	9.152121	18.85337	
22	113.8397	116.1948	109.8156	105.4278	12.50782	85.56395	98.65148	111.739	0	9.152121	18.85337	
23	96.56809	91.26178	104.8475	102.4304	8.583019	85.56395	98.65148	111.739	0	9.152121	18.85337	
24	94.52987	87.65413	113.1535	95.90833	13.42651	85.56395	98.65148	111.739	0	9.152121	18.85337	
25	84.5776	106.2974	92.80382	94.04543	9.32176	85.56395	98.65148	111.739	0	9.152121	18.85337	
26	100.9317	112.7704	114.9584	111.0543	7.831361	85.56395	98.65148	111.739	0	9.152121	18.85337	
27	103.7441	101.2226	92.78095	98.81094	5.47919	85.56395	98.65148	111.739	0	9.152121	18.85337	
28	103.768	109.3918	94.54095	100.2932	8.832906	85.56395	98.65148	111.739	0	9.152121	18.85337	
29	117.9758	97.70074	100.443	109.718	13.69623	85.56395	98.65148	111.739	0	9.152121	18.85337	

Figure 11.2   Results of worksheet calculations.

3. The next screen shows the $\overline{X}$ chart complete with identification for each line, because we included the top identification cells (row 9) in the graphing *range*. Select the Series in Columns option below the chart and click on Next>.

4. Figure 11.3 illustrates the screen with the Chart title and axes labels entered. Add the Chart title (*Xbar Control chart*), identification for the *x*-axis (*Subgroup Number*), and identification for the *y*-axis (*Subgroup Average*), then click on Next>.

5. Select the option button (As Object In:) to place the graph on the sheet with the worksheet calculations and click on Finish.

6. The chart will be placed in the worksheet. Use the left mouse button to drag the chart to a range that is to the right of column Q or below the 45th row.

After placing the graph on sheet 1, double-left-click on the UCLxbar, Xbarbar, and LCLxbar to change the type of lines, thickness, and color, and to eliminate the use of symbols on the lines. Next, double-click on the *x*-axis and *y*-axis and adjust the scales to your preference. The example shows *y*-axis values ranging from 80 to 120 in major units of 10, and major units of 5 for the *x*-axis. Figure 11.4 illustrates the edited X-bar control chart.

Figure 11.3 Chart Wizard step 3 of 4—Chart Options.

Figure 11.4 $\overline{X}$ control chart.

Creating the Sigma Control Chart

The $\overline{X}$ control chart requires a matched sigma control chart. The steps to create a sigma chart are similar to those for the $\overline{X}$ chart except the graphing *ranges* are different. Table 11.4 lists the graphing *ranges* for the sigma control chart. Figure 11.5 illustrates the sigma control chart. The graph requires a graphing *range* that includes three parts: B9:B45, I9:I45, and M9:O45. The Control key must be held down when selecting noncontiguous *ranges*.

To create the sigma control chart, follow these steps:

1. Click on the Chart Wizard icon [icon] .

2. Select the XY (Scatter) type graph, select the subgroup type in the bottom left corner (Scatter with data points connected by lines), and click on Next>.

3. The next screen shows the X-bar chart complete with identification for each line, because we included the top identification cells (row 9) in the graphing range. Select the Series in Columns option below the chart and click on Next>.

4. Add the chart title (*Sigma Control Chart*), identification for the *x*-axis (*Subgroup Number*), and identification for the *y*-axis (*Subgroup Standard Deviation*), then click on Next>.

5. Select option button (As Object In:) to place the graph on the sheet with the worksheet calculations and click on Finish.

6. The chart will be placed in the worksheet below the X-bar control chart. Use the left mouse button to drag the chart to a *range* that is to the right of column Q or below the 45th row.

After completing the Chart Wizard steps, double-left-click on each line and format the lines to match the lines used in the $\overline{X}$ control chart.

Support Capabilities

Formatting Numbers

Excel provides numerous capabilities to format values and check spelling along with other tools. To format the numbers in the worksheet, point to cell C10 and hold the left mouse key down and drag to identify the *range* C10:L45, point and left-click on Format, and point and left-click on Cells. Click on the Number tab and click on Number in the Category dialog list.

Table 11.4   Graphing ranges for the sigma control chart.

X scale	Sigma	LCLs	$\overline{S}$	UCLs
B9:B45	I9:I45	M9:M45	N9:N45	O9:O45

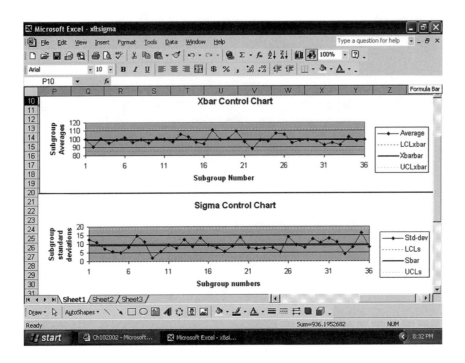

Figure 11.5 $\overline{X}$ and sigma control charts.

The <u>D</u>ecimal Places edit box appears. Using the spinner button, change the number of <u>D</u>ecimal Places to 3, and click on OK. Then, define the *range* N10:N45 and repeat the process. There is no need to format column M (the LCLs) because all the values are zero.

Formatting Text

Often a large font is used for the title of a worksheet. In cell F1 type *Xbar and Sigma Control charts*. With cell F1 the active cell, point with the mouse and left-click on F<u>o</u>rmat, then left-click on C<u>e</u>lls, and finally, left-click on Font to specify a <u>S</u>ize of 16. Figure 11.6 illustrates the results.

Template

Template *x&sigma.xls* is the completed one-page $\overline{X}$ and sigma control charts developed in the previous section. We find the vertical (down the page) layout easier to expand than the horizontal (across the page) layout used in the development of the $\overline{X}$ and range control charts. The $\overline{X}$ and sigma control chart pair may be expanded by copying the last line of the worksheet data down the page.

The screenshot shows a Microsoft Excel window titled "Microsoft Excel - x&sigma" with the spreadsheet "Xbar and Sigma Control Charts":

	A	B	C	D	E	F	G	H	I	J	K	L
1	x&sigma.xls					Xbar and Sigma Control Charts						
2					n=5							
3	Inspector:		A3:		1.43							
4	Process:		B3:		0							
5	Part no:		B4:		2.06							
6	Part name:											
7												
8	Remarks	Subgroup						Subgroup	Subgroup			
9		Identification						Average	Std-dev	LCLxbar	Xbarbar	UCLxbar
10		1	96.86162	94.33281	83.16319	110.0786	114.4275	99.77276	12.5988	85.56395	98.65148	111.
11		2	81.17904	94.77295	81.42317	107.6699	88.29121	90.66724	11.03483	85.56395	98.65148	111.
12		3	96.25705	111.6179	97.36715	103.1771	94.20266	100.5244	7.039987	85.56395	98.65148	111.
13		4	94.01877	91.93807	94.32335	90.35935	104.9145	95.11081	5.713316	85.56395	98.65148	111.
14		5	98.51029	94.79437	95.69621	99.63189	107.137	99.15396	4.881966	85.56395	98.65148	111.
15		6	110.2737	88.23897	105.4773	101.3883	102.3689	101.5494	8.206821	85.56395	98.65148	111.
16		7	108.5159	83.22036	86.44182	85.82228	114.4919	95.69844	14.63221	85.56395	98.65148	111.
17		8	90.44858	93.81987	116.4319	103.5424	90.5409	98.95672	11.13566	85.56395	98.65148	111.
18		9	94.05758	92.84793	95.97833	97.96333	96.0805	95.38553	1.980046	85.56395	98.65148	111.
19		10	100.615	93.10946	108.993	102.893	100.5896	101.24	5.695621	85.56395	98.65148	111.
20		11	88.45147	113.3128	95.00271	98.73854	102.0182	99.50474	9.219694	85.56395	98.65148	111.
21		12	89.7736	90.97055	107.5556	100.6214	94.33679	96.65159	7.409389	85.56395	98.65148	111.

Figure 11.6 Formatting chart title.

Using $\overline{X}$ and Sigma Control Charts

The control chart template provides a tool to examine control chart behavior as a function of changes in the process average and process standard deviation (variation). We know that individually and/or together the average and variation of a distribution can cycle, jump, shift, trend, and go in or out of autocorrelation. No matter what type of control chart analysis one uses, numbers alone do not always lead to the correct decision. Two types of errors may be made when analyzing numbers:

Type I error: Numbers indicate a change when there is none and time and money are wasted in looking for the reasons for the change

Type II error: Numbers do not indicate a change when a change has occurred, causing an opportunity for improvement to be missed

All efforts to reduce the type I error result in an increase in type II errors. Traditionally, three standard deviations are used to set the control chart limits. By selecting three standard deviation limits, we may assume that the two types of errors are balanced.

In addition to type I and type II errors, one may make another critical mistake—measuring the wrong parameter. Usually, the selection of a quality characteristic parameter is based on utilizing the best professional judgment available. It is not unusual to be forced to select the best measure from a series of indirect measurements of the process one wishes to control. For example, it may be difficult to measure customer satisfaction with service received at a fast-food restaurant drive-in window, however, an indirect measure of satisfaction may be the time span between driving into the line and receiving the order.

The procedure for expanding the worksheet to analyze a process is:

1. Expand the worksheet to 50 subgroups and save under the file name *x&s50.xls*.

2. Use part 1 (first 25 subgroups) for the base period; that is, to define the standard for average $\overline{X}$, and standard deviation (variation) to define the upper and lower limits and overall averages.

3. Redefine the graphing *range* to include all the subgroups.

4. Introduce a shift in the average and/or variation beginning with subgroup 26.

5. Examine the results using the pair of control chart graphs of all the data.

Expanding the Worksheet for Additional Observations

Expanding from 36 subgroups to 50 subgroups requires that one identify the *range* B45:O45 and copy the contents of these cells into the *range* B46:O59.

Changing the Average and Standard Deviation of a Range of Subgroups

To change the average and standard deviation for subgroups 26 through 50, begin by entering the following text and values in the following cells:

Row	Column	
	S	T
1	From	26 to 50
2	Average:	120
3	Std Dev:	10

Next, the formula in cell C35 is changed to:

$$=(rand()+rand()+rand()+rand()+rand()+rand()+rand()$$
$$+rand()+rand()+rand()+rand()+rand()-6)*\$T\$3+\$T\$2$$

To change the formula, make cell C35 the active cell by pointing and clicking. Press F2 to go into the edit mode, edit $Q$3 to $T$3 and $Q$2 to

$T$2 by either inserting and deleting or pressing the Insert key and over-typing. Make cell C35 the active cell and click on <u>E</u>dit and <u>C</u>opy. Identify the *range* C35:G59 and click on <u>E</u>dit and <u>P</u>aste, or press Enter.

The example is based on the assumption that management wants to use the first 25 subgroups as the base period. The formulas in cells K10 (xbar) and N10 (sbar) must be changed to:

Cell	Formula
K10	=AVERAGE(H10:H34)
N10	=AVERAGE(I10:I34)

Figure 11.7 illustrates the control chart pair for studying the specified change in the process average after the *y*-axis graphing scale is changed to a maximum of 140. Your work will produce a similar pattern, but unless you use the same exact random number sequence, your results will be slightly different.

Type I error: Numbers indicate a change when there is none and time and money are wasted looking for the change.

Type II error: Numbers do not indicate a change when one occurred and we miss an opportunity to improve the process.

Figure 11.7 Change in process average.

Figure 11.8   Change in process standard deviation.

No Change in the Mean, Two-Sigma Increase in the Variation

Figure 11.8 illustrates the screen after changing the value in cell T3 to 30 and keeping T2 at 100. Wild swings can be seen in the $\overline{X}$ chart and many outliers may be seen in the sigma control chart. The $\overline{X}$ and sigma control chart pair produces similar results to the $\overline{X}$ and range control chart pair studied in chapter 10. When the subgroup size is five or less, the range and sigma control charts produce similar results. The sigma control chart is preferred when subgroups contain more than five observations.

Real Life

Figure 11.9 illustrates $\overline{X}$ and sigma control charts for skin temperature in an ICU patient. The top chart is the $\overline{X}$ chart with temperature in degrees Celsius on the *y*-axis and the subgroup average on the *x*-axis. This chart illustrates a slow trend in the increase in skin temperature, while the sigma chart displays no indication of change. The change seen is minor in terms of skin temperature; that is, the scale on the $\overline{X}$ chart is only a half a degree. The medical records indicate that the patient developed an infection several

Figure 11.9 $\overline{X}$ and sigma chart of skin temperature.

days after the control chart results indicated an increase in skin temperature, as shown in Figure 11.9.

Summary

The $\overline{X}$ and sigma control chart pair is the theoretical correct combination for analyzing variable data. The range chart is a satisfactory substitute for the sigma chart only when subgroups are small—less than six. The worksheet layout and formula structure is similar to that of the $\overline{X}$ and range charts except that the formulas include calculating the standard deviation. Excel includes *=stdvs(range)*, a one-step formula that eliminates all of the complexity in performing standard deviation calculations.

The down-the-page control layout structure is easy to use and expand for calculating and creating $\overline{X}$ and sigma charts. The creation of the control chart starts with creating the page headings and then the column headings. Usually, the first row is unique, while the second row may be copied into the remaining rows. Creating and using $\overline{X}$ and sigma charts is based on a graphical-visual analysis, like most quality control methods. Excel provides the tools to produce quality graphs.

Exercises

11.1   Edit the example worksheet *x&sigma.xls* so that the control chart is across the page rather than down the page.

11.2   Experiment with the mean and standard deviation used to simulate the data in *x&s50.xls*. For the first 25 observations, use a mean of 100 and standard deviation of 10, then for observations 26 through 50, change the average to 105, 110, 115, 120, 125, 130, and 135. At each new value of the mean, run the system 10 times by pressing the F9 key to generate new observations, then count the number of subgroups that occur after the change and before there is an outlier (individually on the $\overline{X}$ and sigma charts) at each level. Record the results. Use Excel to graph the value of the new mean versus the average number of subgroups before an outlier occurs on each control chart separately.

11.3   Replicate problem 11.2 except this time hold the mean constant at 100 and vary the standard deviation from 10, 15, 20, 25, 30, 35, to 40. Replicate the experiment 10 times at each level and calculate the average number of subgroups before an outlier occurs on the $\overline{X}$ and the sigma chart. Graph the *new* standard deviation versus the average number of subgroups before an outlier occurs on each control chart separately.

11.4   Given the data in the problem 10.4 (chapter 10), in Excel create an $\overline{X}$ and sigma control chart pair. Identify outliers, if any. If you performed this problem in chapter 10, compare the two control chart pairs.

11.5   In a textbook on statistical process control, find a sample problem illustrating $\overline{X}$ and sigma charts. Enter that text's data into an Excel worksheet and compare the charts from that text with your results. (For a list of texts refer to the reference section located at the back of this book.)

12

p and *np* Control Charts

OUTLINE

Prior Knowledge

From earlier chapters, you should know how to open files, save files, edit, cut, and copy a *range* of cells from part of a worksheet to another, and use the function =rand().

Why Use *p* and *np* Control Charts?

Quality is often measured as *attribute data* using counts, fractions, and percentages of defective items. A *defective item* is a part or service that is considered unsatisfactory. In many applications, the quality measure may also count satisfactory events or a set of events of particular interest. Attribute data are classified as good or bad and on or off, and may be measured using go/no-go gauges rather than with a measurement instrument. It is usually faster and cheaper to determine if a part fits in a hole (go-gauge) but not in a second hole (no-go gauge), than it is to measure a part with a measurement instrument (ruler or weight). One advantage of using *p* and *np* control charts is that attribute data can measure more than one quality attribute at a time to combine several characteristics into a single analysis. For example, color, weight, and size may be considered simultaneously. However, the primary disadvantage of attribute data is that when they are utilized for process control, more samples must be collected to achieve the same level of control of type I and type II errors as continuous measurement data.

When attribute data are used, *p* and *np* charts are the preferred choice of control charts. The *p* and *np* control charts are used for counts, fractions, and percentages of defective items in a run or lot. The *np* chart is used when data consist of a count of the defective items and the lot size is constant. The *p* chart is used when data consist of fractions or percentages and the lot size may be constant or variable.

The *np* chart uses a simple count of defective items, with the assumption that the sample size (number in the lots or runs) is constant. When using attribute control charts, the inspection record always includes the number of parts inspected and the number of defective parts. If the sample size is constant and the number of defective items is already recorded, the *np* chart is preferred. On the other hand, if there is any chance of variation in sample sizes, then using a *p* chart that examines the fraction or percentage of defective items is preferable.

The *p* chart uses calculations based on the fraction or percent of defective items. When one simply divides the number of defective items by the total number of items inspected, the result is the fraction of defective items. When the fraction of defective items is multiplied by 100, the result is the percentage of defective items. There are no statistical reasons for selecting *fraction defectives* over *percent defectives*. One should select the approach that is the most consistent with past practice.

Defective item: A part that is considered unsatisfactory.

***p* control chart:**   Control chart for attribute data that uses fractions or percentages.

***np* control chart:**   Control chart for attribute data that uses a count.

Attribute data: Measurements of the characteristics of items (components or products) that are classified as either meeting or not meeting specifications (accept or reject; go or no-go).

Variable data: Data representing a quality characteristic that is measured.

Fraction defective: The value derived by dividing the number of occurrences of a defective item by the total number of observations.

Percent defective: The value derived by multiplying the fraction defective by 100.

Creating *p* and *np* Worksheets

Attribute data worksheets may be designed to run either down the page (vertically) or across the page (horizontally). In chapter 9, the $\overline{X}$ and range control chart worksheets were designed across the page. In chapter 11, the $\overline{X}$ and sigma control chart worksheets were designed down the page. For the *p* control chart, a simple worksheet going down the page is utilized. Begin by typing the name of the worksheet, *pchart01.xls*, in cell A1. Note that this worksheet's file name follows the old DOS naming rules. Many organizations are still using some Windows 3.1 systems and have the need to transfer files back to older systems. For those who do not have this limitation, the long file names of later versions of Windows allow you to create more descriptive names for your worksheets. Save the worksheet in the subdirectory of your choice.

p and *np* Chart Formulas

The *p* and *np* charts are based on the binomial distribution. In addition, normal distribution theory is used to establish the control limits. The averages for the control charts are based on the following formulas:

1. For the fraction defective p chart:

$$\bar{p} = \left(\Sigma\# \, defectives\right) / \left(\Sigma\# \, observations\right)$$

2. For the percent defective p chart:

$$\bar{p} = \left(\left(\Sigma\# \, defectives\right) / \left(\Sigma\# \, observations\right)\right) * 100$$

3. For the np chart:

$$n\bar{p} = \left(\Sigma\# \, defectives\right)$$

To calculate the standard deviations for establishing control chart limits, the formulas are:

4. For the fraction defective p chart:

$$S_p = \sqrt{\bar{p} * \left(1 - \bar{p}\right) / n}$$

5. For the percent defective p chart:

$$S_p = \sqrt{\bar{p} * \left(1 - \bar{p}\right) / n * 100}$$

6. For the np chart:

$$S_{np} = \sqrt{\bar{p} * \left(1 - \bar{p}\right) * n}$$

The quantity $(1 - \bar{p})$ is often referred to as $\bar{q}$. The symbol $\bar{q}$ is often used in place of $(1 - \bar{p})$ in the formulas just shown. Like many statistical formulas, the formulas look complex when first examined, but in Excel, all the formulas are simple to use.

Entering Worksheet Text

The first step is to enter the column headings by placing the text in the appropriate cells (Table 12.1).

To adjust the size of the cell to accommodate the text, click on the letter at the top of each column in the worksheet, and when you see the double-sided arrow, hold the left mouse button down and drag to size the columns to fit the text in each column.

Rather than enter *p-bar* in F6, you may enter the more correct notation $\bar{p}$ as the column head using either Text box or WordArt. To use WordArt, select the second icon to the right of the Chart Wizard icon ![icon]—the

Drawing icon ![icon]. The drawing menu appears on the bottom of the screen.

Table 12.1 Text for column headings.

Cell	Text
B5	Number
C5	Number
D5	Fraction
A6	Number
B6	Defective
C6	Observed
D6	Defective
E6	LCLp
F6	p-bar
G6	UCLp
C7	100
C1	Sigma
C2	Z:
C3	3 sigma
D2	3
F1	UCLp
F2	LCLp
H1	Simulated value
H2	P-bar
I2	0.05

Locate the Insert WordArt icon ▲ in the menu. After left-clicking on Insert WordArt icon, the WordArt Gallery appears. Select the style from the upper left corner, as illustrated in Figure 12.1. To type a *p* with a bar over it as the text, type a dash and press the enter key and then type a *p*. Specify a font Size of 9 and click on OK or press Enter. Locate the WordArt by holding down the left mouse key to drag it to cell F6.

Now use Text Boxes to enter *UCLp* and *LCLp* sideways.

1. Click on the Drawing icon 🗗 to start the drawing menu if it is not on the screen.

2. Select the Text Box icon. The Text Box icon 🄰 is just left of the Insert WordArt icon.

3. Draw a text box anyplace on the screen.

Figure 12.1   WordArt options.

4. Type *LCLp* in the text box.

5. Right-click on the corner of the text box and left-click on Format Text Box.

6. Click on the Colors and Lines tab.

7. In the Line section, click on the Color: option and then click on the top selection No Line.

8. Left-click on the Alignment tab near the top of the screen.

9. Click on the Orientation of your choice and click on OK.

10. Delete the text in cell E6.

11. Move the text box to cell E6.

Repeat the process for UCLp. Figure 12.2 illustrates the results. You may resize the column size to fit the new headings.

Each sample (lot) is identified by a consecutive number in column A. To number the lots, follow these steps:

1. Click on cell A7 and type *1* and press Enter.

2. In cell A8 type *+1+*

3. Click on cell A7 and press Enter (*2* should appear in cell A8).

Figure 12.2 Text boxes and WordArt as column headings.

4. Click on cell A8 and click on the Copy button.

5. Holding down the left mouse button, select the *range* A9:A31.

6. Press Enter.

The rows of the worksheet should be numbered consecutively from 1 through 25.

Generating Sample Data

Control charts require large data sets of over 100 numbers. Entering 100 or more numbers individually, without errors, is an unnecessary task. When you are analyzing a real process, then the actual number of defective items in each lot and each lot size must be entered into the worksheet. When you are working sample problems, it is easier to generate random numbers to use as observations. The specific numbers are not important in statistical process control worksheet development, but the numerical patterns are important because it is critical that the patterns can be replicated.

For simplicity, use the normal distribution process generator to generate random numbers. The formula in cell B7 is:

=round(((rand()+rand()+rand()+rand()+rand()+rand()+rand()+rand()
+rand()+rand()+rand()+rand()−6)*sqrt($I$2*(1−$I$2)/100)+$I$2)*100,0)

After entering the formula in cell B7, press Enter, and press the function key F9 to observe the values in cell B7 change. The values should vary around 5. The formula in cell F9 uses a normal distribution process generator, with the data rounded off to the nearest whole number. The average fraction used is the simulated p-bar; *0.05*, the number in cell I2. The standard deviation used is:

$$S_p = \sqrt{\bar{p} * (1 - \bar{p}) / n}$$

Make B7 the active cell and click on the Copy button. Point to cell B8 and hold the left mouse button and drag to define the *range* B8:B31, then press Enter. Random numbers should appear in each cell in column B.

The value of n is set at 100 on the assumption the number observed will always be 100. If n is not a constant, then the n in our formula must be adjusted to match the sample size. Copy the value of 100 found in cell C7 to the remaining cells in column C by clicking on cell C7 and then clicking

on the Copy icon ![icon]. Select the *range* C8:C31 and press Enter. The value 100 should be duplicated in each cell of the column.

The generation of sample data is now complete.

Entering Worksheet Formulas

Now enter the calculations for the average and control chart limits, using the first 25 rows of data (fraction defective calculations in cells D7:D31) as the base period. If the text *#NUM!* is displayed as the formulas are entered, this is a message that the column is too narrow to display the number in the cell. Press the F9 key once or twice to generate new values that can be displayed or adjust the width of the column.

1. p-bar—In cell F7 type the following formula:

=AVERAGE($D$7:$D$31)

and press Enter. This formula calculates the average fraction of defective parts in the base period.

2. Sigma—Sigma is the standard deviation of the sample. In cell D1, type the following formula:

=SQRT((F7*(1-F7))/100)

and press Enter.

3. 3 sigma—Establishes the upper and lower control limits by multiplying sigma by 3. In cell D3, type the following formula:

+D2*D1

and press Enter.

4. Fraction of defective items—To calculate the fraction of defective items, follow these steps:

    a. Click on cell D7 and type +*B7/C7* and press Enter.

    b. Click on cell D7 and click on the Copy icon.

    c. Select the range D8:D31 and press Enter.

The fraction of defective items in each lot is calculated.

5. LCLp—The lowest value possible for the number of defective items is zero; therefore the LCLp is zero. The LCLp is calculated in cell G2 by entering the following formula:

$$+\$F\$7-\$D\$3$$

This formula subtracts three sigmas from the p-bar value. The values in cell G2 should be close to –0.01. The exact value cannot be predicted since the calculations are based on simulated data.

In cell E7 type the following formula:

$$=if(\$G\$2<0,0,\$G\$2)$$

and press Enter. This formula instructs Excel to define the LCLp as zero if the number in cell G2 is negative; otherwise use the value in cell G2.

6. UCLp—If the upper control limit was near one (meaning almost all parts in the lots are defective), a statement that ensures that UCLp is never greater than one is necessary. For this example, we will use the value in cell G1.

The UCLp is calculated in cell G1 by entering the following formula and pressing the Enter key:

$$+\$F\$7+\$D\$3$$

This formula adds three sigmas to the p-bar value. The values in cell G1 should be close to 0.1. The exact value cannot be predicted since the calculations are based on simulated data.

In cell G7 type the following formula:

$$+\$G\$1$$

and press Enter.

To copy the values in cells E7, F7, and G7 into the remaining cells, follow these steps:

1. Select the *range* E7:G7 using the left mouse button.

2. Click on the Copy icon.

3. Select the *range* E8:G31 using the left mouse button.

4. Press Enter.

The values in each column should be entered down the columns as shown in Figure 12.3.

Creating the *p* Control Chart

Hold the left mouse button down and drag to define the *range* A7:A31, and left-click on the Up arrow on the right side of the screen until cell D7 is showing. Next, press and hold down the Control (Ctrl) key and drag to define the graphing *range* D7:G31.

To create the *p* control chart, follow these steps:

1. Click on the Chart Wizard icon .

2. Select XY (Scatter) and the straight line with points Chart subtype and click on <u>N</u>ext>.

3. The next screen shows the *p* chart; select the Series in Columns option below the chart and click on <u>N</u>ext>.

4. On the screen add the chart title *p control chart* and press the Tab key.

5. Type in the label *Lot number* for the *x*-axis and press the Tab key.

6. Type in the label *Fraction defective* for the *y*-axis and click <u>N</u>ext>.

7. Select As <u>O</u>bject In to place the graph on the sheet with the worksheet calculations and click on <u>F</u>inish.

8. The chart is placed on the worksheet; use the left mouse button to drag the chart to a range that is to the right of column H or below the 37th row.

After placing the graph on sheet 1, double-left-click on each of the lines to change the type of lines, thickness, color, and to eliminate symbols on the lines. Use a dashed line with symbols for the control limits, a solid line without symbols for $\bar{p}$, and a straight line with symbols for each lot. Next, double-click on the *x*-axis and *y*-axis and adjust the scales to your own preferences. This example uses *y*-axis values ranging from 0 to 0.15 in major units of 0.05, and major units of 10 for the *x*-axis. Figure 12.4 illustrates the edited *p* control chart.

Template

To save the results, click on <u>F</u>ile, <u>S</u>ave, and save the current worksheet as *pchart01.xls* in the subdirectory of your choice. The current worksheet, pchart01.xls, including the *p* chart illustrated in Figure 12.4, is found on your CD. It needs work to be complete, but this worksheet provides an excellent starting point for creating a *p* chart.

Figure 12.3   Finished worksheet.

Figure 12.4   *p* chart.

Worksheet Design Improvements

The development of the perfect worksheet requires careful planning. At times, as you create a worksheet you may find that changes are needed; however, as you gain experience in creating worksheets, fewer changes will be required.

Examination of Figure 12.4 shows that we failed to name the lines on the chart correctly—that is, Series 1 should be p, Series 2 should be $UCLp$, Series 3 should be p-bar, and Series 4 should be $LCLp$.

1. Using the *right* (not the left) mouse button, click on the body of the graph to display the menu as shown in Figure 12.5.

2. Select Source Data as shown in the figure.

3. Click on the Series tab and make the following changes:

    a. Highlight Series 1 and then click on the typing area next to the right of Name: and type p

    b. Click on Series 2 and then click on the typing area next to the right of Name: and type $LCLp$

    c. Click on Series 3 and click on the typing area next to the right of Name: and type p-bar

    d. Click on Series 4 and click on the typing area next to the right of Name: and type $UCLp$

Figure 12.5   Fix-it menu.

The formula in cell D1 includes the value *100*. Experts recommend that you *never* use a number in a formula, but instead create a cell to record the value. Creating a cell to store a value simplifies the editing process because it takes a great deal of effort to change every occurrence of a number in the formulas of a worksheet. If one occurrence is missed, critical errors are introduced into the worksheet calculations.

To correct this error, create a cell in column C above the text that contains the word *Sigma* by following the steps listed below.

Insert a new row at the top of the worksheet and change the worksheet name:

1. Click on the *1* that identifies row one.

2. Click on Insert and Rows. The entire worksheet moves down a row and all formulas are adjusted accordingly.

3. Click on cell A2 and click on Edit and Cut.

4. Click on cell A1 and press Enter. The name of the worksheet is moved from cell A2 to cell A1.

Because *pchart01.xls* was saved as a template, the worksheet name in cell A1 should be changed to *pchart02.xls*:

5. Click on cell A1, press F2, and change the file name to *pchart02.xls* and press Enter.

6. Click on File, click on Save As, and save the current worksheet as *pchart02.xls* in the subdirectory of your choice.

Insert text and formula for lot size:

1. Click on cell C1 and type *Lot size* and press Enter.

2. Click on cell D1 and type *100* and press Enter.

3. Click on cell D2, press F2 to replace the 100 in the formula with *D1*, and press Enter.

This formula instructs the software to calculate sigma based on the sample size recorded in cell D1, rather than on a particular value.

Place a reference to cell D1 in cell C8, the Number Observed column:

1. Click on cell C8 and type *+$D$1* and press Enter.

2. Click on cell C8 and click on the Copy button.

3. Use the left mouse button to define the *range* C9:C32 and press Enter.

The value 100 is still displayed in column C (see Figure 12.6). To see how easy it is to change lot size, click on cell D1 and type 50 and press Enter. All the values in column C should change to 50 and other values are recalculated based on the new lot size. Now, change the value in cell D1 back to 100 and observe the values in the cells of column D changing back to 100.

Note: Save your worksheet; later in the chapter we will redo pchart02.xls *for variable lot sizes.*

Figure 12.6   Revised *p* chart.

Revising the Worksheet for the *np* Control Chart

Institutions often collect data as counts (number of defects) rather than as fractions or percentages of defects for decision making. The *np* chart is a simple control chart that uses only counts. You could begin by creating a new worksheet; however, we prefer to start with some of the work done, so the completed *pchart02.xls* worksheet will be used as the base for the *np* chart.

To protect the template from change, open the worksheet *pchart02.xls* and use File, Save As to save the worksheet under the name *npchart1.xls*. To change the worksheet, follow these steps:

1. Click on cell A1 and press F2 to edit the text *pchart02.xls* to *npchart1.xls*.

2. Identify the *p* graph by pointing the left mouse button inside the graph and pressing it once. When you see the black boxes on the corners of the graph, press the Delete key to delete the graph.

3. Use the left mouse button to identify the *range* C6:D32.

4. Press the Delete key to delete the numbers and text in these cells.

5. Use the left mouse button to identify the *range* E6:G32.

6. Click on the Cut icon .

7. Click on cell C6 and click on the Paste button.

Due to the changes, some of the formulas are no longer correct. Figure 12.7 illustrates the screen.

Changing Formulas for *np* Chart Generation

Only two formulas must be changed to generate the np chart—the average *np* (np-bar) formula, as well as the formula for sigma.

To change the formula for sigma, follow these steps:

1. Click in cell D8 and type the following formula and press enter:

$$=AVERAGE(\$B\$8:\$B\$32)$$

2. Copy this formula into the *range* D9:D32.

3. Click on cell D2 (the formula in cell D2 is =SQRT(D8*(1–D8)/D1); this formula is incorrect for the binomial distribution.

Figure 12.7 Formula problems.

4. Press F2 to enter the edit mode.

The formula for the standard deviation of a binomial distribution using counts is:

$$S_{np} = \sqrt{\bar{p}*(1-\bar{p})*n}$$

5. Enter this formula:

=SQRT((\$D\$8/D1)*(1–(\$D\$8/D1))*\$D\$1)

6. Press Enter.

After the formula in cell D2 is changed to the standard deviation using counts, all the errors disappear. Figure 12.8 shows the completed worksheet.

Changing Column Labels for the *np* Control Chart

The next step is to change the column headings from a *p* chart to an *np* chart.

1. Double-click on the WordArt $\bar{p}$.

2. Edit the WordArt to $n\bar{p}$.

After changing the WordArt it may be necessary to change the width of the box used to present the WordArt.

3. Click on the WordArt to see the WordArt box; point to the square in the middle of the box on either side when the double arrow appears to stretch the box to accommodate the new text.

4. Edit the Text boxes for UCLnp and LCLnp by double clicking on the text box and inserting an *n* in each.

Creating the *np* Control Chart

Hold the left mouse button and drag to define the *range* B7:E32. To create the *np* control chart, follow these steps:

1. Click on the Chart Wizard icon ▦ .

2. Select XY (Scatter) and the straight line with points Chart subtype and click on Next>.

3. The next screen shows the *np* chart and is Step 2 of 4—Chart Source Data.

4. Select the Series in Columns option below the chart.

5. On the same screen, click on the Series tab.

6. Click on Series1 to highlight the words *Series1*

7. Click on the empty box to the right of <u>N</u>ame and type *np*

Microsoft Excel - npchart1

	A	B	C	D	E	F	G	H	I
1	npchart1.xls		Lot Size:	100					
2			Sigma	2.22027025		UCLp	11.861	Simulated value	
3			Z:	3		LCLp	-1.461	p-bar	0.05
4			3 sigma	6.66081076					
5									
6		Number	LCL	np	UCL				
7	Number	Defective							
8	1	5	0	5.2	11.86				
9	2	6	0	5.2	11.86				
10	3	4	0	5.2	11.86				
11	4	6	0	5.2	11.86				
12	5	8	0	5.2	11.86				
13	6	5	0	5.2	11.86				
14	7	3	0	5.2	11.86				
15	8	3	0	5.2	11.86				
16	9	5	0	5.2	11.86				
17	10	1	0	5.2	11.86				
18	11	5	0	5.2	11.86				
19	12	3	0	5.2	11.86				
20	13	4	0	5.2	11.86				
21	14	6	0	5.2	11.86				
22	15	7	0	5.2	11.86				
23	16	8	0	5.2	11.86				
24	17	6	0	5.2	11.86				
25	18	5	0	5.2	11.86				
26	19	4	0	5.2	11.86				
27	20	3	0	5.2	11.86				
28	21	6	0	5.2	11.86				
29	22	5	0	5.2	11.86				
30	23	7	0	5.2	11.86				
31	24	7	0	5.2	11.86				
32	25	8	0	5.2	11.86				

Figure 12.8 *np* worksheet.

8. Click on Series2, then click on the Name box and type *LCLnp*

9. Click on Series3, then click on the Name box and type *np-bar*

10. Click on Series4, then click on the Name box and type *UCLnp*

11. Click on Next>.

12. On the screen add the chart title *np control chart*, name the *x*-axis *Lot number*, name the *y*-axis *np*, and click Next>.

13. Select As Object In to place the graph on the sheet with the worksheet calculations and click on Finish.

14. The chart is placed on the worksheet; use the left mouse button to drag the chart to a range that is to the right of column F.

After placing the graph on sheet 1, double-left-click on each of the lines to change the type of lines, thickness, color, and eliminate symbols on the lines. Use a dashed line without symbols for the upper control limit, a solid line without symbols for *np*, and a straight line with symbols for each lot. Next, double-click on the *x*-axis and *y*-axis and adjust the scales to your own preferences. This example uses *y*-axis values ranging from 0 to 12 in major units of 1.0, and major units of 10 for the *x*-axis. Figure 12.9 illustrates the edited *np* control chart.

Figure 12.9   The *np* control chart.

p Control Charts Based on Variable Lot Size

Open *pchart02.xls*. Edit cell A1 to *Var-n.xls* and use File, Save As to save the work as *Var-n.xls*. If you did not save *pchart02.xls*, you can start with *pchart01.xls* and make the corrections indicated in the *Worksheet Design Improvements* section.

Revising the Worksheet

A column will be inserted and then Number Observed will be placed in the inserted column.

1. Click on B at the top of column B.

2. Click on Insert, and then click on Column. Column B is now an empty column.

3. Highlight cells D6 and D7 and cut and paste the contents of these cells into C6 and C7.

4. Delete the text in cell D1 and the number 100 in cell E1.

5. Type the following numbers in the cells in column B beginning with B8, and make up numbers for the remaining cells in column B through cell B32.

Cell	Value
B8	100
B9	200
B10	100
B11	33
B12	100
B13	45
B14	85
B15	150

To generate sample data for the number of defective parts:

1. Edit the formula in C8 to:

$$=round(((rand()+rand()+rand()+rand()+rand()$$
$$+rand()+rand()+rand()+rand()+rand()+rand()$$
$$+rand()-6)*sqrt(\$J\$3*(1-\$J\$3)/100)+\$J\$3)*B8,0)$$

Notice that B8 in the formula does not include dollar signs. This is a relative address, not an absolute address.

2. Make cell C8 the active cell, and click on the C̲opy button.

3. Using the left mouse button, identify the *range* C9:C32 and press Enter.

4. Type the heading *Sigma* in cell D7; sigma must be calculated for every lot, because as the lot size varies, sigma will vary for each lot.

5. Delete the text *sigma* in cell D2 and the formula in cell E2.

6. Delete the text and formulas in the *range* G2:H3 and in D4 and E4.

7. In cell E8 type =C8/B8 and press Enter.

8. Copy this formula into the *range* E9:E32.

Revising Formulas for Chart Generation

Revise the formulas to calculate the values for the control chart with variable lot sizes. Four formulas must be revised: p-bar, sigma, LCLp, and UCLp.

1. p-bar—To calculate the average fraction of defectives, follow these steps to revise the formula:

    a. Make cell G8 the active cell and check the formula to ensure that the formula for the averages is correct:

    $$=average(\$E\$8:\$E\$32)$$

    b. Check that this formula is entered into the *range* G9:G32.

    The same value in cell G8 should appear in each cell in column G.

2. Sigma for each lot—To calculate sigma for each lot, follow these steps:

    a. Edit the formula in cell D8 to *=SQRT(G8*((1-G8)/B8))*

    b. Copy this formula into the cells in *range* D9:D32.

3. LCLp—The formula for the LCLp is:

    $$LCLp = \bar{p} - Z * Sigma$$

    for LCLp > 0 and zero if LCLp < 0. The formula for the LCLp must include an If statement preventing it from going below zero.

    a. Make cell F8 the active cell and press F2 to edit the formula to:

    $$=IF(G8-\$E\$3*D8<0,0,G8-\$E\$3*D8)$$

    and press Enter.

    b. Copy this formula into the cells in *range* F9:F32.

4. UCLp—Based on the possible invalid assumption that we will be working with a fraction defective rate near zero, not near 100, use the formula

    $$=G8+\$E\$3*D8$$

    in cell H8 to calculate the UCLp.

    a. Click on cell H8 and type *=G8+\$E\$3*D8* and press Enter.

    b. Copy this formula into the cells in *range* H9:H32.

Figure 12.10 illustrates the completed worksheet *var-n.xls*. Notice how the control limits vary up and down to reflect changes in lot sizes. The standard deviation (sigma) is small for large values of the lot size and large for small values of the lot size.

Figure 12.10 var-n.xls worksheet.

Generating the *p* Control Chart with Variable Lot Sizes

To create the *p* control chart for samples with variable lot sizes, define the *range* E8:H32 and follow the steps described in Creating the *p* Control Chart. Figure 12.11 illustrates the control chart. Notice how the control limits of the process chart go up and down to reflect the changes in lot size and sigma.

Using *p* Control Charts

The primary objective in using control charts is to identify when a change occurs. The control chart indicates *when* a change occurs in a process, but the production manager must identify *why* a change occurs. One method for studying control chart change is to compare a sample of process data to base period data. This can be accomplished by controlling the values of *p* in an exercise that utilizes randomly generated observations. To complete the exercise follow these steps:

Open the worksheet *pchart02.xls* and change the name of the worksheet in cell A1 to *simulate.xls*. Save the worksheet using the new file name *simulate.xls* by clicking on File, clicking on Save As, and following the procedure for saving the files as *simulate.xls*. If you fail to rename the file in cell A1 and save the file under the new name, you will overwrite the original file.

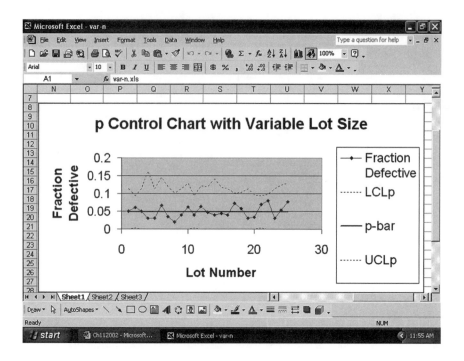

Figure 12.11 *p* control chart with variable lot sizes.

Revising the Worksheet

The next step is to revise the worksheet by adding 25 more lots, for a total of 50 lots. The first 25 lots will serve as the base period. Follow these steps:

1. Use the mouse to identify the *range* A8:G32.

2. Click on the <u>C</u>opy button .

3. Click in cell A33 and click on the <u>P</u>aste button ■.

4. In cell A33 type =+*1*+ and click on cell A32 and press Enter.

The worksheet now has 50 rows of data, with the lots numbered in column A.

5. In cell K2 type *New p*

6. In cell K3 type *0.11*

The value 0.11 is approximately equal to the original simulation p plus three standard deviations. Cell B33 is the number of defectives in the 26th lot.

7. Edit the formula in cell B33 to

$$=\text{round}(((\text{rand()}+\text{rand()}+\text{rand()}+\text{rand()}+\text{rand()}$$
$$+\text{rand()}+\text{rand()}+\text{rand()}+\text{rand()}+\text{rand()}$$
$$+\text{rand()}-6)*\text{sqrt(\$K\$3*(1-\$K\$3)/100)}+\$K\$3)*\$D\$1,0)$$

8. Make cell B33 the active cell, and click on the <u>C</u>opy button

9. Define the *range* B34:B57, and press Enter

10. Identify the cell *ranges* A8:A57 and D8:G57 (remember to hold the Control [CTRL] key while you identify the range with the left mouse button)

11. Using the Chart Wizard 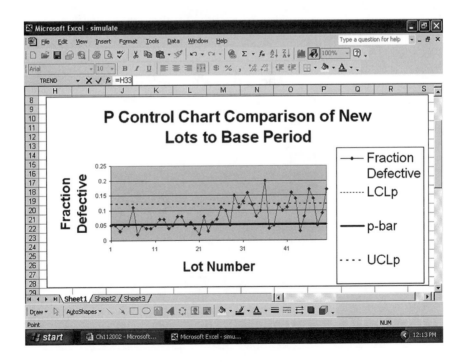, recreate the chart using the same procedures described in the section Creating the *p* Control Chart

An interesting experiment would be to study the number of lots using the "new" quality level needed as the value in cell K3 is adjusted. Figure 12.12 illustrates the control chart for a selected run showing the change.

From the chart, one can see that the fraction of defective items in lots 25 through 50 has increased. The quality control specialist or the production

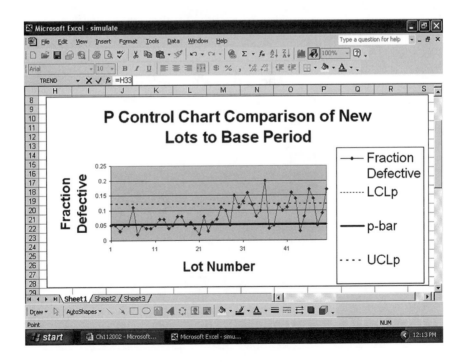

Figure 12.12 Comparing new lots against the base period.

specialist must investigate why the number of fraction of defects has increased. Remember, the control chart informs the specialist that a change has occurred, but does not explain why the change occurred.

Real Life

A printed circuit board (PCB) was identified as the cause of many system failures. Current inspection procedures were not effective in eliminating the problem. The engineering group was considering a board redesign. Rather than a complete redesign of the board, someone suggested that the PCB be inspected by function and only the "bad" function be redesigned. After a short engineering review, the primary functions of the PCB were identified so that each function could be inspected individually. p charts were to be recorded for each function (quality characteristic) to ensure the system was stable before any major engineering redesign project was started.

Five functions were identified (A, B, C, D, and E). Figure 12.13 illustrates a Pareto diagram for the results after two weeks.

The dominant failures were in function D. An Excel worksheet control chart was created for function D. Figure 12.14 illustrates the chart. As soon as the engineers saw the chart, the search for the cause of the problem shifted from engineering design to manufacturing. It was found that there was a manufacturing contamination problem that occurred periodically.

Figure 12.13 Pareto diagram.

Figure 12.14 *p* chart for function D.

Summary

The *p* and *np* control charts are effective procedures for studying quality problems where the measurement produces a count. The *np* chart is used when the data consist of a count of bad items and the lot size is constant. The *p* chart is used when the data consist of a count and the lot size may be constant or variable. Managers sometimes prefer to use the *p* chart for all applications; that is they use the *p* chart even when the lot size is constant.

Attribute control charts help managers improve quality. They require more data than variable charts, but only a count of the number of defective parts or services is needed rather than careful measurements. When attribute data are used, the inspection record includes the number of parts inspected and the number of defective parts, therefore, *p* and *np* charts are the charts of first choice.

Exercises

12.1 Reformat the sample worksheet into a horizontal form.

12.2 Create a worksheet for a *p* chart with random number input. For the first 25 days, use a fraction defective of 0.01. For the second 25 days, vary the fraction defective from 0.05 to 0.02 (use an increment of 0.01) and count the number of days before an outlier occurs in every case. Replicate the experiment five times at each level. Record your results. Graph the average number of groups before an outlier occurs versus incoming quality. Explain your results.

12.3   Create a *p* chart for the following data:

Day	Number Inspected	Number Defectives
1	1000	1
2	1000	0
3	1000	1
4	1000	0
5	1000	2
6	1000	0
7	1000	4
8	1000	0
9	1000	1
10	1000	0
11	1000	3
12	1000	0
13	1000	3
14	1000	0
15	1000	3
16	1000	0
17	1000	1
18	1000	0
19	1000	1
20	1000	0
21	1000	0

12.4   Examine several textbooks on quality control. Find one that gives a
p chart example. Create an Excel worksheet for the problem and
compare your results with the textbook's results. (For a list of texts
refer to the reference section located at the back of this book.)

13

c and *u* Control Charts

OUTLINE

Changes in λ (Lambda)

Prior Knowledge

From earlier chapters, you should know how to open and save files, how to cut and copy a range from part of a worksheet to another, and know what a macro is and how recording a macro can be helpful in completing tasks. You should have the Data Analysis option activated in the Tools menu.

Why Use *c* and *u* Control Charts?

Recall that *p* and *np* control charts use attribute data to illustrate the number, fraction, or percentage of defective items in each lot or batch. At times it is important to track the number of *defects* or *nonconformities* for each single item. *c charts* are useful for counting the number of defects in a single item or unit, while *u charts* are useful for counting the number of defects over a number of units. In other words, a *u* chart is a control chart for controlling an operation using the average number of defects per unit as a measure.

The objective of *c* and *u* charts is the same as other control charts—to identify changes in a process as the changes occur and provide the manager the opportunity to identify defects and stop the output of poor quality so the process can be corrected. *c* and *u* charts help the process manager identify *assignable causes of variation* so that a stable system of chance causes is maintained.

c chart: A control chart for controlling an operation using the number of defects per inspection unit.

Defect: An occurrence of lack of conformity to one or more specifications.

Nonconformities: Defects.

u **chart:** A control chart for controlling an operation using the average number of defects over a selected number of inspection units.

Assignable causes of variation: Influences that can be identified.

The *c* and *u* charts use attribute data that count the number of items with a specific characteristic compared to variable data, which is measured using continuous data. The *c* and *u* charts are based on the Poisson distribution, while the *np* and *p* charts are based on the binomial distribution. The number of possible defects follows a Poisson distribution, which is based on integers and the occurrence of events (defects) is low.

A classic example of c chart data is the number of spelling errors on a page of a newspaper. An example of *u* chart data is the average number of errors per page in a daily edition. *c* chart and *u* chart applications usually have a low probability of an event occurring while the number of opportunities for the event to occur is large. Additional examples include: (a) number of bad rivets in a bridge, (b) number of customers receiving the wrong items in their orders in a fast-food restaurant, and (c) number of imperfections in a bolt of cloth.

The *c* and *u* charts are simply control charts that divide a process output into classifications: within control limits or outside control limits. If the process output is outside the control limits, it assumes that a change in the process has occurred since the limits were set. If a change is bad, managers may search for the reasons for the change and try to eliminate the cause to reduce the number of errors or bad units. If a change is good, managers may then attempt to identify the reasons for the change and try to make the change a part of normal operations.

Poisson Distribution—Random Numbers

This chapter presents two methods for generating Poisson random numbers in Excel. The first method uses the random number generation capability provided in Excel. The second method requires the user to enter the Poisson distribution formula, identify a range name, and write a macro (a mini-program created by the user to complete a simple process). If you are interested in using a process generator without learning the details of how the process generator works, then the built-in Excel process generators are an efficient option. On the other hand, if you would like to understand how process generators are created to simulate data, the second method is preferred. A third option is available to users who have already collected process data. These users can manually enter the data into the worksheet, as the task of data entry is minimal for attribute data.

The Poisson distribution is a discrete distribution that exists in the (statistical) range of zero to infinity; that is, the output from a Poisson distribution starts at zero and goes up in increments of one with no upper limit. The formula for the Poisson distribution is

$$P(x \leq n) = \lambda^n * e^{-\lambda} / n!$$

c Chart Formulas

The formulas for the *c* chart are

$$\text{Average defects (center line): } \bar{c} = \Sigma c_i / n$$

$$\text{Standard deviation: } \sqrt{\bar{c}}$$

$$UCL_c = \bar{c} + 3 * \sqrt{\bar{c}}$$

$$LCL_c = \bar{c} - 3 * \sqrt{\bar{c}}$$

These formulas are easy to enter and use in Excel.

Creating the *c* Chart Worksheet

The data collection for a *c* chart is simply the count of defects on a defined inspection unit. The form for data collection should include three columns: remarks, unit identification, and the number of defects. The control chart requires three additional columns: lower control limit (LCLc), upper control limit (UCLc), and the average number of defects across all sample units ($\bar{c}$).

Entering Worksheet Text

Type the following worksheet identification, headings, and text as indicated. After typing the text in each cell, press Enter, the Tab key, or an arrow key.

Cell	Text
A1	c-chart1.xls (or name of your choice)
B4	Defects Report
A5	Department:
A6	Date:
A7	Unit:
D5	Inspector:
D7	Sigma:
D8	Z:
E8	3
A9	Remarks
B9	Identification

Adjust the width of column B for the word *Identification* by left clicking on the column head. When the double arrow displays, hold down the left mouse button to drag the edge of the column to the right.

B10	Unit
C9	Number of
C10	Defects
D10	LCLc
E10	c-bar
F10	UCLc

Click on File and click on Save and select the subdirectory of your choice to save the file as *c-chart1.xls*.

The next step is to input the unit identification numbers:

1. In cell B11 type *1* and press Enter.

2. In cell B12 type the formula *+1+B11* and press Enter.

3. Copy the formula into the cells in *range* B13:B60.

As shown in Figure 13.1, the rows, beginning in row 11, should be numbered from 1 to 50.

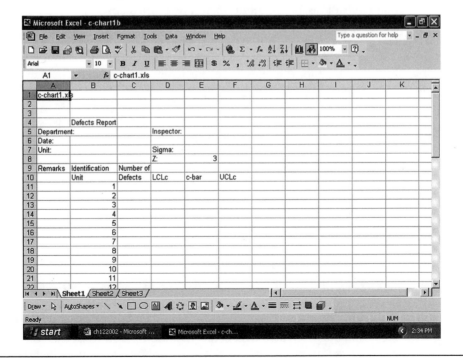

Figure 13.1 Worksheet text.

Generating Sample Data

Recall that there are three ways to generate sample data that fit a Poisson distribution: (1) key the data manually, (2) use the Excel Poisson random number generator, or (3) enter the Poisson distribution formula, identify a range name, and write a macro to generate the data. The worksheet on the disk uses the third alternative—the distribution formula and the macro to generate sample data.

1. Manually Key Data

To enter sample data, type integer values from 0 to 9 into the *range* C11:C60. After the data are entered, you may proceed by skipping to the *Entering Worksheet Formulas* section.

2. Generate Sample Data Using the Excel Poisson Random Number Generator

Excel's random number generator provides a way to easily generate random numbers that fit a particular distribution. This capability is useful when the user understands simulation or is not concerned with how the values of a distribution are simulated. Relying on Excel's random number generator makes it difficult to learn simulation if the user's objective is to learn how to simulate a Poisson distribution.

To use Excel's random number generator to generate random numbers that have a Poisson distribution, follow these steps:

1. Click on Tools, Data Analysis, Random Number Generation (Figure 13.2).

2. Type *1* for the Number of Variables and press the Tab key.

3. Type *50* for the Number of Random Numbers.

4. Click on the arrow to the right of Distribution and select *Poisson.*

5. Type *1* for the value of Lambda.

6. Click on Output Range, type *C11,* and then click on OK.

Fifty random numbers using a Lambda of 1 are generated beginning in cell C11. You may use the procedure for entering random numbers using different values of Lambda.

3. Generate Random Numbers with a Macro

The third option for generating random values using a Poisson distribution is to key formulas and a macro that will generate the random numbers. A *macro* is simply a series of instructions that is recorded to use again and again. This application uses a macro to generate a random number for each cell.

Macros can infect computers with viruses and/or cause other damage to a computer. In Excel xp the default security level set for maximum protection

Figure 13.2   Random number generator dialog box.

guards against destructive macros. It is difficult to run any macros at the High level of security protection. Figure 13.3 illustrates the Excel xp security dialog box, which is displayed from the Tools menu by selecting Options, then the Security tab, and Macro Security button. If you are using the templates provided with this text, you will need to adjust the security level to medium to run the macro in this chapter.

Create the Poisson Distribution Formula

To create the Poisson distribution column headings, type the following text in the appropriate cells:

Cell	Text
N3	Random Number
J4	n
K4	n!
L4	f(x)
M4	F(x)
N4	=rand()

Figure 13.3   Macro Security Level Screen.

The values of *n* start at zero and go up in increments of one. To enter the values for *n* in column J, the steps are:

1. In cell J5 type *0* and press Enter.

2. In cell J6 type *+1+J5* and press Enter.

3. Copy the formula in cell J6 into the cell *range* J7:J27.

In each chapter, the text introduces new worksheet concepts and capabilities as the worksheet examples are created. In chapter 12, the Text Box and WordArt are presented to create unique headings. A Text Box is also useful to add notes or comments to a worksheet. Click on the Drawing icon

. The Draw menu appears.

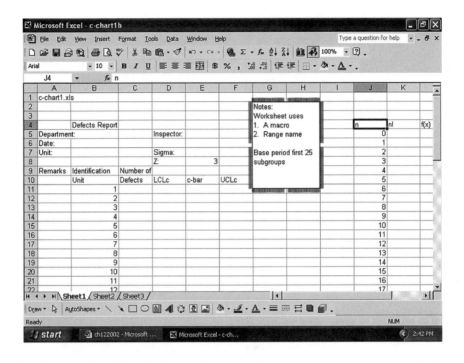

Figure 13.4   Worksheet headings and text box.

Click on Text Box 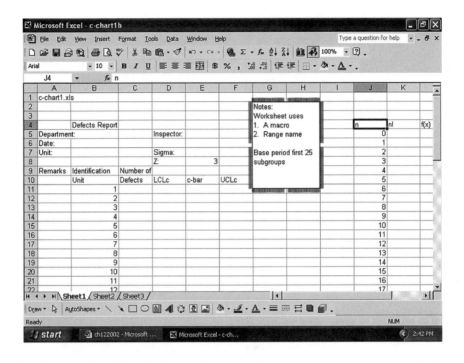 and locate a Text Box in columns G and H, as illustrated in Figure 13.4. In the Text Box type:

Notes:

Worksheet uses

1. A macro

2. Range name

Base period first 25 subgroups

Entering the Poisson Formulas

The *Poisson distribution* is a discrete distribution that exists in the (statistical) range zero to infinity; that is, the output from a Poisson distribution starts at zero and goes up in increments of one. The formula for the Poisson distribution is:

$$P(x \le n) = \lambda^n * e^{-\lambda} / n!$$

To create a macro that will generate data using the Poisson distribution, follow these steps:

1. In cell I1 type | and press Enter (this character is created by holding the Shift key and pressing the \ key).

2. Copy the contents of cell I1 into the cell *range* I2:I27.

3. Resize column I width as small as possible so that only the line shows. This line defines the left position for the Poisson process generator calculations.

Given that λ is in cell K3, *n* is in the *range* J5:J27, and *n!* is in the *range* K5:K27:

4. In cell J3 type *Lambda* and press Enter.

5. In cell K3 type *1* and press Enter.

The values of *n!* must be entered in the *range*: K5:K27. The formula for *n!* is:

$$n! = n * (n-1) * (n-2) * \ldots 1$$

and by definition 0! is 1. The steps needed to enter *n!* are:

6. In cell K5 type *1* and press Enter.

7. In cell K6 type *=+ J6*K5* and press Enter.

8. Copy the formula in cell K6 into the cells in *range* K7:K27.

The values in column K become large. The number 4.79E+08 is scientific notation and means the number is 479,000,000; that is 4.79 times 100,000,000.

Column L includes the probability function *f(x)*.

9. Click on cell L5 and type *+$K$3^J5*EXP(–$K$3)/K5* and press Enter.

10. Copy the formula in cell L5 into the cell *range* L6:L27.

When λ is small (1), the numbers in column L become smaller for large values of *n* (8). The number 7.3E–05 is scientific notation for 0.000073.

Column M includes the cumulative probability function *F(x)*.

11. Click on cell M5 and type *=+L5* and press Enter.

12. Cell M6 is the active cell; type *=+M5+L6* and press Enter.

13. Copy this formula into the *range* M7:M27.

The value of the cumulative probability function is near one when *n* is eight (8). This is how it should be, because the values in *f(x)* are extremely small for *n* equal to eight (8) or above.

The random number placed in cell N4 may be used to select the value of *n*.

14. In cell N5 type *=IF((N4<=M5),j5,"")* and press Enter.

15. Click on cell N6 and type *=IF(AND($N$4<=M6,$N$4>M5),J6,"")* and press Enter.

16. Copy the formula into the *range* N7:N27.

When you press the function key F9, the random number in cell N4 changes, and the selected value of *n* in the *range* N5:N27 changes. There is never more than one number in the *range* N5:N27. Figure 13.5 illustrates the values in the worksheet.

Range Names and Macros

In chapter 3, the difference between relative and absolute addressing in formulas was presented. The default addressing in Excel is relative; however, one can specify absolute addressing by placing dollar signs in front of a cell reference in a formula. However, in an Excel macro, the default addressing is absolute. In the Poisson macro, we need both relative and absolute addressing.

Figure 13.5 Poisson values in the worksheet.

To use relative addressing (for all cell references) in a macro, click on Tools and then on Customize, and then on Toolbars. Next, place a checkmark on Stop Recording and click on Close to activate the Stop Rec box . The Relative Reference box on the right side of the Stop Rec box toggles between relative addressing on and relative addressing off.

To define the Poisson distribution that will be used in the macro, use *absolute addressing* by holding down the left mouse button and defining the *range* N5:N27. Click on Insert, click on Name, click on Define, type *Poisson*, and click on OK.

To create the macro:

1. Click on C11.

2. Click on the relative reference button on the right side of the Stop Recording macro button.

3. Click on Tools.

4. Click on Macro.

5. Click on Record New Macro.

6. Type *rn* for the macro name in the Record Macro screen (as illustrated in Figure 13.6).

Figure 13.6   Macro dialog box.

7. Enter uppercase *R* for the shortcut (Ctrl+Shift R) and click on OK.

8. Click on C11 and type *=max(Poisson)* and press Enter.

9. Click on C11.

10. Click on the Copy button.

11. Click on Edit.

12. Click on Paste Special.

13. Click on Values to place a check in the circle and click on OK.

14. Press Enter.

15. Press Enter once more.

16. Click on Stop Rec button on the left side to end the recording of the macro.

To use the macro, place the cell pointer on cell C11, hold down the Ctrl+Shift keys, and press *R* over and over again until a complete set of defects is generated. The value of *l* may be changed in cell K3 to simulate different levels of defects.

Entering Worksheet Formulas

To enter the formulas to calculate the average and control chart limits, follow these steps:

1. Average number of defects per unit—To calculate the average number of defects per unit:

   a. In cell E11 type *=average($C$11:$C$60)* and press Enter.

   b. Copy the formula into the cell *range* E12:E60.

   The average of all 50 observations should be copied into each cell of the E column.

2. Sigma—To calculate sigma (standard deviation) for this example, type the following formula:

   a. In cell E7 type *=SQRT(E11)* and press Enter.

3. LCLc—The numbers selected may result in a negative number for the LCLc in cell D11. The LCLc cannot be negative. An IF statement that sets the LCLc equal to zero when the lower control limit is negative is required. To calculate the lower control level, type the following formula:

   a. In cell D11 type *=if($E$11–$E$8*$E$7<0,0,$E$11–$E$8*$E$7)* and press Enter.

   b. Copy the statement into the cell *range* D12:D60.

4. UCLc—To calculate the upper control level, type the following formula:

   a. In cell F11 type =+$E$11+$E$8*$E$7 and press Enter.

   b. Copy the formula into the cell *range* F12:F60 .

The *c* control chart calculations are complete. Figure 13.7 illustrates the worksheet.

Creating the *c* Control Chart

Hold down the left mouse key to define the *range* B10:F60. To create the *c* control chart, follow these steps:

1. Click on the Chart Wizard icon 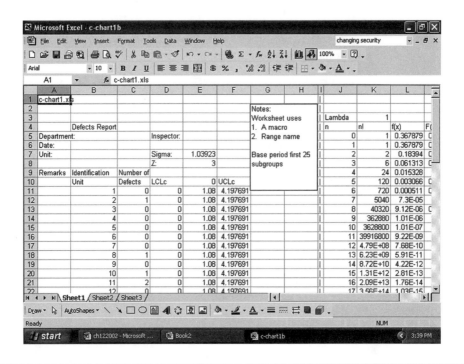.

2. In Step 1 of 4, select the XY(Scatter) and the straight line with data points Chart subtype, and click on Next>.

3. In Step 2 of 4, click on Next>.

4. Enter the chart name *c Control chart*, *x*-axis name *Unit Number*, and the *y*-axis name *Number of Defects per Unit*, and click Next>.

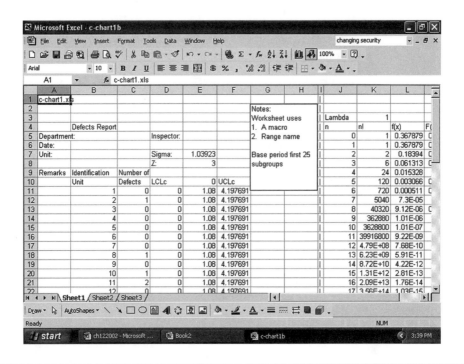

Figure 13.7   The *c* process control worksheet.

5. Select As Object In to place the graph on the sheet with the worksheet calculations and click on Finish.

6. The graph is placed on the worksheet; use the left mouse button to drag the graph to a range of cells below row 60.

7. Using the box tab on the right side of the graph's frame, expand the box to column R to facilitate analysis.

After placing the graph on the worksheet, double-left-click on each of the lines to change the type of lines, line thickness, colors, and eliminate symbols on the lines. Use a dashed line without symbols for the control limits, a solid heavy line without symbols for c-bar line, and a straight line with symbols to connect the number of defects line. Next, double-click on the *x*-axis and *y*-axis to adjust the scales to your own preferences. The example chart uses *y*-axis values ranging from 0 to 5 in major units of 1, and *x*-axis values ranging from 1 to 50 with major units of 10. Figure 13.8 illustrates the *c* control chart.

Changes in λ (Lambda)

Recall that there are three ways to generate sample data to simulate a Poisson distribution: (1) key the data manually, (2) use the Excel Poisson

Figure 13.8   c control chart.

random number generator, or (3) enter the distribution formula, identify a range, and write a macro to generate the data. Depending on which method you selected to generate the data in your spreadsheet, use the corresponding approach to change the values of λ in your observations.

1. Manually Key Data

If you manually key the data into the worksheet, you can simulate a change in the number of defects by rekeying the data using a different set of numbers. Use units 1 through 25 to represent the base period and change the number of defects for units 26 through 50.

2. Generate Sample Data Using the Excel Poisson Generator

If you used the Excel random number generator, you can revise the worksheet data to represent a base period (units 1 through 25) to compare to a sample (units 26 through 50) by making three changes in the random number generation menu:

1. Change the number of random numbers from 50 to 25.

2. Change the value of lambda to a 3 or any other integer.

3. Changing the Output Range from cells C11 to C36.

The 25 observations representing the base period data will remain in cells C11 through C35 and new data will be generated beginning in cell C36. When the values are revised, Excel will provide a warning that if you proceed, your previous values will be replaced and will give you the option to continue. After the data are entered, you may generate a new *c* control chart to analyze the results.

3. Generate Poisson Values with the Distribution Formula

If you generated the observation values using the Poisson formula and a macro, in order to simulate a change in the level of defects (λ), use the macro with *1* in cell K3 to generate values for the range C11:C35. Then change the value in cell K3 to 3, click on cell C36, and hold the Ctrl-Shift key down as you press *R* to enter a new value in cell C36. Continue pressing Ctrl-Shift and R to complete the data set. Figure 13.9 illustrates a *c* chart for a shift from λ = 1 to λ = 3.

u Chart Formulas

Calculations required to create a *u* chart include:

*   Number of units inspected

*   Number of defects in each unit

*   Average number of defects in all units

- Lower control limit (LCLu)

- Upper control limit (UCLu)

The formulas for the u chart are:

$$LCL_u = \bar{u} - 3\sqrt{\bar{u}/n_i}$$

$$UCL_u = \bar{u} + 3\sqrt{\bar{u}/n_i}$$

$$u = \sum c_i / \sum n_i$$

c_i = number of defects found in each group

n_i = number of units inspected in each group

Creating the *u* Chart Worksheet

When the sampling unit is not constant, a u chart must be used rather than a c chart. The u chart requires knowledge of the number of units in each sampling group. The defects per unit are calculated by dividing the number of units in a sample by the number of defects in the sample. The overall average u is calculated by dividing the total number of defects across all samples by the number of units in the samples.

Figure 13.9 c control chart with a shift in lambda from 1 to 3.

Entering Worksheet Text

Text is entered by making the cell the active cell and then typing the text and pressing Enter. Listed here are the cells and the text required in each cell.

Cell	Text
A1	U-chart1.xls
A3	Inspector:
A4	Process:
A12	Remarks
B5	Number inspected:
B6	Number defects:
B8	Z:
C8	3
B12	Lot
C11	Number
C12	Units
D3	Part number:
D4	Part name:
D11	Number
D12	Defects
E12	Defects/unit
F12	Sigma* (Sigma is a function of subgroup size)
G12	LCLu
H12	Ubar
I12	UCLu

According to Table 13.1, there are 25 lots in the sample. Each row in column B should be numbered consecutively by following these steps:

1. In cell B13 type *1* and press Enter.

2. Cell B14 is now the active cell; type *+1+ B13* and press Enter.

3. Copy the formula into the cell *range* B15:B37.

Entering Sample Data

Table 13.1 is a table of data for the u chart. The data includes both the number of units inspected and the number of defects found in all of the units inspected.

Table 13.1   Sample data for the u chart.

Lot	Number of Units	Number of Defects
1	10	1
2	8	1
3	12	1
4	7	1
5	10	0
6	1	0
7	11	2
8	5	0
9	9	0
10	2	0
11	6	1
12	5	0
13	1	0
14	2	0
15	6	0
16	10	0
17	7	0
18	8	3
19	6	0
20	3	0
21	5	0
22	4	0
23	6	0
24	9	0
25	9	0

Entering Worksheet Formulas

Enter the formulas for calculating the average, sigma, and control chart limits by following these steps:

1. The defects per unit are calculated by dividing the number of units in a group by the number of defects in the group.

   In cell E13 type =*D13/C13* and press Enter.

2. Number inspected: In cell D5 type =*SUM(C13:C37)* and press Enter.

3. Number of defects: In cell D6 type =*SUM(D13:D37)* and press Enter.

4. *u:* The overall average is calculated by dividing the total number of defects in all the samples by the number of units in all of the samples. This is a common way of performing this type of calculation when the number of units per lot is not constant.

   In cell H13 type =*$D$6/$D$5* and press Enter.

5. LCLu: The calculations for the LCLu may result in a negative number. The minimum true value of the LCLu is zero. We may use an IF or a MAX statement to select the larger of two values.

   In cell G13 type =*MAX(H13–$C$8*F13,0)* and press Enter.

6. UCLu: In cell I13 type =*+H13+$C$8*F13* and press Enter.

7. Sigma: In cell F13 type =*SQRT(H13/C13)* and press Enter.

The manner in which the formulas were entered in row 13 makes it possible to copy columns E through I in one step.

1. Define the *range* E13:I13; click on the Copy icon .

2. Define the *range* E14:I37 and press Enter.

The *u* chart calculations are complete. Figure 13.10 illustrates the completed worksheet.

Be careful to save the worksheet using the name in cell A1, *u-chart.xls* in the subdirectory of your choice.

The graphing is identical to the *c* chart, except that the graphing range includes columns E, G, H, and I. Graphing the *u* control chart is left as an exercise for the reader, however, a completed *u* control chart is illustrated in Figure 13.11.

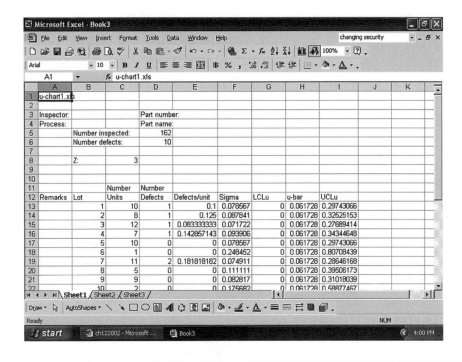

Figure 13.10   Complete *u* chart worksheet.

Figure 13.11   *u* control chart.

Figure 13.12   Real data in a *u* chart.

Real Life

The molding of large objects such as 15- or 16-foot-long fiberglass kayaks may result in a few small nonstructural defects, such as surface blemishes or blowholes. These defects may often be repaired with no ill effect on the final product. If, however, the number or size of the defects increases, then the imperfections may have a negative effect on the product and in some cases the product may have to be declared a second. A *second* is a unit that must be sold at a reduced price because of imperfections. These types of production problems are a classic application for a *c* or *u* chart.

Figure 13.12 illustrates a real *u* chart in which the number of defects per unit is increasing. The real problem with this chart is that the change is taking place during the base period. It is difficult to know if the number of defects is increasing if quality standards are not created using base period data.

Summary

The *c* and *u* charts help the manager prevent the production of poor quality products or services. The charts illustrate the number of defects so that the manager can track the process and investigate sources of defects. These charts are most useful when the probability of a defective occurrence is small. The Poisson distribution is the best theoretical model for the process.

Exercises

13.1 Set up a *c* chart for 50 items. Assume that Lambda for the first 25 items is 2. Adjust Lambda for the second 25 items from 0.5 to 1 to 1.5 . . . to 4 and count the number of items before an outlier appears on the *c* chart. Replicate five times at each level; graph the results.

13.2 Given the following data, create a *c* chart. Evaluate the results.

Item	Number of Defects	Item	Number of Defects
1	5	26	0
2	3	27	0
3	2	28	0
4	4	29	1
5	6	30	0
6	4	31	0
7	3	32	0
8	2	33	2
9	2	34	0
10	0	35	0
11	3	36	2
12	2	37	0
13	4	38	1
14	6	39	1
15	2	40	0
16	8	41	1
17	6	42	0
18	3	43	1
19	3	44	0
20	3	45	0
21	11	46	0
22	5	47	0
23	9	48	1
24	3	49	0
25	7	50	0

13.3 Find a textbook with a *c* chart example. Enter the data into a *c* chart and compare your results with the textbook. (For a list of texts refer to the reference section located at the back of this book.)

14

Process Capability

KEY TERMS

Control	Specification limit
Goodness-of-fit test	Stable system of chance causes
Lower natural tolerance limit (LNTL)	Upper natural tolerance limit (UNTL)
Process capability study	Visual test
Significance test	

OUTLINE

Prior Knowledge

From earlier chapters, you should know how to open and save files, cut and copy a range from part of a worksheet to another, and how to create and edit a graph. You should have the ToolPak option activated in the Tools menu.

Capability of a Process

The *capability* of a process is the ability of a process to perform a given task, such as the production of parts within some set of specified limits. In order to assess the capability of a process, the quality control specialist must perform *process capability analyses*. A common measure of process capability is the number of standard deviations of the process output that fit between two given limits, assuming that the average of the process output is centered between the two limits.

A *process capability study* assumes that the system is stable and that the data are normally distributed. A stable process is critical to performing a process capability study because it is impossible to estimate process parameters when a process is unstable. You may recall that an unstable process is subject to unidentified external forces that result in nonrandom changes. Therefore, the parameters of an unstable process can take on an infinite number of values at anytime. It is common practice to use indices to measure process capability, however, if the system is not stable or if the data are not normally distributed, the use of indices and ratios may lead to incorrect decisions that result in errors and increased costs.

The steps in a process capability study are:

1. Establish a stable system of chance variation using control chart methods.

2. Perform *goodness-of-fit tests:* visual and statistical.

3. Calculate the probability of being outside the *specification limits.*

4. Calculate selected indexes and ratios, including:

    a. The standard deviation of the population

    b. The upper and lower natural tolerance limits

A good method for establishing a stable system is to use control charts. The concept of *control* informs us that a system is in control if it is reproducible within limits. The procedure for establishing control is:

1. Collect control chart data for at least 20 to 25 subgroups.

2. Examine each point outside the control limits for possible assignable causes.

3. Remove from the sample all the subgroups with assignable causes.

4. Recalculate the limits and use these limits as the basis for making decisions.

The control charts created in the previous chapters are used to identify process parameters. The authors assume that stability has been established using the material in prior chapters and, therefore, will not spend time on this effort here. This chapter covers steps 2, 3, and 4.

Control: Reproducibility within limits.

Goodness-of-fit test: Statistical procedure to test if observations could have come from a specified distribution.

Process capability study: Analysis of the capability of a process to produce results in terms of percent defective.

Specification limit: The results required.

Stable system: A system working in an environment in which only normal random variation is present.

Testing for the Normal Distribution

Process capability analysis may be conducted using visual tests or statistical goodness-of-fit tests for any known distributions. Process capability analysis is based on the assumption that the data generated by the process are normally distributed. Although manual calculations to conduct statistical goodness-of-fit tests could require many hours, a test, such as the *Kolmogorov-Smirnov (KS)* test for normality, can be completed using an Excel worksheet in a few seconds. Excel also allows the user to make a simple visual test with minimum effort. The worksheets for both tests are created in the following sections.

The central limit theorem indicates that as the sample size increases, the average of a random sample will approximate a normal distribution regardless of the distribution of the individual variables. Excellent tables and formulas are available to test for a normal distribution. The assumption of normality is common in quality control applications, so the goodness-of-fit tests in this chapter will test for the normal distribution.

All goodness-of-fit tests involve the comparison of observed data to a theoretical distribution. The authors recommend that the cumulative distribution should be used to compare continuous distributions; however, a histogram of data superimposed over the normal distribution's probability density function provides an excellent visual comparison. Both a cumulative distribution graph and probability density function graph are presented in this chapter. Other methods are available for conducting goodness-of-fit tests. The important point is to compare your data against a theoretical distribution to ensure that your data fit the distribution that you are using. If your data are not distributed according to the particular distribution that is guiding your decisions, your statistical tests may not be valid.

Creating a Process Capability Worksheet

Entering Worksheet Text

Assume a data set contains 25 subgroups, each with five observations. Start by creating a worksheet complete with headings and simulated data. Type the text or numbers into the cells as indicated in Table 14.1. After typing the content in each cell, press Enter, the Tab key, or an arrow key.

Figure 14.1 illustrates the completed headings. Notice that the columns have been sized to accommodate the text. Notice also that there are no labels for columns J and K; these labels will be added later.

The next step is to number the subgroups:

1. Click on cell A10 and type =+1+A9 and press Enter.

2. Copy this formula into the cells in the *range* A11:A33.

The rows of the worksheet, beginning with row 10, should be numbered from 1 through 25.

Creating Observations Using the Normal Random Number Generator

There are two ways to generate sample observations that conform to a normal distribution: (1) use the Excel normal random generator, or (2) enter a formula that conforms to a normal distribution. Both methods are demonstrated in this chapter.

1. Generating Sample Data Using the Excel Normal Random Number Generator

Excel's random number generator provides a way to easily generate random numbers that fit a particular distribution. This capability is useful when the user understands simulation or is not concerned with how the

Table 14.1   Process capability worksheet text.

Cell	Text Input	Notes
A1	Pcap-01.xls	Worksheet name
A8	Subgroup	
B2	Simulated input data	
B3	Average:	
B4	Std. Dev.:	
B8	1	
C3	100	Simulation value
C4	10	Simulation value
C8	2	
D8	3	
E8	4	
F8	5	
G2	Results of Simulation	
G3	Average:	
G4	Std. Dev.:	
H8	Z	
I8	Z*sd+avg	Column heading for the reverse Z transformation
J3	Count:	
K6	Observed--------------------------------------	
K7	Count:	
L8	Frequency	
M8	Cum. Freq.	
N6	Expected--------------------------------------	
N8	Cum. Normal	
O8	Count Exp.	
P8	Spec. limits	
A9	1	

Figure 14.1   Worksheet text.

values of a distribution are simulated. Relying on Excel's random number generator makes it difficult to learn simulation if the user's objective is to learn how to simulate a particular distribution.

To use Excel's random number generator to enter random numbers that have a normal distribution, follow these steps:

1. Click on Tools, Data Analysis, Random Number Generation (Figure 14.2).

2. Type *5* for the Number of Variables and press the Tab key.

3. Type *25* for the Number of Random Numbers.

4. Click on the arrow to the right of Distribution: and select *Normal*.

5. Type *100* for the Mean.

6. Type *10* for the Standard deviation.

7. Click on Output Range, type *B9*, and then click on OK.

After the random observations are generated, proceed to the Define the *z* Scale section.

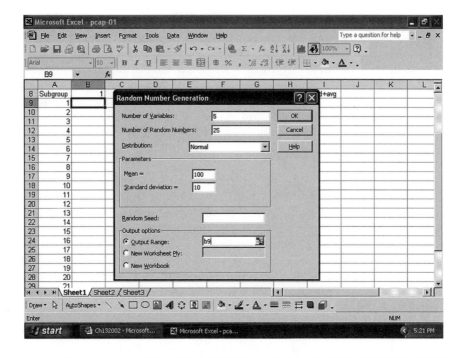

Figure 14.2   Random Number Generation dialog box.

2. Generating Normal Values with the Distribution Formula

The second option for generating random values using a normal distribution is to key a formula that will generate the random numbers. To generate random numbers for each observation in the subgroup, follow these steps:

1. Click on cell B9 and type the normal process generator equation:

    =round((rand()+rand()+rand()+rand()+rand()+rand()+rand()
    +rand()+rand()+rand()+rand()+rand()–6)*$C$4+$C$3,2)[1]

2. Copy this formula into the cell *range* B9:F33.

Observations should be created for each cell in the *range* B9:F33.

---

[1]The normal distribution process generator includes: (1) A round statement to fix the number of values to the right of the decimal point; (2) 12 uniform random numbers; (3) A minus 6 to center the distribution near zero; and (4) a reverse Z transformation (multiplying the sum by the standard deviation plus the mean) to obtain numbers as if they were generated by a distribution with an average equal to the number in cell C3 and a standard deviation equal to the number in cell C4.

Using a process generator with one average and one standard deviation throughout the range means that the results of both the visual test and the Kolmogorov-Smirnov (KS) test should indicate that the observations have a normal distribution. After you complete the two tests, you may wish to introduce a change in the data so that you can examine situations where changes in the distribution occur. That is, change the observations so that you expect to reject the null hypothesis that the distribution is normal.

Defining the *Z* Scale

The next step in the visual test is to define the Z scale for analysis. This scale will provide a smooth line showing the normal distribution. The subgroup observations will be compared to this line to assess normality of the data. The traditional Z scale translates observations into standard deviations. This translation indicates how far each observation is from the sample mean. In a normal distribution, most of the observations (98 percent) will fall between plus/minus three (3) standard deviations. For this graph, plus/minus 4.5 sigma with a cell change (increment) of 0.25 sigma was selected.

To generate the Z scale, follow these steps:

1. Click on cell H9 and type *−4.5* and press Enter.

2. Cell H10 should be the active cell; type *+0.25+H9* and press Enter.

3. Copy the formula in cell H10 into cell in the *range* H11:H45.

The values in the *range* H9:H45 should be displayed in increasing increments of .25.

Enter the following formulas into the appropriate cells:

Cell	Formula	Notes
H3	=average(B9:F33)	Sample mean
H4	=stdev(B9:F33)	Sample standard deviation
I9	=H9*$H$4+$H$3	Reverse Z transformation

The reverse Z transformation changes the Z score (number of standard deviations away from the mean) to a score that is consistent with the data in this example.

To complete the scale:

4. Copy the formula in cell I9 into the cells in the *range* I10:I45.

The next step is to create a histogram of the reverse Z values from the data. Tools, Data Analysis, . . . are needed to count the number of random numbers in each bin as defined by the Z scale. The Bins column simply displays a histogram of the data points. If Data Analysis is not available when you click on Tools, click on Add-Ins and check Analysis ToolPak to activate the Data Analysis option.

1. Click on Tools.

2. Click on Data Analysis.

3. Click on Histogram, and then click on OK.

4. With the cursor blinking in the Input Range: identify the *range* B9:F33 with the mouse (or type in the range).

5. Click in the Bin Range box and define the *range* I9:I45.

6. Click on Output range.

7. Click on the Output range box and type *J8*

8. Click on OK.

Figure 14.3 illustrates the results. When you press F9, all the random numbers change. To update the cell counts in columns J and K, you must select Tools, Data Analysis, and complete steps 1 through 8 to recalculate the revised count.

Figure 14.3 Bins defined, count complete.

For the cumulative distribution analysis, the count in column K must be converted to a frequency (for this application, Excel's use of the word *Frequency* in cell K8 is misleading). To convert a count to a frequency, one must divide the count by the number of observations. To calculate the frequencies and the cumulative frequencies, follow these steps:

1. Click on cell K3 and type *=count(B9:F33)* and press Enter.

2. Click on cell L9 and type *=K9/$K$3* and press Enter.

3. Copy the formula in cell L9 into the cells in the *range* L10:L45.

4. Click on cell M9 and type *=+L9* and press Enter.

5. Click on cell M10 and type *=+M9+L10* and press Enter.

6. Copy the formula in cell M10 into the cells in the *range* M11:M45.

This completes the creation of the observed data. The next step is to define the process expectations by following these steps:

1. Make cell N9 the active cell; click on the fx icon .

2. From the Or Select a Category drop down list, click on Statistical and use the arrow key in the Select a Function window to page down to NORMDIST. Figure 14.4 illustrates the dialog box.

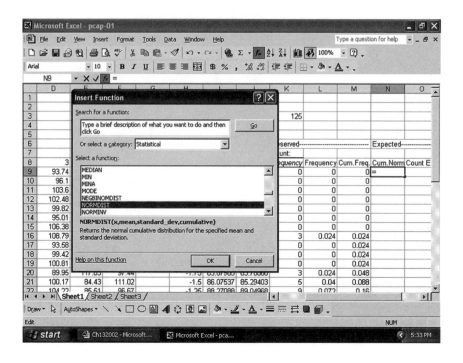

Figure 14.4   Insert Function dialog box.

Notice that the normal distribution function requires

NORMDIST(x,mean,standard_dev,cumulative)

Where

x is the bin cell value from column I

Mean is the average of the data found in cell H3

Standard_dev is the standard deviation of the data found in cell H4

Cumulative is true; that is, we wish to use the cumulative distribution as noted by the column head

3. Type *I9* in the window to the right of x and press the Tab key.

4. Type *$H$3* in the window to the right of Mean and press the Tab key.

5. Type *$H$4* in the window to the right of Standard Deviation and press the Tab key.

6. Type *true* in the window to the right of cumulative.

7. Click on OK.

The selection of the mean and standard deviation is not limited to the average of the data. We could have selected to test against the simulated values in cells C3 and C4 or any other average and standard deviation. The selection of the average and standard deviation determines the parameters of the normal distribution that are being tested.

8. Copy the formula in cell N9 into the cell *range* N10:N45 and press Enter. (This is a good select checking point. The values in column N should go from near zero to near one.)

9. Click on cell O9 and type *=+(N10–N9)*$K$3* and press Enter. [(N10–N9) is the probability of being in a given bin H9, and (N10–N9)*K3 is the count expected in the bin.]

10. Copy the formula in cell O9 into the cells in the *range* O10:O45.

11. Assume that the lower specification limit is near Z=–3.75; click on cell P12 and type *=max(K9:K45,O9:O45)+1* and press Enter.

12. Assume that the upper specification is near Z=3; click on cell P39 and type *+P12*

This step completes the data entry for the worksheet.

Graphing Data for a Visual Test

Visual tests are conducted by comparing the graphs of two or more data sets to determine if the data are from the same type of distribution. As previously noted, two types of graphs may be examined depending on whether the variables are continuous or discrete: (1) A cumulative graph of the observed and expected data for continuous variables; and (2) a probability density graph for discrete data showing in terms of frequencies the expected, observed, and specification limits.

Cumulative Graph

To create the cumulative graph, follow these steps:

1. Using the left mouse button while holding down the Control (Ctrl) key, identify the following graphing ranges:

Purpose	Range
X	H8:H45
(Observed) Cumulative frequency	M8:M45
Cum. Normal	N8:N45

2. Click on the Chart Wizard icon .

3. Click on XY(Scatter) and select the graph subtype of smoothed lines without markers, and click on Next>.

4. In step 3 of 4, name the Chart *Cumulative Observed and Expected*, name the x-axis Z, name the y-axis *Cumulative Frequency*, and then click on Finish.

The graph in Figure 14.5 shows that the generated data appear to be distributed in a normal distribution; however, the best way to test for a normal distribution is to run a Kolmogorov-Smirnov (KS) test.

Lower natural tolerance limit (LNTL):   The normal lower limit of the output of a process.

Upper natural tolerance limit (UNTL):   The normal upper limit of the output of a process.

Visual test: Comparing the graphs of two or more data sets to determine if the data sets are from the same type of distribution.

Expected, Observed, and Specification Limits

To convert all the data points into frequency counts, use the data in columns K, O, and P. Using the Control key with the left mouse button, identify the graphing ranges while holding down the Control key:

Purpose	Range
Observed count	K8:K44
Expected count	O8:O44

1. Click on the Chart Wizard icon 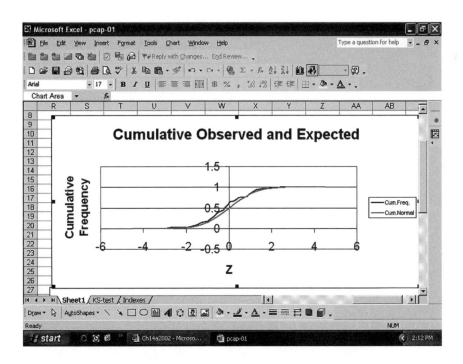 .

2. Click on the Custom Types tab and use the arrow key to locate and select the Line–Column selection.

3. In step 3 of 4, label the graph *Observed/Expected*, label the *x*-axis *bins*, label the *y*-axis *Count*, and click Finish.

4. Double click on the Count Expected line and change the type to a style without symbols.

Figure 14.6 illustrates the results. This test is appropriate for discrete variables. Examination of the frequency counts suggests that the data are distributed normally. A normal distribution has the largest counts near the peak of the curve and the fewest counts near the tails of the curve.

Kolmogorov-Smirnov (KS) Test

The Kolmogorov-Smirnov (KS) test is one of the more popular tests for goodness-of-fit for a normal distribution. It is a simple test, but requires a massive amount of calculation—a perfect job for a worksheet. To conduct the KS test, a sheet 2 is created in the current worksheet workbook. To create sheet 2, click on Sheet2 tab at the bottom left of the worksheet.

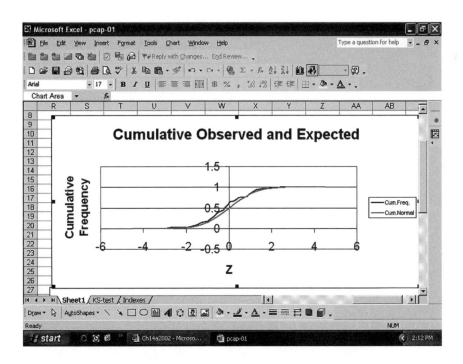

Figure 14.5 Cumulative visual test.

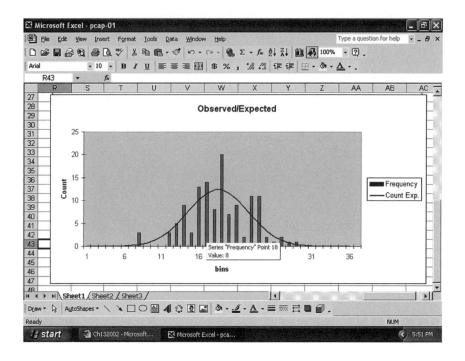

Figure 14.6   Visual test and specification limits.

Double-click on the sheet's name, change the name to *KS-test*, and press Enter. The steps for conducting the KS test are:

1. Rename Sheet2 to KS-test.

2. Set up column heads.

3. Transfer data from Sheet1 to KS-test sheet.

4. Reorganize data into a single column of 125 observations.

5. Number the observations 1 to 125.

6. Edit, Copy, Edit, Paste-Special values.

7. Sort low to high, using the A–Z sorting icon ![A-Z icon].

8. Calculate Z, using a Z transformation.

9. Calculate the expected normal frequency.

10. Calculate the absolute differences.

11. Find minimum difference.

12. Perform KS test.

13. Graph.

To enter the data in the worksheet, follow these steps:

1. Click on cell A11 and type + .

2. Click on Sheet1.

3. Click on cell A9 and press Enter (the KS-test sheet—Sheet2—should now be active).

4. On sheet 2, click on cell A11, click on Edit, and then click on Copy.

5. Identify the *range* A12:F35 and press Enter.

6. Click on cell A10 and type *Number* and press the right-arrow key (→).

7. In cell B10 type *Data* and press Enter.

The next step is to reorganize the data.

8. Identity the *range* C11:F35 and click on the Cut button.

9. Click on cell B36 and press Enter (the entire block of cells should be pasted below the first 25 data observations).

10. Identify the *range* C36:E60 and click on the Cut button.

11. Click on cell B61 and press Enter.

12. Identify the *range* C61:D85 and click on the Cut button.

13. Click on cell B86 and press Enter.

14. Identify the *range* C86:C110 and click on the Cut button.

15. Click on cell B111 and press Enter.

All the data should be pasted from row 11 through row 135 in column B. To number each observation:

1. Click on cell A36 and type *+A35+1* and press Enter.

2. Copy the formula in cell A36 into the cell *range* A37:A135.

Column A should contain the numbers 1 to 125, and column B contains the transferred data.

In order to sort the values in column B, the values must be copied to column C because random numbers cannot be sorted.

1. Click on cell C10 and type *Ordered* and press Enter.

2. Identify the *range* B11:B135, click on Edit, and click on Copy.

3. Click on Edit, click on Paste Special, check Values, click on OK, click on cell C11, and press Enter. Column C contains fixed numbers that can be sorted.

The range C11:C135 is identified. Click on the ⬚ icon and the data are sorted from low to high.

Enter the following text into the cells indicated:

Cell	Text
A3	Average:
A4	Std. Dev.:
A5	Count:
D10	Z
E10	Obs. Cum. Frequency
F10	Exp. Normal Distribution
G10	Difference

The reasons for the long titles in cells E10 and F10 are for graphing. Complete the worksheet as follows:

1. In cell C3 type =*AVERAGE(C11:C135)* and press Enter.

2. In cell C4 type =*STDEV(C11:C135)* and press Enter.

3. In cell C5 type =*COUNT(C11:C135)* and press Enter.

4. In cell D11 type +*(C11–$C$3)/$C$4* and press Enter.

5. Copy the formula in cell D11 into the cell *range* D12:D135 (the normal distribution Z column was placed in column D for graphing considerations).

6. In cell E11 type +*A11/$C$5* and press Enter (this formula determines the frequency of observations up to the value of Z found in column D).

7. Copy the formula in cell E11 into the cell *range* E12:E135.

8. In cell F11 type =*NORMDIST(D11,0,1,true)* and press Enter.

9. Copy the formula in cell F11 into the cell *range* F12:F135.

10. In cell G11 type +*ABS(F11–E11)* and press Enter.

11. Copy the formula in cell G11 into the cell *range* G12:G135.

12. In cell H5 type *Maximum difference* and press Enter.

13. In cell H6 type =*MAX(G11:G135)* and press Enter.

The value in cell H6 is the KS statistic. The KS statistic must be compared to a KS table to determine the probability of obtaining this value by chance. This is a test of significance. A *significance test* uses statistical information to aid in making a decision. In this example, the significance test indicates the probability of obtaining a particular statistic by chance alone. The KS table lists the values (factors) that must be obtained to determine the significance level of a particular KS statistic. For sample sizes over 100, the formula *Factor* / $\sqrt{n}$ may be used for calculating the KS critical values. Table 14.2 lists the factors for selected significance levels.

Type the following text and formulas into the cells indicated:

Cell	Text/Formula
H8	Sign. Level
H9	0.20
H10	0.15
H11	0.10
H12	0.05
H13	0.01
I8	n>100
I9	+1.07/SQRT(C5)
I10	+1.14/SQRT(C5)
I11	+1.22/SQRT(C5)
I12	+1.36/SQRT(C5)
I13	+1.63/SQRT(C5)
J7	Pointer
J8	=IF(P5<I9,"← ","..")
J9	=IF(AND($P$5<I10,$P$5>I9),"← ","..")

The right arrow is typed as a *less than* symbol (<) followed by two dashes (- -). Copy the contents of cell J9 into the cell *range* J10:J14. The formulas in cells J8 and J9 instruct Excel to print an arrow in column J in the cell to the right of the KS value that indicates the significance level of the KS test. If the KS value does not indicate a significant difference, no arrow will be printed in these cells. Figure 14.7 illustrates the results of the KS analysis.

The maximum difference in this example is 0.0504, which is less than 0.0957037. Whenever the value of the maximum difference is less than the required value at a particular significance level, we can conclude that the sample data are normally distributed. If the maximum difference value is greater than the values found in column I, we can conclude that sample data do *not* represent a normal distribution. Remember that if the data are

Table 14.2   KS significance level for sample sizes > 100.

Significance level:	0.02	0.15	0.10	0.05	0.01
Factor:	1.07	1.14	1.22	1.36	1.63

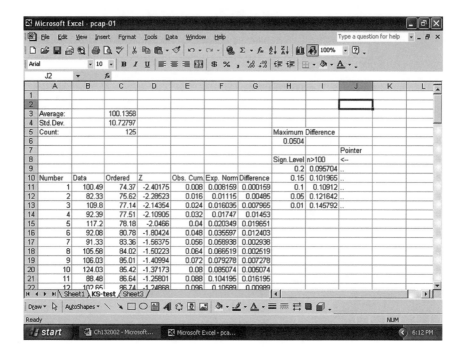

Figure 14.7 KS results.

not from a normal distribution, the use of control charts or indices that are based on the assumption of normality are likely to result in incorrect decisions and increased costs.

Significance test: A test that uses statistical information to aid in making a decision.

Kolmogorov-Smirnov (KS) Graph

The authors believe that graphs are an excellent tool for assessing quality. One can also create an Observed/Expected graph for the KS test by following these steps:

1. Identify the *range* D10:F135 and click on the Chart Wizard icon 📖.

2. Select the XY(Scatter) with smoothed lines without markers.

3. In step 3 of 4, add the chart title *Observed/Expected KS test*, label the *x*-axis *Z*, and the *y*-axis *Frequency*. Click on Finish.

4. Adjust the font sizes and color of the lines to suit your preferences. Figure 14.8 illustrates the results.

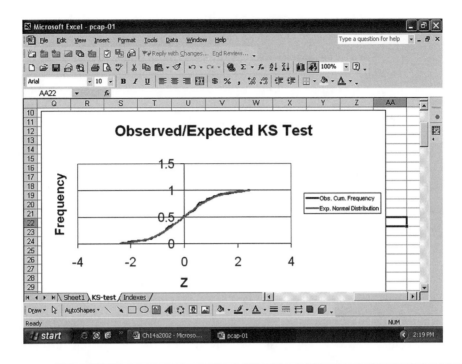

Figure 14.8 KS graph.

The KS graph in this example supports the conclusion of the KS test. The observed line closely fits along the line that illustrates the expected values. The similarity of the lines suggests that the data fit the normal distribution.

Issues in KS Testing

Some quality control professionals like to use both a left and right KS test analysis. This example shows only the left side of the curve. The right side test is left as an exercise.

In addition, other tests for goodness-of-fit have been suggested. The authors have used the KS test for many years and are confident in its results. We caution readers not to assume that data are normally distributed, and suggest that users conduct both visual and statistical tests for normality.

Indexes and Ratios

The objective of a process capability study is to analyze the relationship between the output of a process and the specification limits. Specification limits establish a range for specific parameters of a product. In other words, the specification limits set the required results. Usually, specification limits are set so that only a small fraction of parts or products will fall outside the upper and lower specification limits.

Two types of limits are of interest to the quality control specialist, *specification limits* and *natural tolerance limits*. Specification limits are often set by designers or production specialists as production goals, without regard to the mean or standard deviation of the process. On the other hand, natural tolerance limits are calculated based on the capabilities of the process, using the standard deviation of the data. The upper and lower natural tolerance limits are the normal upper and lower limits of the output of a process. Recall that in a normal distribution, approximately 98 percent of the observations will fall within 3 standard deviations above and below the mean. Therefore, the upper natural tolerance limit (UNTL) and the lower natural tolerance limit (LNTL) are calculated using the following formula:

$$\overline{X} \pm 3 * \sigma$$

An *index* is a number that represents a relative relationship. Indexes are calculated to aid the quality control specialist. When an index falls outside of a predetermined limit, then the process is tagged as out of limits and requires the attention of managers or quality specialists to identify the reason for the change. Indexes are useful for comparing the performance within a plant or department for two different time periods. Because indexes are so simple to calculate, there is a danger of generating misleading information if one compares information from different departments rather than one department at two points in time.

A popular method of studying process capability uses three indexes. One index to measure the relative distance of the sample mean from the target mean, and two indexes (CpL and CpU) that measure the distance of the sample mean from the upper and lower specification limits. The formulas for these indexes are shown below.

Index	Formula
Center	$\left|X_o - \lambda_o\right| / \text{Minimum}\left(\overline{X}_o - LSL, USL - \overline{X}_o\right)$
CpL	$\left(\lambda_o - LSL\right) / \left(3 * \sigma'\right)$
CpU	$\left(USL - \lambda_o\right) / \left(3 * \sigma'\right)$

Where:

X_o is the target mean

λ_o is the grand mean or $\overline{\overline{X}}$

σ' is the standard deviation of the population

LSL is the lower specification limit

USL is the upper specification limit

The center index and the CpL and the CpU indexes are often production goals set for an organization. When the value of the index exceeds the established number, the process is flagged for management action. When CpL and CpU are greater than one (1), we know that the natural tolerance limits are wider than the specification limits. This situation indicates that the specification limits are requiring a level of precision that is beyond the capability of the process. Conversely, when the CpL and CpU are less than one (1), we know that the natural tolerance limits are within the specification limits. Therefore, the probability of producing defective parts or products is low.

Figure 14.9 illustrates a perfectly centered six-(6) sigma distance from both the lower and upper specification limits. The probability of a defective part at 6-sigma distance is almost zero. If a distribution is perfectly centered, then $|\overline{X}_o - 1_o|$ is zero and the center index is zero. For our example, using a standard normal distribution with a mean of zero (0) and a standard deviation of one (1), the value of the CpL and CpU would both be two (2).

Index calculations are simple on a worksheet. Figure 14.10 illustrates the worksheet for calculating indexes. The value of the LSL, USL, and Center were selected by a production engineer and written in the worksheet. The average and standard deviation were transferred from the KS-test sheet. The formulas for the indexes are:

Index	Excel Formula
Center	=ABS(B10–B6)/MIN(B10–B4,B5–B10)
CpL	=(B10–B4)/(3*B11)
CpU	=(B5–B10)/(3*B11)

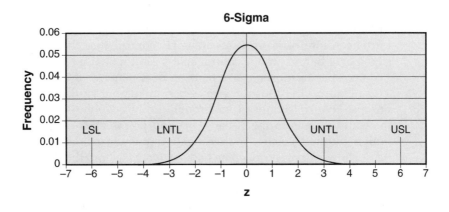

Figure 14.9 Specification limits are not restricted by distribution.

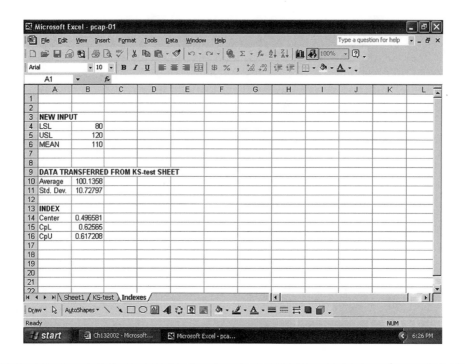

Figure 14.10   Calculating indexes.

The indexes calculated in this worksheet illustrate that for this process the natural tolerance limits are within the specification limits and are therefore producing high quality products.

Real Life

In order for statistical process control analysis to be meaningful, processes must be in control. If processes are not in control, then the use of X-bar and sigma or X-bar and range control charts cannot be used.

The specification on a dimension of a manufactured part is 1.35″ ± .002″. Figure 14.11 illustrates an X-bar and sigma worksheet for 100 subgroups. Five collections of subgroups produced points above and below the control limits in the X-bar chart and points above the upper control limit in the sigma chart. An investigation of the machine used to stamp the items showed that the machine had a defective clamp that held the mold in place. Whenever the clamp became loose, the operator simply tightened it down again. The clamp had been defective for such a long time, and the operator had no idea that it was causing the defective parts to be produced.

After the clamp was replaced, the quality problem was eliminated. The five subgroups were dropped from the data set. Figure 14.12 shows the control charts without the data generated when the clamp was loose.

Figure 14.11 Worksheet for X-bar and sigma.

Figure 14.12 X-bar and sigma control charts after the clamp was replaced.

Summary

A *process capability study* is the analysis of the capability of a process to produce results in terms of percentage of defective items. A *goodness-of-fit test* is a statistical procedure to test if a data set could have come from a specified distribution. Before performing tests on a data set, control is critical. *Control* exists when the results of the process are reproducible within control limits. Distributions can be tested using both visual and significance tests. A *visual test* compares two distributions by examining graphs of each distribution. A *significance test* is a test that uses statistical information to assist in analyzing the distribution of the data.

The results of a process capability study include the calculation of the probability of defective units, and the natural tolerance limits. The *upper natural tolerance limit* is the normal upper limit of the output of a process, while the *lower natural tolerance limit* is the normal lower limit of the output of a process.

Exercises

14.1 Use the worksheet created in Figure 10.3 in chapter 10. Edit the worksheet to include X-barbar, sigma (RMS), and counts. Transfer the data from the worksheets created in this chapter to complete the following tasks:

a. A visual test for normality

b. A KS test for normality

c. A process capability study using a target mean of 115 ± 8

14.2 Use the worksheet created in Figure 10.2 in chapter 10. Edit the worksheet to include X-barbar, sigma (RMS), and counts. Transfer the data from the worksheets created in this chapter to complete the following tasks:

a. A visual test for normality

b. A KS test for normality

c. A process capability study using a target mean of $\pm$

14.3 Complete the KS test for the right side in the example KS worksheet.

15

Pareto and Fishbone Diagrams

KEY TERMS

Fishbone diagram   Pareto diagram

Pareto analysis

OUTLINE

Prior Knowledge

From earlier chapters, you should know how to open and save files, enter text, cut and copy a range from part of a worksheet to another, sort worksheet data, and create and edit graphs.

Why Use Pareto Analysis?

The purpose of *Pareto analysis* is to identify the sources of defects and order the sources of the defects according to frequency or costs associated with each cause. The foundation of many quality control techniques is management by exception. The *Pareto diagram* is a management-by-exception technique that helps the quality control specialist identify the primary causes of selected events. The Pareto diagram is a combination bar chart and line graph. The bars represent the frequency or the costs associated with each cause, and the lines show the cumulative contribution of each cause. The classic Pareto diagram requires that all sources of quality problems be identified and that causes of each defective unit be recorded on the inspection form. Pareto diagrams are simple charts that are fun to create in Excel and are powerful analytical tools, despite their simplicity.

Pareto analysis: Analysis for identifying the sources (types) of defects and ordering the sources according to cost or frequency of occurrence so that corrective action may be taken.

Pareto diagram: A combination bar and line graph illustrating the frequency of sources (types) of defects.

Creating a Worksheet for a Pareto Diagram

The creation of a Pareto diagram begins with the collection of data manually on a form similar to that shown in Figure 15.1, or electronically in a computer file that makes it easy to create output on a form similar to the form in Figure 15.1. The form may be revised according to the data collection sampling scheme and the preferences of the users; however, most inspection reports are similar.

The steps required for a Pareto analysis are:

1. Collect and summarize inspection data, such as number of defects, number of reworks, or number of customer complaints for a period of time.

2. Calculate the cost or the value of each cause of the defects or reworks.

3. Sort the data according to frequency of causes or by cost.

4. Prepare the Pareto diagram.

Figure 15.1   Inspection Report.

Entering Worksheet Text

Since text is easy to enter and move, it is recommended you start by entering text. Table 15.1 contains a list of the cells and the text you should type into each cell.

You may wish to adjust the number of dashes in cell B10 and the number of equal signs in cell B12 to line up to the width of the column.

Entering Worksheet Formulas

Enter the following formulas into the worksheet to calculate the total sum of all the defects, the frequencies of each defect cause, and the cumulative frequencies:

1. In cell B11 type *=SUM(B5:B9)* and press Enter.

2. To calculate the percentage (frequency) for each cause, in cell D5 type *=B5/$B$11* and press Enter; copy this formula into the *range* D6:D9.

3. To calculate the cumulative frequency, in cell E5 type *=+D5* and press Enter; in cell E6 type *=+E5+D6* and press Enter; copy the formula in cell E6 into the cell *range* E7:E9.

Table 15.1   Text for Pareto worksheet.

Cell	Contents	Notes
A1	Pareto1.xls	Name of the worksheet
B4	Count	Column label
C4	Source	Column label
D4	Frequency	Column label
E4	Cum. Freq.	Column label
B5	123	Number of defects due to size
C5	Size	Cause of defect
B6	155	Number of defects due to weight
C6	Weight	Cause of defect
B7	22	Number of defects due to number
C7	Number	Cause of defect
B8	213	Number of defects due to roundness
C8	Roundness	Cause of defect
B9	54	Number of defects due to shape
C9	Shape	Cause of defect
B10*	'------------------	Line showing between number and sum
B12*	'------------------	Line underlining total number of defects

*NOTE: Begin these lines with a single quotation mark to avoid an error.

To ensure that your worksheet is correct, check the value in cell E9. The sum of the frequencies must be one, therefore, the value in cell E9 should be one.

Notice that the order of the data is Count and then Source. Using this order makes sorting easy. There are two sorting icons: [icon] for Ascending and [icon] for Descending. Block off the *range* B5:C9 and click on the Descending icon. Figure 15.2 illustrates the results. Save the worksheet using the file name in cell A1, *pareto1.xls*.

Creating the Pareto Diagram

To create a Pareto diagram, follow these steps:

1. Hold down the left mouse button and drag to identify the *range* B4:E9.

2. Click on the Chart Wizard icon [icon].

3. Select the Custom Types Tab option.

4. Click on the down arrow until the Line–Column is shown; highlight the Line–Column option and click on <u>N</u>ext>.

5. In step 3 of 4, type the following labels:

    a. Type the chart ţitle *Pareto*

    b. Label the *x*-axis *Source*

    c. Label the *y*-axis *Frequency* and click on <u>N</u>ext>.

6. In step 4 of 4, select the default option As Object <u>I</u>n and click on <u>F</u>inish.

Locate and resize the graph. Figure 15.3 illustrates the completed Pareto diagram.

The Pareto diagram indicates that if time is invested in correcting the roundness problems, the facility can obtain the biggest reduction in quality problems. The data also suggest that after the roundness problem is corrected, the facility can further reduce quality problems by correcting the process so that units are produced with accurate weight.

Revising the Pareto Worksheet to Include Costs

The Pareto diagram is not limited to counts. Since managers are most interested in costs, the count data can be converted to cost data. Then, one can focus on correcting the problems associated with the greatest costs.

Figure 15.2   Worksheet results.

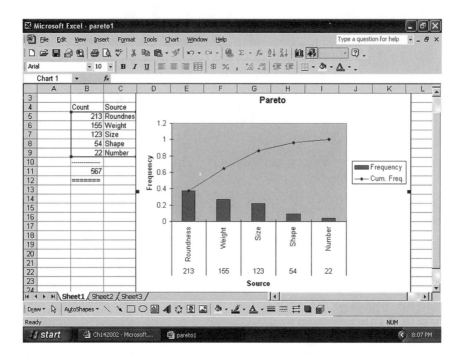

Figure 15.3   Pareto diagram.

Change the name of the worksheet in cell A1 to *Pareto2.xls* and save the worksheet in the subdirectory of your choice and follow these steps to revise the worksheet.

Type the following text in the appropriate cells:

Cell	Text	Note
F4	Repair Cost	Column label
F5	25	Cost of repairing a roundness defect
F6	50	Cost of repairing a weight defect
F7	15	Cost of repairing a size defect
F8	10	Cost of repairing a shape defect
F9	3	Cost of repairing a number defect
G4	Total Cost	Column label
H4	Cum. Cost	Column label
I4	Percent $ Volume	Column label
J4	Cum. % of Cost	Column label

Enter the following formulas in the appropriate cells:

1. Total cost—To calculate total cost, multiply the count of defects by the repair cost of each defect. In cell G5 type *=B5*F5* and press Enter; copy the formula in cell G5 into the cell *range* G6:G9.

2. Sort the order of the data by clicking on any cell in the *range* G5:G9, then click on the Sorting icon ![Sort icon].

3. Revise the formulas in cells E5 and E6 to reflect the new order. In cell E5 type *+D5* and press Enter; in cell E6 type *=+E5+D6* and press Enter. Copy the formula in cell E6 into the cell *range* E7:E9.

4. Cumulative cost—In cell H5 type *+G5* and press Enter; in cell H6 type *=+H5+G6* and press Enter. Copy the formula in cell H6 into the cell *range* H7:H9.

5. Percent $ volume—In cell I5 type *=G5/$H$9* and press Enter; copy the formula in cell I5 into the cell *range* I6:I9.

6. Cumulative percentage of cost—In cell J5 type *=H5/$H$9* and press Enter; copy the formula in cell J5 into the cell *range* J6:J9.

Figure 15.4 shows a redesigned version of the Pareto worksheet to calculate the costs associated with each cause of poor quality.

Figure 15.4 Cost associated with each defect.

Creating the Pareto Cost Diagram

To create the Pareto diagram that shows the relative costs of the causes of defects, follow these steps:

1. Highlight the following *ranges* using the left mouse button, while depressing the Control (Ctrl) key: C4:C9, I4:I9, J4:J9.

2. Click on the Chart Wizard icon .

3. Select the Custom Types tab option.

4. Use the down arrow button to advance to the Line–Column option; point and click on this chart type to select this option and then click on <u>N</u>ext>.

5. In step 3 of 4, type the following labels:

   a. Type the chart title *Pareto Cost Diagram.*

   b. Label the *x*-axis *Source.*

   c. Label the *y*-axis *Frequency* and click on <u>N</u>ext>.

6. In step 4 of 4, select the default option As <u>O</u>bject In and click on <u>F</u>inish.

Locate and resize the graph. Figure 15.5 illustrates the completed Pareto Cost diagram.

Analysis of the cost diagram shows that the greatest cost savings can be obtained by correcting the weight problems. The second greatest savings can be realized by correcting the causes of the roundness problems.

Why Use a Fishbone Diagram?

The *fishbone diagram* gets its name because it often looks like a fish skeleton. It is also called the *cause-and-effect* diagram. The fishbone diagram helps managers organize information about a process or a quality problem. The diagram provides a picture of how inputs are related to outputs.

Fishbone diagram: A graph illustrating the relationships between inputs and outputs that is used to identify possible sources of quality problems.

Creating a fishbone diagram starts with input and output identification. In general, the factors of production in economic/business terms are *land* (raw materials), *labor* (men and women), *capital* (money and machines), and the *business enterprise* (management system). The factors of production represent inputs to every business. Using the factors of production, Table 15.2 lists sources of quality problems.

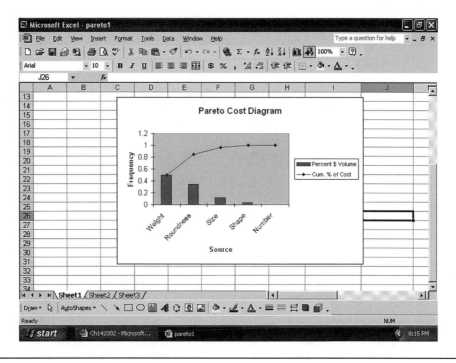

Figure 15.5   Pareto Cost Diagram.

Table 15.2   Sources of quality problems.

Sources	
Primary	*Secondary*
Land (Raw materials)	Power Steel Plastic
Labor	Machinists Assemblers
Capital	Milling machines Grinders
Business enterprise	Sales Marketing Production management

Creating a Fishbone Worksheet

Entering Worksheet Text

Using a simple approach, enter the text from Table 15.2 into a worksheet, as illustrated in Figure 15.6 (and save the worksheet using the name in cell A1, *fish01.xls*).

Entering Worksheet Art

To create a fishbone (cause-and-effect) diagram, transfer the text listed along the left side of the worksheet to selected locations on the worksheet.

The locations were selected so that you can use the Draw line   to connect

the boxes. To draw the lines, click on the Drawing icon   if the drawing options are not showing at the bottom of the screen. Click on the diagonal

line   in the AutoShapes menu and place the ± at the point where the line begins and hold the left mouse button as you drag the mouse across the cells to draw the line. Release the mouse button to end the line. To move the line, point to the line and click on the left mouse button. Circles will appear at each end of the line. You may shift the entire line or adjust one end by clicking the left mouse button on the square at the end of the line and adjust the line as you wish.

The title *Cause-and-Effect Diagram* was placed on the top of the diagram to complete the exercise. Figure 15.7 illustrates the completed worksheet.

Summary

A *Pareto diagram* is a combination line and bar graph that shows the frequency and importance of sources of defects. *Pareto analysis* orders the causes of defects according to frequency or costs so that quality control specialists can concentrate on correcting the causes of quality problems that will yield the greatest improvements in the process or output.

A *fishbone diagram* illustrates relationships among the causes and effects in a process. The fishbone diagram helps quality specialists identify the sources of quality problems. Although the fishbone diagram can increase understanding of the causes of quality problems, to obtain maximum value from the fishbone analysis, one should quantify the problem as well as the causes that may be affecting the problem. The fishbone diagram is a valuable tool for facilitating discussions and brainstorming among quality specialists.

Figure 15.6   Fishbone worksheet—getting started.

Figure 15.7   Fishbone diagram.

Exercises

15.1 A molding operation for small plastic parts identified four possible causes for defective parts: heat, cold, dirt, and inaccurate measurements that result in parts being too large or too small. A part molded from plastic that is overheated becomes too brittle and is scrap. A part molded from plastic that is too cold does not meet the strength requirements and may be recycled. A part that is molded in a dirty mold may be reworked by sanding off the dirt. Parts that are too small must be scrapped, while parts that are too large may be reworked by filing and sanding. Using the data listed in Table 15.3, create an inspection report and conduct a Pareto analysis.

15.2 Using the inspection report and the data in Table 15.4, conduct a Pareto cost analysis.

Table 15.3 Causes of defective parts.

Source of Defect	11/1	11/8	11/15	11/22	Date 11/29	12/6	12/13	12/20	12/27
Hot	0	0	0	1	1	0	1	0	1
Cold	2	0	0	2	4	1	2	0	2
Sludge	4	1	8	1	2	0	4	3	2
Large	2	1	0	2	0	1	1	1	1
Small	1	1	1	0	0	0	0	0	0

Table 15.4 Causes of and costs for defective parts.

Source of Defect	9/2	9/3	9/4	9/5	Date 9/6	9/7	9/8	9/9/	Cost
A	0	0	0	1	1	0	1	0	12.00
B	2	0	0	2	4	1	2	0	10.00
C	4	1	8	1	2	0	4	3	3.00
D	2	1	0	2	0	1	1	1	2.50
E	0	0	0	0	0	1	0	1	5.60
F	1	2	0	0	1	2	2	0	1.50
G	1	1	1	0	0	1	0	0	10.00

16

Cumulative Sum (CuSum) Charts

KEY TERMS

Operating characteristic curve   V-mask

OUTLINE

Prior Knowledge

From previous chapters, you should know how to open and save worksheets, enter text and formulas, copy the contents of a cell or group of cells to another part of the worksheet, and create and edit graphs using the Chart Wizard. You should have an understanding of type I and type II errors. You should have knowledge of $\overline{X}$ and range control charts or $\overline{X}$ and sigma control charts (discussed in chapters 10 and 11). An understanding of operating characteristic curves discussed in chapter 7 is also helpful.

What Is a Cumulative Sum (CuSum) Chart?

A Cumulative Sum (CuSum) Chart is a control chart that is more likely to detect subtle or sudden changes in the process mean more quickly than other types of control charts, such as the average ($\overline{X}$) chart and to pinpoint more accurately the time when the change occurred.[1] One of the reasons that cumulative sum charts indicate changes in the process more readily is that the chart is based on *all* the data collected within a time frame and not just the last few data points; therefore, the decision rule of determining if a significant change in the process has occurred is based on the cumulative sum of the differences between the cumulative observed mean of the sample and the mean of the process when the process is in control. Generally, CuSum charts result in fewer false alarms than $\overline{X}$ or range charts.

CuSum charts are useful for identifying differences from expected or forecast outcomes and observed outcomes, for example, increases in the amount of scrap, material usage, characteristics of manufactured parts such as diameter or weight, water content, or survival rates following surgeries. CuSum charts may be calculated based on the number or the proportion of observations that do not meet specifications, or on sample statistics such as the mean, the range, or the standard deviation.[2]

Cumulative sum charts are most appropriate in situations where data are collected slowly and in small samples, or cumulative sum charts can also be based on individual observations rather than sample statistics. This chapter demonstrates the creation of CuSum charts based on individual observations; however, an exercise at the end of the chapter requires the use of small subgroups to produce the CuSum chart.

Cumulative sum charts can be constructed to detect two-sided, as well as one-sided, differences between observations and the mean. For example, a CuSum chart can be constructed that detects only increases or decreases in the parameter of interest; such a chart would be a one-sided chart. In this chapter, the two-sided procedure to detect both increases and decreases in the mean, using both upper and lower control limits, is demonstrated. The two-sided procedure uses a V-shaped control chart, which is usually referred to as the "V-mask," as shown in Figure 16.1.

V-mask: The V-shaped control chart that graphs the cumulative sum. The upper control limit is the bottom line of the V and the lower control limit is the upper line of the V. The V-mask must be recalculated every time a new observation is collected.

---

1. Duncan, Acheson J. *Quality Control and Industrial Statistics.* Homewood, IL: Richard D. Irwin, 1974.
2. Mitra, Amitava. *Fundamentals of Quality Control & Improvement.* Upper Saddle River, NJ: Prentice-Hall, 1998.

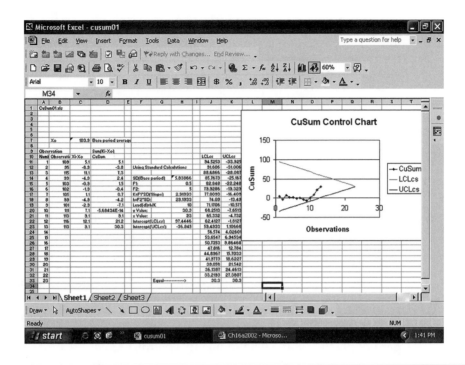

Figure 16.1   Cumulative sum chart.

After each sample is taken, the V-mask must be redrawn using the last cumulative sum as the base point for the new V-mask. With each redrawing, the location of the V-mask can change radically. If any of the previously plotted points fall outside the control limits of the V-mask, the process is assumed to be out of control and the reason for the change in the process should be identified and corrected.

In Figure 16.1 the calculations are shown along with the CuSum chart. Three standard values are calculated to determine the location of the control limits. These values include h, k, and the lead. The constant h is the control limit for the CuSum chart when $X_t < h$, the process is in control or when $X_t > h$ the process is beyond the control limit. The three values are selected to minimize Type I errors, false alarms that indicate the process is out of control, when it is in control. When manually drawing CuSum charts it is necessary to calculate the angle in order to draw the control limits, but when we use Excel to create the graph, once we know the slope of the line and one point on a line, we do not have to calculate any angles. In addition, when creating a manual CuSum chart the vertical and horizontal chart scales must match; this is not necessary when using Excel because Excel automatically scales the axes.

One significant difference in the cumulative sum chart is that the upper control limit (UCLcs) of the CuSum is on the bottom of the graph, while the lower control limit (LCLcs) is on the top. Therefore, a point graphed below the bottom line indicates an upward shift of the quality indicator and a point above the top line indicates a downward shift of the quality indicator. When observations (or subgroups) are within the V-mask the quality indicators are assumed to be in a state of statistical control. The control chart illustrated in Figure 16.1 is in control. The last observation was changed by one-half of a standard deviation. This CuSum control chart did not identify the change in the process.

Why Use the CuSum Chart?

CuSum charts work. The classic design of the CuSum chart tests if the mean of the observations are the same as the population mean, $H_0: \mu = \bar{x}_0$. The value of μ may be estimated by using the average of the data collected in a base time period. When μ is estimated from a sample average, the CuSum chart identifies changes in the process as fast as or faster than other control charts in many applications, with fewer false alarms.

A measure of control chart performance is the operating characteristic curve (OC curve), which shows the relationship of the probability of acceptance of the hypothesis that no change has occurred for a given level of the average of the incoming data. Because the use of the OC curves is the standard of practice in the field of quality control, OC curves are presented in chapters 20 and 22. Using a random number generator, we can generate an operating characteristic curve for the CuSum chart.

Operating characteristic curve: Graph of the probability of accepting a lot given various levels of incoming quality.

Figure 16.2 illustrates an OC curve for the CuSum chart. Because the CuSum chart is a two-sided chart, that is it tests for increases and decreases in the process average, the probability of acceptance of the lot decreases as the average of the sample moves further from the population mean. As the sample mean moves closer to the population mean, the probability of acceptance of the lot increases to the point where the sample mean and population mean are equal (in this example, when $\bar{x} = 100$); then the probability of acceptance of the lot is 99 percent. Type I error is the probability of looking for a change when no change has occurred and is one minus the value of the OC curve (type I error = $1 - .99$), that is 0.01.

When the sample mean is two standard deviations lower than the expected mean, ($\bar{x} = 80$), the probability of acceptance is 0.37. When the input data are two standard deviations above the expected mean, ($\bar{x} = 120$), the probability of acceptance is 0.42. To create the operating characteristics curve, 200 control chart runs were simulated for each input level. As the number of simulations increases, the true OC curve is approached.

Figure 16.2 Operating characteristic curve for a CuSum chart.

Disadvantages of the CuSum Chart

The primary weakness of the CuSum chart is that the control chart must be redrawn after each sample or observation is collected. When data are collected at a rapid pace, the CuSum chart is probably not the best control chart to use. The CuSum chart's advantages are strongest when data are collected slowly and one needs to obtain maximum information from a small set of slowly collected data.

Creating the CuSum Worksheet

Entering Worksheet Text

Table 16.1 includes the cell location and text needed for the CuSum worksheet. To enter the worksheet text, click on the appropriate cell and type the text as indicated in Table 16.1.

To enter observation numbers click in cell A11 and type *1*, and press Enter. The active cell is now A12. Type *=1+* and click on cell A11 and press Enter. The value 2 appears in A12. Copy the contents of A12 into the *range* A13:A33.

Table 16.1   CuSum worksheet text.

Cell	Text Notes	
A1	CuSum01.xls	Name of spreadsheet
B7	Xo	Base value for comparison, average used
D7	Base period average	Label
A9	Observation	Column head for observation number
A10	Number	Column head for observation number
B10	Observation	Column head for observations
C10	Xi-Xo	Column head for Sum calculation
D9	Sum(Xi-Xo)	Sum of sum calculations
D10	CuSum	Title for graph
F12	Using Standard Calculations	Standard factors to be used
F14	SD(Base period):	Standard deviation of data in base period
F15	F1:	Standard factor
F16	F2:	Standard factor
F17	K=F1*SD (Slope):	Slope calculations
F18	h=F2*SD:	
F19	Lead (d) = h/K:	Lead distance on graph
F20	y Value:	y value of last calculation of Cusum
F21	x Value:	x value at end of graph
F22	Intercept (LCLcs):	Intercept of LCLcs
F23	Intercept (UCLcs):	Intercept of UCLcs
J10	LCLcs	Column head
K10	UCLcs	Column head
G33	Equal ----------------→	Label

Entering Worksheet Values

Enter the values in Table 16.2 in the worksheet. The numbers in *range* B11 through B23 are the observation values. Later in the chapter these values are replaced with randomly generated numbers. The values in cells H15 and H16 are the standard CuSum numbers, which control the slope of the control limits and the amount of lead distance between the last observation and where the control limits meet.[3] You may wish to experiment with values other than the default values after you have successfully created the CuSum chart.

[3]Farnum, Nicholas R. *Modern Statistical Quality Control and Improvement.* Belmont, CA: Duxbury, 1994: 202.

Table 16.2   Values.

Cell	Value	Notes
B11	109	Observations
B12	95	
B13	115	
B14	99	
B15	103	
B16	102	
B17	105	
B18	99	
B19	101	
B20	111	
B21	113	
B22	116	
B23	113	
H15	0.5	One of the CuSum standard values
H16	5	The second of the CuSum standard values

Entering Worksheet Formulas

For the individual observation CuSum chart there are no special formulas. The calculations include: subtraction, summations, an average, a standard deviation, and some multiplication and division. For the subgroup CuSum chart there are some additional calculations needed for the subgroup average. The worksheet formulas are listed in Table 16.3.

The formulas in cells C7 and H14 depend on the number of observations in the base period. Since we defined the base period as observations 1 through 10, the average calculated in C7 is the average of the observations in cells B11 through B20.

In cell H14 we used the formula for the population standard deviation rather than the formula for the sample standard deviation. If one assumes that the data set contains measurements of the entire population, then the population formula is correct. On the other hand, if one assumes that the data are samples taken from the population, then the sample standard deviation is the best statistic. The population standard deviation formula results in a slightly smaller standard deviation than the sample standard deviation formula; therefore, using the population standard deviation results in a slightly higher probability of an observation being above or below the control limits.

Table 16.3   Worksheet formulas.

Cell	Formula	
C7	=AVERAGE(B11:B20)	
C11	=B11–$C$7	
D11	=C11	
D12	=D11+C12	
H14	=STDEVP(B11:B20)	Population standard deviation
H17	=H15*H14	Slope of the control limits
H18	=H16*H14	
H19	=H18/H17	
H20	+D23	A point on both control limits
H21	=A23+H19	
H22	=H20+H17*H21	Formula for the control limit lines
H23	=H20–H17*H21	Formula for the control limit lines
J11	=$H$22–$H$17*A11	Control limits
K11	=$H$23+$H$17*A11	Control limits

Copy the formula in C11 into the *range* C12:C23 and copy the formula in D12 into the *range* D13:D23. Copy the formulas in J11 and K11 into *range* J12:K33.

Note the following values in the worksheet:

A. The *y* value is the last value in column D. Every time the number of observations is changed, the location of the last value in column D changes.

B. The first value in cell H21 depends on the number of samples. Every time the number of observations is changed, the location of this value changes.

C. The two formulas in cells H22 and H23 are formulas for a straight line. The value in cell H17 is the slope of the control limits. The upper control limit is minus this value while the lower control limit is this value.

D. The value in cell H30 is where both control limits meet. The slope and a value define a straight line. We can calculate any point on the control limits with the above information.

E. In cells H22 and H23 we calculate the intercept value of the two control limits. This observation is the key to using a spreadsheet for the CuSum calculations.

F. In cells J11 and K11 are the formulas for the control limits depending on the values in column A. Note that the last value in column J, column K, and the value in H20 are identical.

Creating the CuSum Chart

The steps to create a CuSum chart are:

1. Select the *range* A10:A33.

2. Hold the control key down and select the *range* D10:D33.

3. Continue holding the control key and select the *range* J10:K33.

4. Click on the Chart Wizard icon .

5. Select the XY (Scatter) chart in the Chart Wizard—Step 1 of 4.

6. Select straight lines without markers in the Chart subtype:

7. Click on <u>N</u>ext>.

8. Click on <u>N</u>ext> again.

9. Add the Chart title: *CuSum Control Chart;* Value of *x*-axis: *Observations*, and the Value of *y*-axis: *CuSum*, in Step 3 of 4.

10. Click on <u>F</u>inish.

11. On the graph, right-click on the CuSum series line.

12. Select the F<u>o</u>rmat data series option.

13. Click on the Patterns tab.

14. In the Marker area, click on the A<u>u</u>tomatic radio button.

15. Click OK.

This example includes the column labels in the range selection to provide series names in the graph. When the column labels are included, Excel may identify the X scale values (A10:A33) as an additional series. If this happens, left-click on the chart, then right-click to display the chart menu. Left-click on <u>S</u>ource Data. . . and then click on the Series tab. Select the series that is causing the problem and click on the <u>R</u>emove button. Another way to eliminate this problem is not to include the column labels in the selected ranges and add them as Series names in step 2 of 4 in the Chart Wizard.

Summary

The CuSum control chart is similar to all other quality control charts. It has upper and lower control limits; however, the CuSum V-mask does not look exactly like other control charts. One disadvantage is that new observations cannot be graphed without redrawing the entire V-mask. An advantage of the CuSum chart is the technique's ability to handle both individual observations and sparse data sets with as few as three or four observations. Another advantage of the CuSum chart is its ability to quickly detect changes in a process. Just like other quality control charts, if the CuSum statistic is beyond the control limits, then the process is considered changing and the quality control specialist should attempt to identify the reasons for the change. If the Cusum statistic is within the limits, then the process is considered to be in statistical control.

Real Life

A team of volunteer data collectors take water samples for a variety of purposes around Mobile Bay. The fecal content of the water is one of the parameters measured. The volunteer is required to use a sterilized bottle to collect water from the bay. The bottle is placed on ice and must be delivered to a local laboratory within 3 hours.

Because individuals volunteer their time to support the project there are many gaps in the data collection process. In addition, it is known that the fecal measurement will go up after a rain due to runoff. Figure 16.3 illustrates an Excel worksheet with a complete CuSum chart. In this example, the base period was set equal to all the data available.

Exercises

16.1 Examination of the following data set indicated that there was a gap in time between observation 5 and 6. Discussion of the situation with the area supervisor indicated that a number of changes were made in the process between observations 5 and 6.

Number	Date	Observation
1	12/01	13.45
2	01/07	12.33
3	02/03	11.12
4	03/04	12.34
5	04/13	13.65
6	09/04	15.65
7	10/03	16.34
8	11/04	15.32

Figure 16.3 Mobile Bay fecal data worksheet.

Select a base period and an add-on period and use the CuSum to analyze the data. What conclusions can you draw based on the results? Comment on the number of observations available. Use the sample standard deviation for your analysis.

16.2 Given the following data set organized as individual observations on the left and as subgroup data on the right:

a. Make a CuSum analysis of the individual observations using the first 24 observations as the base period data. Use the sample standard deviation.

b. Make a CuSum analysis of the subgroup data using the first six subgroups as the base period data. Use the sample standard deviation.

c. Compare the results. Which scheme provides better control information? Why?

Both CuSum charts indicated that a change has occurred. In the individual analysis almost all the observations were out of limits, while in the subgroup data analysis only a single subgroup was out of limits.

Number	Observation	Subgroup	1	2	3	4
1	35.44	1	35.44	34.77	34.97	40.87
2	34.77	2	42.06	41.95	37.77	34.27
3	34.97	3	39.98	39.55	41.56	33.89
4	40.87	4	41.25	37.07	42.54	33.28
5	42.06	5	33.91	39.22	36.27	34.64
6	41.95	6	33.09	40.61	35.37	34.61
7	37.77	7	48.77	44.42	46.07	43.33
8	34.27	8	46.14	49.82	50.36	52.60
9	39.98					
10	39.55					
11	41.56					
12	33.89					
13	41.25					
14	37.07					
15	42.54					
16	33.28					
17	33.91					
18	39.22					
19	36.27					
20	34.64					
21	33.09					
22	40.61					
23	35.37					
24	34.61					
25	48.77					
26	44.42					
27	46.07					
28	43.33					
29	46.14					
30	49.82					
31	50.36					
32	52.60					

16.3   This exercise is to identify the minimum number of observations that can be handled by the CuSum chart. Using the simulation methods outlined in the chapter, generate the operating characteristic curve for a CuSum chart with three observations in the base period and the addition of two additional observations. For the base period use an average of 100 in cell B5 and a standard deviation of 10 in cell B6. For the additional period use an average from –3 standard deviations (70) to an average of +3 standard deviations (130) in steps of 5. Use the random generator:

=((rand()+rand()+rand()+rand()+rand()+rand()+rand()+rand()
+rand()+rand()+rand()+rand()+rand()+rand()–6)*$B$6+$B$5)

Using a macro similar to the one in chapter 22, simulate 200 cycles at each input average. Review the significance of your results.

16.4   Use the spreadsheet created in problem 16.3. Maintain the average over the simulation at 100, but vary the standard deviation from 5, 6, 7, 8, 9, 10, to 16.

17

Individual, Moving Average, and Moving Range Control Charts

<table>
<tr><td colspan="2" align="center">**KEY TERMS**</td></tr>
<tr><td>autocorrelation</td><td>moving range chart</td></tr>
<tr><td>individual control chart</td><td>outlier</td></tr>
<tr><td>moving average chart</td><td></td></tr>
</table>

OUTLINE

Graphing the Moving Average Control Chart

Using Individual, Moving Range, and Moving Average Control Charts

Real Life

Summary

Exercises

Prior Knowledge

From previous chapters, you should know how to open and save worksheets, enter text, copy the contents of a cell or group of cells to another part of the worksheet, and create and edit charts and graphs using the Chart Wizard.

Individual control chart: A control chart for controlling central tendency (average) using individual measurements.

Moving average and moving range charts: A pair of control charts for controlling both the central tendency (average) and variation of a process using variable limits.

Introduction

For variable data, the rate of data generation/collection versus the timing of decision making often determines which control chart pair should be used. For example, if one collects only a single datum point once a day and makes daily decisions, each datum point collected must be analyzed as it is collected. In some processes, the time required to produce one unit is lengthy. In these situations, the collection of data may be too slow for the average control chart to be meaningful. $\overline{X}$ and range or sigma control chart pairs cannot be used because these charts require at least two data points to calculate a mean and range. One possible solution is a combination of three control charts: *individual, moving average,* and *moving range control charts.* The individual or moving average charts and moving range charts are not as powerful as the $\overline{X}$ and range/sigma control chart pair due to the reduced amount of data.

One solution might be collecting more data points for each time period; however, collecting more data may not be possible due to costs or other considerations. Generally, costs should not be the only issue. If the decision is important, then the most appropriate data collection schedules should be identified and the additional costs of collecting the data should be justifiable. However, other considerations may present real limitations, for example, the researchers have been involved with volunteer data collection groups in which collecting multiple samples at the same time is beyond the time limits or the motivation of some of the individuals in the group. Many of the volunteers may simply record one observation twice rather than taking two measurements. In another application, each datum point represented an accident that resulted in a death. Therefore, the number of observation points was limited by the accidents that resulted in death. In other situations where the researchers are relying on historic data, the number of observations available for analysis will be limited.

Why Use Individual Control Charts?

Individual charts are utilized in situations in which a decision is made based on one datum point. In situations in which the managers are experienced with their process and are comfortable making decisions based on a single observation, the individual chart can provide information for a quick reaction time. Individual control charts graph each individual datum point, compared to an average line and 3-sigma limit.

If data are collected at a rate that allows a mean to be calculated, the authors recommend using a moving average chart over an individual control chart. The moving average calculation provides confidence that type I and II errors are controlled. The key to selecting between the individual and the moving average chart is the rate of data collection. If the data collection rate is fast enough to allow the calculation of a mean and standard deviation, then the moving average and moving range control charts are preferred.

The first step in creating a moving average is to calculate the average of all the observations in the base period. These values provide the process average (the chart centerline) and the upper and lower control limits. The observation means and ranges are calculated by dropping off the oldest data point as a new data point is added. For example, if the following number of defects were counted each day for eight days:

	Day 1	Day 2	Day 3	Day 4	Day 5	Day 6	Day 7	Day 8
Number of defects	3	5	2	4	6	1	2	3

The average for the first three days is $(3 + 5 + 2)/3 = 3.33$

The average for the fourth day is $(5 + 2 + 4)/3 = 3.67$

The average for the fifth day is $(2 + 4 + 6)/3 = 4.00$

The average for the sixth day is $(4 + 6 + 1)/3 = 3.67$

The average for the seventh day is $(6 + 1 + 2)/3 = 3.00$

The average for the eighth day is $(1 + 2 + 3)/3 = 2.00$

The moving **range** is calculated as the difference between the highest and lowest observations for a number of data points. When data collection rates are slow, the difference is likely to be the difference between two consecutive observations. The moving **range** and moving standard deviation control chart are used to study changes in variation. For subgroup sizes of two, the two types of charts produce identical results. The range chart becomes less and less efficient as the subgroup size increases due to its use of only two data points, compared to the standard deviation control chart, which uses all the data points in the calculation of the standard deviation. Usually, the moving range chart is used for subgroups sizes of $n = 2$ or $n = 3$. Seldom is the moving range chart used for n greater than 3.

The **ranges** for the example just shown for $n = 3$ are:

The **range** for the first three days is $5 - 2 = 3$

The **range** for the fourth day is $5 - 2 = 3$

The **range** for the fifth day is $6 - 2 = 4$

The **range** for the sixth day is $6 - 1 = 5$

The **range** for the seventh day is $6 - 1 = 5$

The **range** for the eighth day is $3 - 1 = 2$

Assumptions of Normality

The control limits for individual control charts depend on the assumption that the data conform to a normal distribution. When the normality assumption is valid, the probabilities relative to the selection of 3-sigma limits will match the probabilities of a normal distribution. If the assumption of normality is not valid, the individual control chart may be of reduced value, and in some situations may provide misleading information. The closer the data in the samples match the normal distribution, the more accurate the results. Our sample worksheet applications use a nonnormal distribution to generate the data. In general, symmetrical distributions yield better results than nonsymmetrical distributions. We recommend that you do not assume the data are normally distributed; we prefer to use the testing methods detailed in chapter 14 on process capability to test for the appropriate distribution.

The objective of a control chart is to identify change. When the normal assumption is not valid, the relative values of the type I and II errors change. The type I error is looking for a change when no change has occurred. When the type I error becomes large, time is wasted looking for problems when there are none. When the type II error becomes large, changes in a process are overlooked. One way to control type I error is to widen the sigma control limits from 2 to 6 sigma. Another way to control errors is to use a cumulative data analysis approach rather than the individual control chart.

Creating Individual Process Control Worksheets

Entering Worksheet Text

Figure 17.1 illustrates the top of the worksheet with the worksheet name in cell A1. Table 17.1 contains a list of the cells and the text to be typed into each cell.

The next step is to enter the row labels that identify the subgroups. Use the following commands to number the rows.

1. Click on cell A10 and type *1* and press Enter.

2. In cell A11 type *+1+A10* and press Enter.

3. Copy the formula in cell A11 into the *range* A12:A59.

Entering Observation Data

Generating Random Numbers for Observations

The random number formula that was introduced in chapter 8 will be used to generate random numbers for the simulated observations. The function rand() generates a uniform distribution. This nonnormal distribution was selected to demonstrate what happens when the assumption of normality is violated.

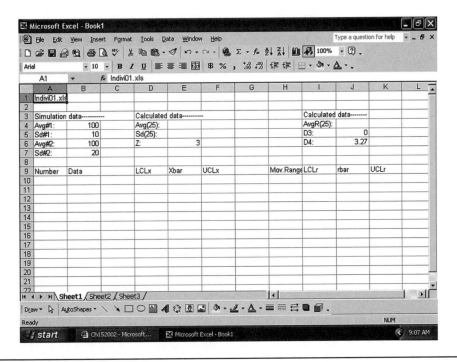

Figure 17.1   Starting the worksheet.

Table 17.1   Text for cells.

Cells	Text	Notes
A1	Indivi01.xls	Name of the worksheet
A3	Simulation data--------------	
A4	Avg#1:	Average for the first 25 observations
A5	Sd#1:	Standard deviation for the first 25 observations
A6	Avg#2:	Average for observations 26–50
A7	Sd#2:	Standard deviation for observations 26–50
A9	Number	Observation number
B4	100	Value representing the average to simulate first 25 observations
B5	10	Value representing the standard deviation to simulate first 25 observations
B6	100	Value representing the average to simulate second 25 observations
B7	20	Value representing the standard deviation to simulate second 25 observations
B9	Data	
D3	Calculated data--------------	
D4	Avg (25):	Calculated average for first 25 observations
D5	Sd(25):	Calculated standard deviations for first 25 observations
D6	Z:	Number of standard deviations for limits
D9	LCLx	Lower control limit for the average
E6	3	Number of standard deviations
E9	Xbar	Average of all observations
F9	UCLx	Upper control limit for the average
H9	Mov. Range	
I3	Calculated data--------------	
I4	AvgR(25):	Average range for first 25 observations
I5	D3:	Factor label
I6	D4:	Factor label
I9	LCLr	Lower control limit for the range
J5	0	D3 factor for range charts $n=2$
J6	3.27	D4 factor for range charts $n=2$
J9	Rbar	Average for all the ranges
K9	UCLr	Upper control limit for the range

To generate random numbers for the first 25 observations, follow these steps:

1. In cell B10 type =*(rand()–0.5)*$B$5+$B$4* and press Enter.

2. Click on cell B10 and copy this formula into the *range* B11:B34 by pointing to the + on the bottom right corner of the cell and dragging the symbol across the *range* B11:B34. When the left mouse button is released, random numbers are entered into each cell.

To generate random numbers for the second 25 observations, follow these steps:

1. In cell B35 type =*(rand()–0.5)*$B$7+$B$6* and press Enter.

2. Click on cell B35 and copy this formula into the *range* B36:B59 by pointing to the + on the bottom right corner of the cell and dragging the symbol across the *range* B36:B59.

Entering Worksheet Formulas

The calculations for the average and standard deviation for the first 25 observations are entered into cells E4 and E5 respectively. These observations are used as the base period for the analysis.

1. In cell E4 type =*average(B10:B34)* and press Enter.

2. In cell E5 type =*stdev(B10:B34)* and press Enter.

3. In cell E10 type +*$E$4* and press Enter.

4. In cell D10 type +*$E$10–$E$6*$E$5* and press Enter.

5. In cell F10 type +*$E$10+$E$6*$E$5* and press Enter.

6. Copy the contents of cells D10, E10, and F10 into the range D11:F59.

These steps complete the calculations for the individual control chart. Figure 17.2 illustrates the results.

Graphing the Individual Control Chart

To create the graph of the individual control chart, follow these steps:

1. Hold down the Control (Ctrl) key and identify the graphing *ranges* A9:B59 and D9:F59.

2. Click on the Chart Wizard icon .

3. Click on the XY(Scatter) selection.

4. Select the option at the bottom left (Scatter with data points connected by lines).

5. Click <u>N</u>ext>.

6. In step 3 of 4, type the chart title *Individual Control chart*, *x*-axis title *Observation Number*, and *y*-axis title *Observation Value*.

7. Click <u>N</u>ext>.

8. Click <u>F</u>inish.

9. Position the chart on the worksheet and size the chart according to your own preferences.

10. Click on the *y*-axis (scale) and change the scale minimum value to 90, the maximum to 120, and the major unit to 10.

11. Click on each of the lines to change the line style and to remove the symbol as desired; Figure 17.3 illustrates the results.

Revising the Worksheet for the Moving Range Control Chart

Individual control charts are utilized when decisions are made at a rate approximately equal to the rate of data collection. To demonstrate a moving range control chart, a two-period moving range chart is selected. Basing decisions on only two data points provides for maximum response

Figure 17.2   Worksheet calculations.

Figure 17.3   Individual control chart.

time. Since the moving range is calculated as the absolute difference between two consecutive observations, the absolute value function =*abs(x1–x2)* is appropriate.

1. In cell H10 type =*abs(B11–B10)* and press Enter.

2. Copy the formula in cell H10 into the *range* H11:H59.

3. In cell J4 type =*average($H$11:$H$34)* and press Enter.

4. In cell J10 type +*$J$4* and press Enter.

5. In cell K10 type +*$J$10*$J$6* and press Enter.

6. In cell I10 type +*$J$10*$J$5* and press Enter.

7. Copy the contents of I10:K10 into the *range* I11:K59.

This completes all the calculations for the moving range chart.

Graphing the Moving Range Control Chart

The steps to create the moving range chart are similar to those for the individual control chart. Its creation is left as an exercise. The graphing ranges for the chart are A9:A58 and H9:K58. *Note that the last row of data is omitted from the chart.* Figure 17.4 illustrates the results.

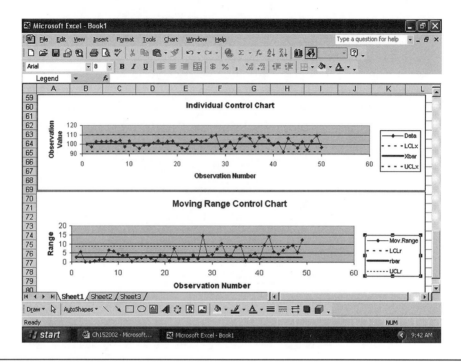

Figure 17.4 Individual and moving range control chart pair.

Revising the Worksheet for the Moving Average Control Chart

To revise the worksheet to create a moving average control chart, save the current worksheet, *Indiv01.xls*, and then edit the name in cell A1 to *Individ02.xls* and save the worksheet as *Indivi02.xls*, using the Save <u>A</u>s option in the <u>F</u>ile menu. Table 17.2 contains a list of the cells and the text to be typed into each cell.

Copy the contents in columns M10 through P10 into the *range* M11:P59. This completes the worksheet calculations.

Graphing the Moving Average Control Chart

To graph the moving average control chart, identify the graphing *range* A9:A58 and M9:P58

1. Click on the Chart Wizard icon ![icon].

2. Select the Line with markers displayed at each data value.

3. Add the titles *Moving Average Control Chart, Observation #,* and *Average.*

4. Position the graph on the worksheet.

Table 17.2   Worksheet labels and formulas.

Cells	Text	Notes
A1	Indivi02.xls	Name of worksheet
N6	A2	Factor label
O6	1.88	A2 factor for subgroup size of 2
M9	Moving Avg	
M10	=average(b10:b11)	Formula for calculating the average of two observations
N9	LCLxb	Lower control limit label
N10	+$O$10–$O$6*$J$4	Formula for calculating the lower control limit
O9	Xxbar	Average label
O10	=average($M$11:$M$34)	Formula for calculating the average of 25 observations
P9	UCLxb	Upper control limit label
P10	+$O$10+$O$6*$J$4	Formula for calculating the upper control limit

Click on each line to eliminate the symbols and change the line color and style to your own preferences. Figure 17.5 illustrates the results.

Using Individual, Moving Range, and Moving Average Control Charts

The procedures for using the individual, moving range, and moving average control charts are similar to those for other control charts. The charts show the probability that a change has occurred. The danger in using the individual control chart is the need to assume the existence of a normal distribution. Similarly, the moving range and moving average charts look like other control charts, but since time lapses between the collection of each data point, the sampling scheme does not offer a high probability of change between subgroups and a low probability of change within a subgroup. These control charts are a management-by-exception technique and should be used only when other control charts cannot be applied.

The control chart data were simulated using the same average for the entire data set with a standard deviation of 10 for the first 25 observations and a standard deviation of 20 for the second 25 observations. In Figure 17.5, each control chart indicates outliers. An *outlier* is an observation above the upper control limit or below the lower control limit. Both the individual and

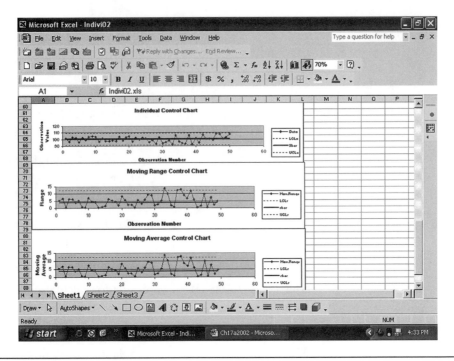

Figure 17.5   Moving average control chart.

moving average control charts indicate outliers above and below the control limits. The moving range chart shows outliers above the UCLr. These results are logical since the standard deviation for observations 26 through 50 is twice that for observations 1 through 25.

Experiment with another value for the standard deviation of the second 25 observations and examine the changes. Remember the data were generated using a nonnormal (uniform) process generator. What are your own judgments regarding the value of these control charts for this particular nonnormal distribution?

Outlier: A point above the upper control limit or below the lower control limit.

Real Life

For a number of years we have worked with a local volunteer group collecting water data on the health of Mobile Bay, Alabama. One of the parameters being measured is the amount of oxygen in the bay water. The data are collected once a week at a number of locations. The data for one data collection location are listed in Table 17.3.

Table 17.3   Mobile Bay oxygen data.

Count	Data	Count	Data	Count	Data
1	115	13	64	25	320
2	210	14	92	26	28
3	170	15	500	27	16
4	100	16	47	28	80
5	88	17	153	29	130
6	64	18	10	30	280
7	138	19	136	31	270
8	220	20	104	32	68
9	108	21	80	33	145
10	199	22	15	34	800
11	310	23	600	35	7
12	470	24	524	36	83
				37	409

Figure 17.6 illustrates an individual and moving range control chart for oxygen in Mobile Bay water.

Autocorrelation may be a concern when using environmental data such as oxygen in bay water. *Autocorrelation* occurs when a given measurement is dependent on a prior measurement or measurements. Our weekly data control charts do not display any of the characteristics we associate with autocorrelation; however, using Excel, it is simple to calculate autocorrelation. Figure 17.7 illustrates the top of the second sheet of our worksheet (*BAYOXY*).

Using Tools, Data Analysis, and Correlation, the correlation between the *n*th observations (column B) and the *n+1* (column C) observations were calculated and the result is displayed in cell E3: *0.010239*. Autocorrelation varies from zero to one. In the authors' opinions, an autocorrelation value less than 0.50 indicates that autocorrelation is not a serious concern in most production data sets. The graph in Figure 17.7 illustrates the autocorrelation present. If there were 100 percent autocorrelation, all values would fall on the line that defines the relationship between columns B and D. Column D is simply a duplication of column B created for the purpose of drawing the line.

Autocorrelation: An observation is related to or a function of previous data behavior.

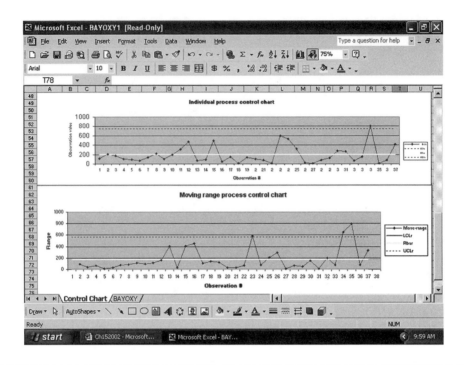

Figure 17.6 Oxygen levels in Mobile Bay.

Figure 17.7 Autocorrelation.

Summary

When the data collection rate is fixed and only one observation is collected over a relatively long period of time, for example, once a day, then an *individual control chart* may be the only option for recording and analyzing the data. Individual control charts show managers when an adjustment or repair may be necessary and the repair or adjustment should be made as quickly as possible after the datum point is collected, for example, an adjustment in a chemical processing facility.

Moving average and *moving range charts* are a variation of the $\overline{X}$ and range or sigma chart pairs. Moving average and moving range charts are appropriate when the subgroup size is two ($n = 2$). These charts are the only realistic option when data collection costs are high or data collection rates are limited, or when historical data are utilized. For example, these charts would be appropriate to track the gas mileage of a company vehicle.

When managers use individual control charts or the moving average and moving range charts, these charts should be the only realistic option available. When data collection rates are faster, other charts presented in this book are more useful.

Exercises

17.1 Create a worksheet following the procedures presented to create the worksheet *individ01.xls*, except generate the sample observations using Excel's normal random number generator. Compare the results.

17.2 Use a normal distribution process generator and replicate the example worksheet for individual, moving average, and moving range control charts in this chapter. Examine the control charts for your worksheet and the sample worksheet from the chapter. Make a histogram of the data. Explain your results.

17.3 Use the exponential process generator $=-average*LN(rand())$ to generate your data and replicate the example worksheet for individual, moving average, and moving range control charts in this chapter. Examine the control charts for your worksheet and the sample worksheet from the chapter. Make a histogram of the data. Explain your results.

18

Exponential Weighted Moving Average Control Charts

OUTLINE

Prior knowledge

From previous chapters, you should know how to open and save worksheets, enter text and formulas, copy the contents of a cell or group of cells to another part of the worksheet, and create and edit graphs using the Chart Wizard. You should also have an understanding of moving average charts (discussed in chapter 17) for comparison with the exponential weighted moving average charts.

Why Use EWMA Charts?

The exponential weighted moving average (EWMA) chart is a process control chart that may be substituted for either the traditional Shewhart X-bar or individual process control charts when *autocorrelation* is present. From chapter 10 you may recall that *autocorrelation* occurs when an observation is a function of the prior observation. When data are autocorrelated, observations are not independent but are related to each other, thus increasing the number of type I errors or false alarms. EWMA charts are based on the idea that when autocorrelation is present, the process is in control when the data fit a time series model.[1] Time series models are based on the calculation of residuals which are differences in values between the observations.

You may recall from chapter 17 that one technique for controlling type I errors is to use moving average and moving range charts. EWMA charts are based on a cumulative data analysis technique similar to the moving average and moving range charts. The primary difference is that weights are assigned to observations, with the most recent observations assigned greater weight than earlier observations. The EWMA chart can detect small shifts in the process average faster than the traditional Shewhart X-bar process control charts because the EWMA chart uses information from all previous subgroups but applies greater weight to the most recent observations. The weights of earlier observations decrease geometrically as new observations are collected.

Autocorrelation: An observation is related to or a function of previous data behavior.

Residual: A residual is the difference between the value of an observation and the value of the previous observation.

Type I error: Numbers indicate a change when there is none and time and money are wasted looking for a change.

Type II error: Numbers do not indicate a change when one has occurred and we miss an opportunity to improve the process.

---

1. Douglas, C. Montgomery and Christina M. Mastrangelo. "Some Statistical Process Control Methods for Autocorrelated Data." *Journal of Quality Technology* 23, no. 3 (1991): 179–193.

The exponential weighting scheme for the EWMA control chart is illustrated by the following formula:

$$G_t = r\overline{X}_t + r(1-r)\overline{X}_{t-1} + r(1-r)^2 \overline{X}_{t-2} + \dots + (1-r)^t G_0,$$

where

r is a weighting constant $(0 < r \le 1)$

G_t is the exponential weighted moving average

G_0 is $\overline{\overline{X}}$

$\overline{X}$ is the average of the subgroup

t and $(t-1)$ . . . represent the time periods, with t representing the current period and $(t-1)$ the time period preceding t

The EWMA chart has a wide range of uses. The EWMA chart is an alternative to the X-bar chart when the subgroup size is greater than one, is an alternative for the individual (or moving average) chart when the subgroup size is one, or is an alternative to the CuSum chart.

The chief disadvantages of the EWMA chart are:

1. The title can be intimidating and misleading to students and quality professionals with limited statistical experience.

2. There is no straightforward method for selecting alpha (alpha is also referred to as lambda), the weighting factor.

There are two types of EWMA charts:

1. Smoothed limits (flattened limits) chart

2. Wandering limits chart

The primary difference between the two charts is in the calculation of the control limits. The control limits in the smoothed limits or flattened limits chart are recalculated for each value of the weighted moving average; however, the limits are smoothed by a constant (alpha), which adjusts the number of periods included in the calculation of the average. For the smoothed limits EWMA chart, recommended values of alpha (the smoothing constant) are between 0.2 and 0.4. Values in this range balance older observations with newer observations. These values are based on the assumption that the residuals are statistically independent.

The control limits in the wandering limits EWMA control chart are also recalculated for each value of the weighted moving average; however, the limits are not smoothed, but follow the time series trend.

Figure 18.1 illustrates a smoothed limits (flattened) EWMA control chart and Figure 18.2 illustrates a wandering limits EWMA control chart.

Both types of control charts are relatively easy to create using Excel. Experts disagree on the proper method used to create the wandering EWMA chart. The authors experimented with several methods before selecting the method presented in this chapter.

Figure 18.1 Smoothed limits (flattened) EWMA control chart.

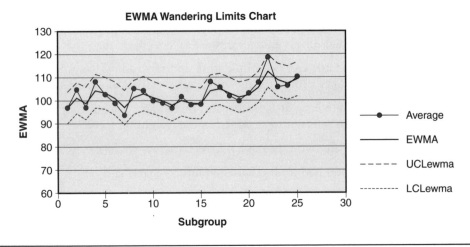

Figure 18.2 Wandering limits EWMA control chart.

The authors believe that the EWMA is no more difficult to create and interpret than any other Shewhart process control chart; however, the title can be intimidating for students, managers, and other professionals such as physicians. To reduce the level of intimidation, we often refer to the EWMA chart as simply a "weighted average" control chart.

The EWMA chart helps the user control the process average. It does not help in the control of variation. Common practice is to use either a range or standard deviation (sigma) chart to control variation along with the EWMA chart.

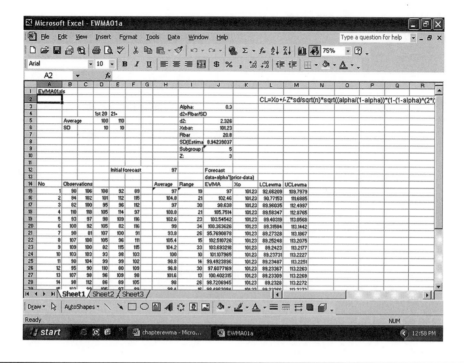

Figure 18.3 EWMA worksheet.

Creating the Smoothed Limits EWMA Worksheet

In the worksheet illustrated in Figure 18.3, the first 20 subgroups are the base period and subgroups 21 through 25 are the additional periods.

Entering Worksheet Text

Enter the text and values from Table 18.1 into the new worksheet.

The formula for the control limits was entered as text into cell L2. This formula is complex and is entered in this manner to help you enter the formula into cells L15 and M15 later in the development of the worksheet.

Entering Observation Values

Fixed values are used for observations rather than random numbers so that you may check the accuracy of your formulas and calculations. Later in the chapter these values are replaced by random numbers to do simulations. The values are shown in Table 18.2. The first column is the subgroup number. The observations are in the *range* B15:F39.

Table 18.1 EWMA worksheet text.

Cell	Text	Explanation
A1	EWMA01.xls	Spreadsheet name
A14	No	Column heading
B5	Average	Average value used to simulate data
B6	SD	Standard deviation value used to simulate data
B14	Observations	
D4	1st 20	
E4	21+	
E12	Initial forecast	
H14	Average	Column for subgroup average
I14	Range	Column head subgroup range
I3	Alpha:	
I4	d2=Rbar/SD	Formula explanation
I5	d2:	
I6	Xxbar:	Average of the averages during base period
I7	Rbar	Average of the ranges during the base period
I8	SD (Estimate):	Identifies calculation of standard deviation
I9	Subgroup (n):	
I10	Z:	Number of standard deviations
J5	2.326	Value for D_2 from the appendix
J12	Forecast	
J13	data+alpha*(prior-data)	Formula explanation
J14	EWMA	Column head
K14	Xo	Column head for center line of control chart
L2	CL= Xo +/− Z * sd/sqrt(n)* sqrt((alpha/(1–alpha))* (1–(1–alpha)^(2*i)))	
L14	LCLewma	Lower control limit for the EWMA chart
M14	UCLewma	Upper control limit for the EWMA chart
J3	0.3	The smoothing constant alpha = 0.3
J10	3	The number of standard deviations

Table 18.2   Observations values for the EWMA worksheet.

			Columns		
A	B	C	D	E	F
1	90	106	108	92	89
2	94	102	101	112	115
3	82	100	95	96	112
4	110	118	105	114	97
5	93	97	98	109	116
6	100	92	105	82	116
7	90	81	107	100	91
8	107	108	105	96	111
9	109	100	82	115	115
10	103	103	93	98	103
11	90	104	99	99	102
12	95	90	110	80	109
13	107	98	96	109	98
14	98	112	86	89	105
15	102	99	105	97	89
16	115	97	100	114	115
17	112	117	93	106	100
18	106	104	97	96	107
19	106	87	97	102	106
20	98	97	102	108	110
21	101	106	109	102	120
22	116	118	135	109	114
23	115	121	105	110	78
24	111	114	113	103	90
25	93	126	114	111	106

Entering Worksheet Formulas

The only two complex formulas in the EWMA chart calculate the upper and lower control limits. The formulas for the worksheet are shown in Table 18.3.

We used absolute addressing in the lower control limit formula in cell L15 to make it easier to copy the formula into cell M15. The only adjustment to change the lower limit formula to the upper limit formula is to change the first negative sign to a positive sign.

Copy the formulas in the following cells into the appropriate ranges:

Cell	Range
H15	H16:H39
I15	I16:I39
J16	J17:J39
K16	K17:K39
L15	L16:L39
M15	M15:M39

Table 18.3 Formulas.

Cell	Formula	Note
H12	=H15	Average of first subgroup used as initial forecast
H15	=AVERAGE(B15:F15)	Copied into the range H16:H39
I15	=MAX(B15:F15)–MIN(B15:F15)	Copied into the range I16:I39
J15	=H15	Average of first subgroup used as initial forecast
J16	=H16+$K$3*(J15–H16)	The EWMA forecast calculation
		Copied into the range J17:J39
J6	=AVERAGE(H15:H34)	Average of the subgroup averages in the base period
J7	=AVERAGE(I15:I34)	Average of the subgroup ranges in the base period
J8	=J7/J5	Calculation for the standard deviation
J9	=COUNT(B15:F15)	Size of subgroup
K15	=J6	Transfer value of average
K16	=K15	Copied to the range K16:K39
L15	=$K15–$J$10*$J$8/SQRT($J$9)*SQRT($J$3/(1–(1–$J$3))*(1–(1–$J$3)^(2*$A15)))	
M15	=+$K15+$J$10*$J$8/SQRT($J$9)*SQRT($J$3/(1–(1–$J$3))*(1–(1–$J$3)^(2*$A15)))	

Creating the Smoothed Limits EWMA Control Chart

Hold the left mouse button down and drag to define the *range* A14:A39, press the control key, and select the *range* J14:M39.

1. Click on the Chart Wizard icon ▦ .

2. Select the XY (Scatter) and the smoothed limits without markers and click on Next>.

3. Click on Next> again.

4. Type the Chart title as *EWMA Smoothed Limits Chart*; type the Value *x*-axis as *Subgroups*; and type the Value *y*-axis as *EWMA* and click on Next>.

5. In Step 4 of 4 click on Finish; the graph is shown in Figure 18.4.

The graph in Figure 18.4 shows one subgroup outside the control limits. The simulated observation average for the subgroup was 110, that is, one standard deviation above the average during the base period. As expected, the EWMA chart detected the small shift in the process average.

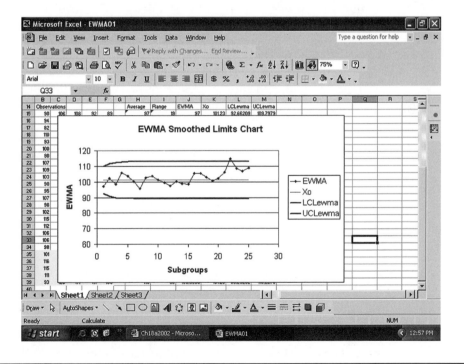

Figure 18.4   EWMA smoothed limits chart.

Revising the Worksheet for the Wandering Limits EWMA Control Chart

The wandering limits EWMA chart does not use a smoothing constant to flatten the control limits; therefore, the performance characteristics may differ from the smoothed limits EWMA chart. Figure 18.5 illustrates an Excel worksheet for the wandering limits EWMA chart using the same data that was used earlier in the chapter to create the smoothed limits EWMA chart.

The data used in the smoothed limits EWMA chart (Figure 18.4) and the wandering limits EWMA chart (Figure 18.6) are identical. In both cases, the EWMA chart indicates one subgroup that is beyond the upper limit. In fact, the same subgroup is out of limits in both charts.

Changing the Worksheet Text

To save time and keystrokes, it is recommended that you copy EWMA01.xls to EWMA02.xls using the Save <u>A</u>s option in the <u>F</u>ile menu. In the File <u>n</u>ame: dialog area change the name of the file to EWMA02 and click on the Save button.

Edit the name in cell A1 from EWMA01.xls to EWMA02.xls.

Make the following changes to the worksheet.

1. In cell I14 change the text to *Std Error* and press Enter.

2. Delete column K by clicking on the K at the top of the worksheet, click on <u>E</u>dit, and click on <u>D</u>elete. The contents of the columns L and M are moved into columns K and L respectively.

3. In cell J3 type *0.45* and press Enter.

4. In cell I4 type *Sqrt(a/(2–a))* and press Enter.

5. Delete the text in the *range* I5:I8.

6. Delete the text and formulas in the *range* J5:J8.

7. Delete the formula in cell K2.

8. Delete the text in cell J12.

9. In cell J13 replace the text with *Centerline/EWMA* and press ENTER.

Changing the Worksheet Formulas

In the range H15:H39 and in the range J15:J39 the formulas for both the flattened limits and wandering limits EWMA charts are identical. Type the additional formulas in the appropriate cells as indicated below.

Cell	Formula
J4	=SQRT($J$3/(2–$J$3))
I15	=STDEV(B$15:F15)
K15	=$J15–$J$10*$I15/SQRT($J$9)*$J$4
L15	=+$J15+$J$10*$I15/SQRT($J$9)*$J$4

Copy the formulas from I15:L15 into the *range* I16:L39.
The completed worksheet is shown in Figure 18.5.

Creating the Wandering Limits EWMA Control Chart

Hold the left mouse button down to define the *range* A14:A39, press and
hold the control key and select the *range* H14:H39 and the *range* J14:L39.

1. Click on the Chart Wizard icon ![icon].

2. Select the XY (Scatter) and the smoothed limits without markers
   and click <u>N</u>ext>.

Figure 18.5 Worksheet for the wandering limits EWMA chart.

3. Click Next> again.

4. Type the Chart title as *EWMA Wandering Chart*; type the Category *x*-axis as *Subgroups*; and type the Value *y*-axis as *EWMA* and click on Next>.

5. In Step 4 of 4 click on Finish; the graph is shown in Figure 18.6.

The performance of both types of EWMA charts was identical for the data set selected. The change between the base period and additional periods was one standard deviation and both charts indicated one change in the process average.

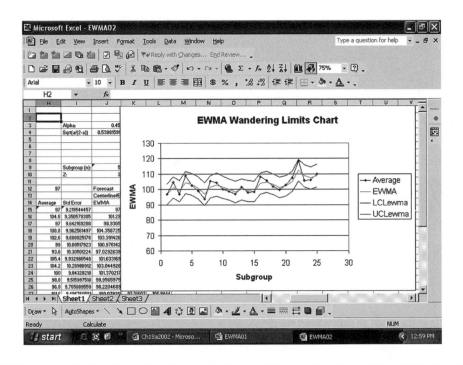

Figure 18.6   Wandering limits EWMA chart.

Real Life

The CuSum chart and the EWMA charts are alternative methods for solving similar problems. The fecal data from the CuSum charts in chapter 16 are used again in this chapter to illustrate the EWMA charts. The CuSum charts did not detect any observations beyond the control limits. The flattened limits EWMA indicated that there were four (4) observations beyond the control limits while the wandering limits EWMA chart indicated that there were nine (9) observations beyond the control limits. Figures 18.7 and 18.8 illustrate the results.

Figure 18.7 Flattened limits EWMA fecal process control chart.

Figure 18.8 Wandering limits EWMA fecal control chart.

Three process control charts, one set of data, and three different indicators are relative to possible indicators of change. Which is correct? We know that the increases in fecal matter may be caused by rain after a period of no rain. Fecal matter is a measure of human and animal waste. Animal waste is expected to wash into a body of water after a rain. If the amount of animal waste has had time to collect then the rain may be expected to result in a peak in the observations.

By referencing weather data, we know that some of the peaks were due to rain. If we want our control chart to help us determine when the peaks are related to rainfall then the CuSum chart is not the best choice because it must be recalculated after each sample is collected. Better choices are the flattened limits or wandering limits EWMA charts. The wandering limits chart identifies more observations as out of limits than the flattened limits EWMA chart. We would select the flattened limits EWMA chart because it seems to have the best balance between type I and type II errors.

Summary

The exponential weighted moving average (EWMA) chart may be substituted for either the traditional Shewhart X-bar or individual process control charts to reduce type I errors or false alarms when observations are autocorrelated.

EWMA charts are based on a cumulative data analysis technique similar to the moving average and moving range charts. The primary difference is that weights are assigned to observations, with the most recent observations assigned greater weight than earlier observations. The EWMA chart can detect small shifts in the process average faster than the traditional Shewhart X-bar process control charts because the EWMA chart uses information from all previous subgroups but applies greater weight to the most recent observations. The weights of earlier observations decrease geometrically as new observations are collected.

There are two types of EWMA charts, the smoothed limits (flattened limits) chart and the wandering limits chart. The primary difference between the two charts is in the calculation of the control limits. The control limits in the smoothed limits or flattened limits chart are recalculated for each value of the weighted moving average; however, the limits are smoothed by a constant (alpha) which is generally recommended to be between 0.2 and 0.4. The control limits in the wandering EWMA control chart are also recalculated for each value of the weighted moving average; however, the limits are not smoothed, but follow the time series trend.

The EWMA charts are alternatives to the X-bar chart when the subgroup size is greater than one, to the individual (or moving average) chart when the subgroup size is one, and to the CuSum chart with subgroup size of greater than one or individual observations.

Exercises

18.1   Use the following data set to create a smoothed limits EWMA chart and review the results. Assume the first 15 observations are from the base period. Use an alpha of 0.35. Review the results.

99.4

95.0

99.0

94.2

102.2

104.8

104.2

102.4

98.4

97.8

97.6

108.4

108.4

106.6

97.8

109.6

104.4

111.2

111.8

106.2

18.2   Given the following data set organized as individual observations on the left and as subgroup data on the right:

a.   Make a flattened limits EWMA analysis of the individual observations using the first 24 as the base period data.

b.   Make a flattened limits EWMA analysis of the subgroup data using the first six subgroups as the base period data.

c.   Compare the results. Which method of data organization is better, why? This is the same data used in a similar assignment for the CuSum chart. If you were assigned that problem, compare the CuSum results with the EWMA results.

Number	Observation	Subgroup	1	2	3	4
1	35.44	1	35.44	34.77	34.97	40.87
2	34.77	2	42.06	41.95	37.77	34.27
3	34.97	3	39.98	39.55	41.56	33.89
4	40.87	4	41.25	37.07	42.54	33.28
5	42.06	5	33.91	39.22	36.27	34.64
6	41.95	6	33.09	40.61	35.37	34.61
7	37.77	7	48.77	44.42	46.07	43.33
8	34.27	8	46.14	49.82	50.36	52.60
9	39.98					
10	39.55					
11	41.56					
12	33.89					
13	41.25					
14	37.07					
15	42.54					
16	33.28					
17	33.91					
18	39.22					
19	36.27					
20	34.64					
21	33.09					
22	40.61					
23	35.37					
24	34.61					
25	48.77					
26	44.42					
27	46.07					
28	43.33					
29	46.14					
30	49.82					
31	50.36					
32	52.60					

18.3   Recalculate problem 2 using a wandering limits EWMA chart.

Part V

Acceptance Sampling

19

Binomial and Hypergeometric Distributions

OUTLINE

Prior Knowledge

From previous chapters, you should know how to open and save worksheets, enter text, copy the contents of a cell or group of cells to another part of a worksheet, and create and edit charts and graphs using the Chart Wizard.

Introduction

Quality inspections for the purpose of acceptance sampling utilize continuous sampling and/or lot-by-lot acceptance sampling. *Acceptance sampling* is the process in which samples are taken from a product lot and the products in the sample are inspected for quality using either attribute or variable measurement. Each lot is accepted or rejected based on the number of defective items found in the sample. An alternative to attribute sampling is 100 percent inspection of each item in the lot; however, this option is rarely cost effective.

When quality characteristics can be measured with continuous variables, X-bar and range or sigma charts may be used in coordination with variable acceptance sampling plans. The variable approach is limited to one quality characteristic at a time. A part may be classified as poor quality due to a variety of reasons. Attribute control charts along with attribute acceptance sampling plans may be used for these parts. Sometimes the quality of a product cannot be measured using variable measurements, but must be measured using attributes. In these situations acceptance sampling is the only option.

Attribute sampling plans are often based on the *binomial* and/or *hypergeometric distributions*. When acceptance sampling is used, care should be taken to ensure the identity of each lot so the sources of poor quality can be analyzed. As much as possible, each lot should contain the output of a single machine or process for a specific time period. It is also important that the sample be drawn at random, meaning that every item or part has an equal chance of being included in the sample.

Cumulative distribution function (cdf):   Shows the cumulative probability of all events from negative infinity up to the point specified.

Probability density function: Shows the probability that the value of any random variable will fall between any two points. Frequently shown with a histogram for discrete values and a curve for continuous values.

Binomial distribution: A distribution based on attribute measures that assume only two values of outcomes are possible (for example, good–bad, on–off, or small–large). This distribution is for large populations in which sampling does not affect the probability of obtaining a given result.

Hypergeometric distribution: A distribution based on attribute measures that assume only two values of outcomes are possible (for example, good–bad, on–off, or small–large). This distribution is for small populations in which taking a sample affects the probability of selecting an item with a particular value.

This chapter presents the procedure for calculating the probability density function (pdf) and the cumulative distribution function (cdf) associated with the binomial and hypergeometric distributions. The theoretical background provided in this chapter is essential for understanding the incoming and outgoing quality calculations presented in chapters 20 and 21.

The *probability density function* (pdf) is a graph of a distribution, which is usually shown with a histogram. A *histogram* is a bar chart of the frequencies of each value in a group of measurements. Recall from chapter 5 that the graph of the normal distribution is a bell-shaped curve. The *cumulative distribution function* (cdf) is a function of the area under the probability density function (the area under the distribution curve); therefore, the cdf for most distributions is an ever-increasing curve.

Binomial Distribution

The binomial distribution is for large lots in which sampling does not affect the probability of obtaining a given result. For example, if the lot is large and the probability of finding a defective item is small, taking an item from the lot will not significantly change the probability of finding a defective item among the remaining items. The binomial distribution is based on attribute measures and assumes only two outcomes are possible, such as heads–tails, on–off, or good–bad. The formula for the binomial distribution is

$$\text{Prob}(x) = \begin{bmatrix} n \\ x \end{bmatrix} * p^x (1-p)^{(n-x)}$$

where

n is the lot size

x is the sample size

p is the probability of the event of interest

The symbol 　　　　　$\begin{bmatrix} n \\ x \end{bmatrix} = \dfrac{n!}{X! * (n-x)!}$

where 　　　　　　　$n! = n * (n-1) * (n-2) \ldots 1$

　　　　　　　　　　$0! = 1$

The symbol

$$C_x^n$$

is often used in place of the symbol $\begin{bmatrix} n \\ x \end{bmatrix}$ since both symbols represent the same thing. The variables $n!$ and $x!$ are factorials. Although calculating factorials may become complex, Excel's worksheet program provides a simple and effective method for calculating factorials.

Hypergeometric Distribution

The hypergeometric distribution is for small lot sizes, in which taking the sample affects the probability of selecting a defective item. We recommend that if the sample size is greater than 10 percent of the lot size, the hypergeometric distribution should be used over the binomial distribution. Other experts do not require the use of the hypergeometric distribution until the sample size exceeds 20 percent of the lot size. With the use of Excel there is less reason to use an approximation than was necessary in the past. The hypergeometric distribution is also based on attribute measures and assumes two values of outcomes such as good–bad, on–off, or small–large. The formula for the hypergeometric distribution is

$$P(r{:}N,B,n) = \frac{\begin{bmatrix} B \\ r \end{bmatrix}\begin{bmatrix} N-B \\ n-r \end{bmatrix}}{\begin{bmatrix} N \\ n \end{bmatrix}}$$

where

n is the sample size

N is the lot size

r is the number of "bad" items in the sample

B is the number of "bad" items in the lot

Creating the Binomial and Hypergeometric Worksheet

Entering Worksheet Text

The calculations for the binomial and hypergeometric cases are similar. The following text and numbers should be entered into the indicated cells.

Cell	Text	Notes
A1	binom-01.xls	Name of the worksheet file
A6	Binomial Distribution	
A8	Sample size	
A9	Probability	
B8	5	
B9	0.5	

continued

continued

Cell	Text	Notes
B10	as a decimal	
D6	# Defective	Number of defective items in the sample
D7	0	
E6	pdf	Probability density function
F6	cdf	Cumulative distribution function
H6	Hypergeometric Distribution	
K6	# Defective	
L6	pdf	
M6	cdf	
K7	0	
H8	Sample size	
H9	Bad in lot	
H10	Lot Size	
I8	5	
I9	25	
I10	50	

Generating Observation Data

Binomial Distribution Data

The observation data for both the binomial and hypergeometric distributions can be generated using Excel's random number generator. One of the limitations of using the Excel random number generator is that the user does not learn how to simulate data for the various distributions; however, using the random number generator saves time. The binomial distribution function is

$$=BINOMDIST(x,n,p,TRUE/FALSE)$$

where x is the number of bad items in the sample, n is the sample size, p is the probability of a bad item, and *True* outputs the cumulative distribution function and *False* outputs the probability density function. To generate the probability density function and the cumulative distribution function, follow these steps:

1. In cell D8 type +1+D7 and press Enter.

2. Copy the formula in D8 into the *range* D9:D13.

3. In cell E7 type =BINOMDIST(D7,$B$8,$B$9,FALSE) and press Enter.

4. Copy the formula in cell E7 into the *range* E8:E13.

5. In cell F7 type +E7 and press Enter.

6. In cell F8 type +F7+E8 and press Enter.

7. Copy the formula in cell F8 into the *range* F9:F13.

In cells E13 and F13, the symbol *#NUM!* appears, which indicates a calculation error. The error is that it is impossible to have six defective items in a sample lot of five. The *#NUM!* message will appear whenever the number of defective items is larger than the sample size. You may expand the worksheet to handle sample sizes of 20, 30, 40 or more.

Hypergeometric Distribution Data

The hypergeometric distribution function is

$$=\text{HYPGEOMDIST}(r, n, B, N)$$

where r is the number of defective items in the sample, n is the sample size, B is the number of defective items in the lot, and N is the lot size. To generate the probability density function and the cumulative distribution function, follow these steps:

1. In cell K8 type +1+K7 and press Enter.

2. Copy the formula in cell K8 into the *range* K9:K13.

3. In cell L7 type =HYPGEOMDIST(K7,$I$8,$I$9,$I$10) and press Enter.

4. Copy the formula in cell L7 into the *range* L8:L13.

5. In cell M7 type +L7 and press Enter.

6. In cell M8 type +L8+M7 and press Enter.

7. Copy the formula in cell M8 into the *range* M9:M13.

The result is shown in Figure 19.1.

Self-Checking

The reason why $n = 5$ and $p = 0.5$ were selected as input is that you can easily check the results using these numbers. The cumulative function

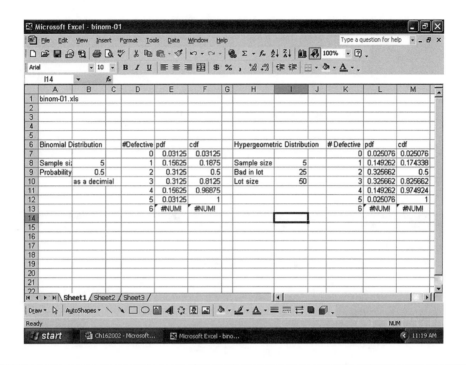

Figure 19.1   Complete worksheet calculations.

becomes 1 for $x = 5$ or whenever $x = n$. Having checkpoints in your worksheet design helps prevent inaccurate decisions and the submission of erroneous reports to managers.

Graphing the Binomial and Hypergeometric Distributions

The binomial and hypergeometric graphs look similar. The bars represent the probability density function (pdf) and the lines connected by squares represent the cumulative distribution function (cdf). The graphs of the probability density functions are symmetrical because the probability of occurrence was set at 0.5 for the binomial distribution and the number of bad items in each lot was set at 25 for a lot of 50 in the hypergeometric distribution. These numbers were selected to help you check your work. Using these numbers, the distributions should be symmetrical; if they are not, there is an error.

To graph the binomial distribution, follow these steps:

1. Highlight the *range* E6:F12.

2. Click on the Chart Wizard icon [image].

3. In step 1 of 4, click on the Custom Types tab.

4. Select the custom type Line–Column and click on Next>.

5. Type the chart title *Binomial pdf and cdf*, name the *x*-axis *Number Defective*, name the *y*-axis *Probability*, and click on Next>.

6. Click on Finish.

7. Size and position the chart on the worksheet.

The steps to create the hypergeometric graph are the same as those for the binomial except the graphing *range* is L6:M12. Both graphs are shown in Figure 19.2.

Figure 19.2   Binomial and hypergeometric probability and cumulative distribution.

Summary

Quality inspections, which utilize lot-by-lot acceptance sampling, require the use of the *binomial* and *hypergeometric distributions*. These distributions are based on attribute data with dichotomous outcomes such as good/bad, defective/nondefective, or go/no-go. *Acceptance sampling* is the process in which samples are taken from a product lot and the products in the sample are inspected for quality using either attribute or variable measurement. Each lot is accepted or rejected based on the number of defective items found in the sample. An alternative to attribute sampling is testing each item; however, this option is rarely cost effective.

When quality specialists use acceptance sampling, care should be taken to ensure that each lot contains only output from a single machine or a single process for a specific period of time. Such clarity allows the quality specialist to investigate and hopefully correct the sources of poor quality. Care should also be taken to ensure that all samples are drawn at random, meaning that every item in the lot has an equal chance of being tested.

The binomial distribution should be used when the sample is small relative to the size of the lot (for example, when selecting an item from the lot does not change the probability of selecting a defective item when the next item is chosen). The hypergeometric distribution should be used when the sample size meets or exceeds 10 percent of the lot size (for example, when selecting an item from the lot does change the probability of selecting a defective item when the next item is chosen). The formulas for estimating the binomial and hypergeometric distributions use factorials, which are easily calculated using an Excel worksheet.

Exercises

19.1   Use the worksheets developed in this chapter to find the probability function for the experiment. Toss a fair coin 12 times and count the number of heads. Use the worksheets developed in this chapter to find the probability function for the following experiment: From a bowl with 10 black and 10 white balls, remove 12 balls and count the number of white balls in the selection. Why are the numbers different for the two experiments?

19.2   The probability of a defective part is 0.001. There are 100 items in the lot. Assume that you take a sample of 10 items (without returning them to the lot). How far off would you be if you used the binomial approximation rather than the hypergeometric model?

19.3   Repeat the calculations in problem 19.1 for a lot of $n = 200$ and $n = 300$. Comment.

19.4   Repeat the calculations in problem 19.2 for defective rates of 0.005, 0.01, and 0.02. Comment.

20

Operating Characteristic and Power Curves (Measuring Average Incoming Quality)

Prior Knowledge

From previous chapters, you should know how to open and save worksheets, enter text, copy the contents of a cell or group of cells to another part of a worksheet, and create and edit charts and graphs using the Chart Wizard. You should also know under what conditions it is most appropriate to use the binomial and hypergeometric distributions presented in chapter 19.

The Operating Characteristic Curve and Power Curve

Incoming quality is the quality of the product or raw material when it arrives at the plant or the business where it is to be inspected before being accepted. At the location, the material is sampled, the quality of the sample is measured, and the lot is accepted or rejected depending upon the quality of the sample. At the receiving location, a sampling plan must be created so that the accept or reject decision may be made. The *operating characteristic (OC) curve* is a graphical analysis of a sample plan that helps the quality control manager select sampling plans that provide the desired consumer (user of the product) and producer (manufacturer of the product) risks. The producer's risk is the probability that good quality lots will be rejected and the consumer's risk is the probability that low quality lots will be accepted. An OC curve is a plot of the probability of acceptance of a lot versus different levels of incoming quality, given an acceptable quality level. The producer's risk and consumer's risk can be identified on the OC curve.

Developing a sampling plan consists of the following steps:

1. Decide on the appropriate acceptable quality level.

2. Decide on the appropriate sample size n, given the probability of type I and type II errors.

3. Consult a table to determine the acceptance level (the maximum number of defective items that will allow the lot to be accepted).

4. Take a sample of n items from the lot.

5. If the number of defective items in the sample is less than the maximum number acceptable, then accept the lot; if the number of defective items in the sample is greater than the maximum number of acceptable items, then reject the lot.

Acceptance number: In an attribute acceptance sampling plan, an acceptance number is a nonnegative value that represents the maximum number of defective items that should be found in a sample. If the number of defective items found in a sample is less than or equivalent to the acceptance number, then the lot is accepted.

Acceptance sampling: The procedure of taking a sample of observations from a lot of product or material and making a decision about whether to accept or reject the lot.

Acceptable quality level: A fraction of defective items specified by the producer and/or customer as the maximum percentage of defective items considered acceptable in a sampling plan.

Lot tolerance percent defective: A fraction of defective items specified as the poorest level of quality that the customer is willing to accept in a given lot.

Operating characteristic curve: Graph of the probability of accepting a lot given various levels of incoming quality.

Power curve: Graph of the probability of rejecting a lot given various levels of incoming quality.

Sampling plan: The specification of how a lot is identified, the size of the lot, how a sample is selected from the lot, the sample size, the basis according to whether a lot is accepted or rejected, and what happens to the lot when the sample is accepted or rejected.

Acceptance sampling is the procedure that offers assurance of the risk of accepting lots containing various levels of quality. The purpose is to guide decision making. When acceptance sampling is utilized, all quality tests are performed on a sample drawn from the lot, and all decisions regarding the lot are made based on the sample. The objective is to be able to accept lots according to the specified *acceptable quality level* (AQL) 95 percent of the time. Using a sample size of $n = 40$ and an acceptance number of $c = 3$, Figure 17.1 illustrates the classic shape of the operating characteristic curve as quality varies from good to poor along the x-axis. A sample size of $n = 40$ means that 40 items are selected from a large lot (assuming the binomial model) and inspected. An acceptable quality level (AQL) of 3 means that if zero, one, two, or three defectives are found, the lot is accepted as "good" quality. Given a sample of 40 and an AQL of 10 percent, if 10 percent of the items in the lot are defective, the probability of accepting the lot, based on a sample of three items, is 40 percent. If 15 percent of the items in the lot are defective, the probability of acceptance drops to approximately 12 percent.

The *lot tolerance percent defective* (LTPD) is the fraction of defective items specified as the poorest level of quality that the customer is willing to accept in a given lot. The objective is to have the *sampling plan* accept lots with the LTPD only 10 percent of the time. The *indifference quality level* (IQL) is the quality in which the probability of acceptance is 50 percent.

Guidelines for developing sampling plans are provided by the American British Canadian Standards (ABC-STD 105). These guidelines are indexed on the acceptable quality level (AQL). To develop a sampling plan, one specifies the desired AQL and sample size required, and then consults a table to determine the appropriate acceptance number. These standards were originally developed at Columbia University during World War II to assist the military in assessing incoming quality. The military standards were originally named *MIL-STD 105*. These plans were modeled after the Dodge-Romig plans developed for internal use by the Bell Telephone Laboratories. ABC-STD have been adopted by numerous nations as guides to quality standards. The foundation of the plans is the operating characteristic curve.

The procedures presented in this chapter demonstrate a series of calculations that will produce a series of operating characteristic curves, which are dependent on the acceptable quality level. For a given level of quality, the probability of acceptance goes up as the acceptance number increases. In other words, as the company allows a larger number of defective parts to be found in the sample, and still identifies the lot as "good," the probabilities of accepting samples with a larger percentage of defective items increases (see Figure 20.1).

Alternatively, a *power curve* is a plot of the probability of rejection given different levels of incoming quality. The power curve is simply one minus the OC curve. Most quality control managers use the operating characteristic curves while many statisticians prefer to use the power curve. The sum of the probability of acceptance and probability of rejection equals one.

Figure 20.1   Operating characteristic curve.

Creating an Operating Characteristic Worksheet

An operating characteristic curve presents the cumulative distribution function as a function of the quality of incoming product. There is a family of operating characteristic curves for each acceptance level. The probability of accepting a lot that does not meet specifications is compared to a measure of incoming quality (percentage of defective items in the population or the number of defective items in a lot). The worksheet for the binomial distribution in this chapter is designed to handle acceptance numbers from zero to 10. The worksheet may be expanded to handle increased levels of incoming quality.

Entering Worksheet Text

Enter the following text into the indicated cells.

Cell	Text
A1	Ocbin-01.xls
A9	c
A10	Acceptance
A11	Number
B2	Sample size n:
B3	Low:
B4	High:
B5	Num of Cells:
B6	Increment
C10	Probability of acceptance, the OC curve
A25	Power curve calculation
A26	c
A27	Acceptance
A28	Number
C27	Probability of rejection, the Power Curve
D2	5
D3	0.001
D4	0.66
D5	20
E4	As a decimal

Double-click on the Sheet1 tab at the bottom of the screen. When the text is highlighted, type *OC-Curve*.

Entering Worksheet Formulas

1. In cell A12 type *0* and press Enter.

2. In cell A13 type *+1+A12* and press Enter.

3. Copy the formula in cell A13 into the *range* A14:A22.

4. In cell D6 type *+(D4–D3)/(D5–1)* and press Enter.

5. In cell C11 type *+D3* and press Enter.

6. In cell D11 type *+C11+$D$6* and press Enter.

7. Copy the formula in cell D11 into the *range* E11:V11 (across the row).

8. In cell C12 type *=BINOMDIST($A12,$D$2,C$11,TRUE)* and press Enter.

9. Click on cell C12 and click on the Copy button.

10. Using the left mouse button, highlight the *range* C12:V22 and press Enter.

The worksheet is shown in Figure 20.2.

This completes the calculations for the worksheet for acceptance numbers from zero to 10. Only acceptance numbers from zero through three

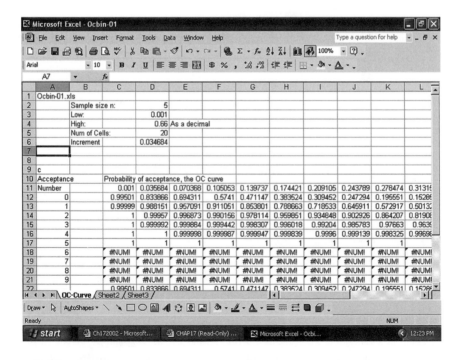

Figure 20.2 OC curve worksheet.

will be graphed in the following example. Notice that in rows 18 through 21 the symbol #*NUM!* is displayed in each cell. This is due to the sample size entered in cell D2 ($n = 5$). The symbol is showing that if the sample size is five, the maximum number of defective items cannot exceed five. If the sample size is increased, the #*NUM!* symbol is replaced with probabilities.

Adding the Power Curve Observations to the Worksheet

Recall that the power curve is equal to one minus the OC curve. To calculate the probabilities of rejection for the power curves, add the following cells to the worksheet:

1. In cell C28 type +*C11* and press Enter.

2. Copy the formula in cell C28 into the *range* D28:V28.

3. In cell A29 type +*A12* and press Enter.

4. Copy the contents in cell A29 into the *range* A30:A38 to number the rejection numbers.

5. In cell C29 type +*1-C12* and press Enter.

6. Copy the formula into the *range* C29:V38.

Figure 20.3 shows the probabilities of rejection.

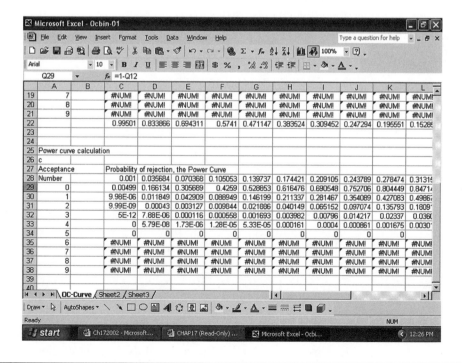

Figure 20.3 Power curve worksheet.

Graphing the Operating Characteristic Curve

To create the graphs for the OC curves, follow these steps:

1. Identify the graphing *range* C11:V15 (remember only acceptance numbers 0, 1, 2, and 3 are included in the sample graph).

2. Click on the Chart Wizard icon .

3. Select the XY Scatter chart and select the sub-graph type (Scatter with data points connected by smoothed lines without markers) and click on Next>.

4. In step 2 of 4, click on the Series tab at the top of the screen and enter the following series labels by clicking on each series, and then typing the text in the box to the right: Series1: ($c = 0$), Series2: ($c = 1$), Series3: ($c = 2$), and Series4: ($c = 3$) and click on Next>.

5. In step 3 of 4, enter the chart title *Operating Characteristic Curves*, the *x*-axis title *Incoming Quality*, and the *y*-axis title *Probability of Acceptance*, and click on Next>.

6. Click on Finish.

7. Locate and size the graph as desired.

Change the sample size in cell D2 to see how a change in the sample size affects the curves.

The operating characteristic curves are shown in Figure 20.4.

Graphing the Power Curve

The steps required to create the power curve graph are identical to those for the operating characteristic curve graph, except the graphing *range* is C28:V32. This task is left as an exercise. Figure 20.5 illustrates the results.

Hypergeometric Operating Characteristic Curves

All operating characteristic curves are similar. Once a worksheet is created for one such curve, it is usually easier to edit an existing worksheet to create a second operating characteristic curve worksheet. The input data for the binomial distribution are: (1) sample size *n*; (2) lowest number of defects possible; and (3) highest number of defects acceptable. The input data for the hypergeometric distribution are: (1) lot size *N*; (2) sample size *n*; (3) lowest number of defects possible; and (4) increment. Use the worksheet OCBIN-01.xls created earlier in the chapter and save the worksheet as *OCHPER01.xls*. The steps to revise the worksheet are:

1. Double-click on the OC-Curve tab at the bottom of the screen.

2. When the text is highlighted, type *OCHY-Curve* and press Enter.

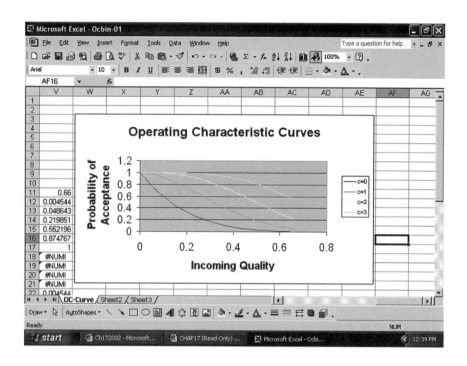

Figure 20.4 Operating characteristic curves graph.

Figure 20.5 Power curves graph.

3. Delete the text in the *range* B2: E6 and enter the following text:

Cell	Text
B2	Lot size n:
B3	Sample size n:
B4	Low:
B5	Increment
D2	50
D3	5
D4	0
D5	2
C10	Number of defectives in the OC curves

Change the following formulas:

1. In cell C11 type +$D$4 and press Enter.

2. In cell D11 type +C11+$D$5 and press Enter.

3. Copy the contents of cell D11 into the *range* E11:V11.

4. In cell C12 type =HYPGEOMDIST($A12,$D$3,C$11,$D$2) and press Enter.

5. Copy this formula into the *range* D12:V12.

6. In cell C13 type =IF(C12>=1,1,+HYPGEOMDIST($A13,$D$3,C$11, $D$2)+C12) and press Enter.

7. Copy the formula in cell C13 into the *range* C13:V22.

8. In cell C29 type =1–C12 and press Enter.

9. Copy the contents of cell C29 into the cell *range* C29:V39.

The reason the formula in cell C13 is different from the formula in cell C12 is that there is no function for the cumulative hypergeometric distribution. Because the hypergeometric function produces an error when the number of defectives in a sample is greater than the number in the lot, an IF statement is required to work around the calculation error. Figure 20.6 illustrates the hypergeometric operating characteristic worksheet.

Graphing the Hypergeometric Operating Characteristic and Power Curves

To graph the hypergeometric operating characteristic curve, use the graphing *range* C11:V15. The graphing *range* for the power curves is C28:V32. The

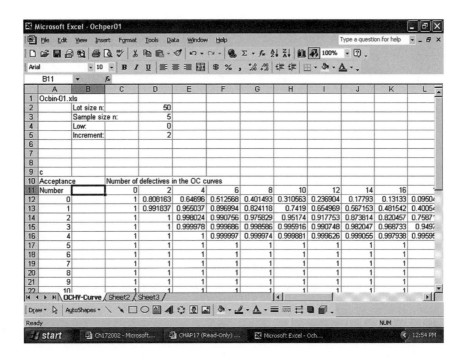

Figure 20.6 Hypergeometric operating characteristic worksheet.

procedures for creating these curves for the hypergeometric distribution are identical to the procedures for creating the curves for the binomial distribution. The results for the hypergeometric operating characteristic curves are illustrated in Figure 20.7. Figure 20.8 illustrates the results for the hypergeometric power curves.

Deming's All-or-None Inspection Rule

W. Edwards Deming's all-or-none inspection rule offers guidance for minimizing the cost of incoming inspections, given the average percent of defective items in incoming lots. The rule is based on the assumption that the process for producing the part is stable and that the average percentage of defective parts is based on a substantial history. The decision rule requires three variables:

p = the average percent of defective items in incoming lots

k_1 = the cost to inspect each part

k_2 = the costs of repairing a product that is faulty due to a defective part

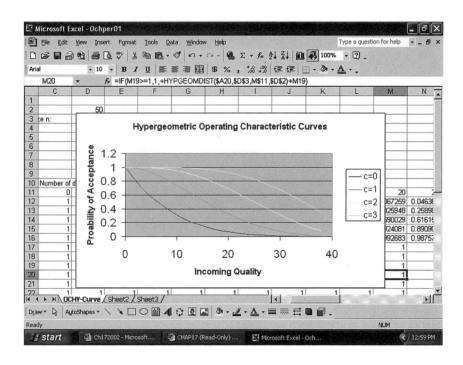

Figure 20.7   Hypergeometric operating characteristic curves.

Figure 20.8   The hypergeometric power curves.

No inspection should be conducted if $k_1/k_2 > p$. In other words, if the percentage of defective incoming parts is low and the cost of including the defective parts in the products is low, then no inspection is necessary. On the other hand, if k_1/k_2, $<p$, every part in each lot (100 percent) should be inspected, because the cost of inspection is low, but the percentage of defective parts is high.

One example is provided. The cost to screen all incoming defective parts is \$10 per part ($k_1 = \$10$). The cost of correcting a bad unit if a defective part is included in the manufacture is \$150 ($k_2 = \$150$). Past history shows that the percentage of incoming defective parts is one in 600 ($p = 1/600 = .00167$). Since $k_1/k_2 = .067$ is greater than .00167, to minimize total cost the company would not inspect incoming parts. To illustrate the cost savings, the cost for correcting the defect due to the one defective part is \$150 in one out of 600 parts, which means that the average cost of corrective action is [\$150 × (1/600) = \$0.25] or 25 cents per part. By eliminating the incoming inspection, the company will save (\$10.00 − \$0.25 = \$9.75) per part. If the company purchases 180,000 parts per year, the annual cost savings is \$1,755,000 (180,000 × \$9.75 = \$1,755,000). For more information concerning Deming's inspection rule, refer to *Quality, Productivity, and Competitive Position*, published by the Massachusetts Institute of Technology, 1982.

Real Life

Acceptance sampling procedures are often part of a purchasing contract. One requirement is often to work with a legal team to evaluate any acceptance sampling procedure suggested by the customer and to be prepared to explain to the attorneys the significance of all the suggested plans for acceptance sampling.

The customer proposed that the producer deliver the product once a week in lots of 1,000. To test the quality of each lot, the customer would use the sampling plan $n = 10$ with an acceptance number of zero or $n = 100$ with an acceptance number of three to accept or reject a lot. All rejected lots were to be returned to the producer at the producer's expense for 100 percent inspection which would be paid by the customer.

The producer knew that the maximum fraction defective was 0.1 (10 percent). The producer prepared the following operating characteristic curves. Figure 20.9 is for a sample size of 10 and an acceptance number of zero. Figure 20.10 is for a sample size of 100 and an acceptance number of three. The quality specialists working for the producer advised the legal team that the probability of accepting lots with fraction defectives under 0.1 using the sample size of 10 was high while the probability of accepting lots with a sample size of 100 was near zero.

In this decision, the producer was not concerned with the cost of sampling, because by contract the customer was responsible for the costs incurred for inspections.

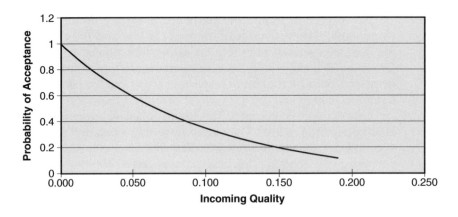

Figure 20.9   Lot size of 10 and an acceptance number of zero.

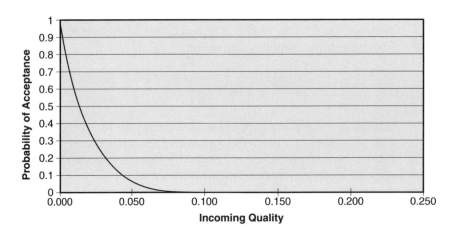

Figure 20.10   Sample size of 100 and an acceptance number of three.

Summary

Operating characteristic curves illustrate the probability that a lot will be accepted given various levels of quality. Operating characteristic curves are based on the binomial and hypergeometric distributions, which use attributes rather than continuous variable data. As items from a lot are sampled, each item is classified as defective or nondefective. If the number of defective items exceeds the acceptance number, the lot is rejected and the causes for the high number of defective items should be identified. OC curves help quality specialists balance the risk of rejecting a good lot against the risk of accepting a lot with quality levels below the *lot tolerance percentage defective*

(LTPD). The objective is to accept lots with the specified *acceptable quality level* (AQL) 95 percent of the time or to accept lots with the lot tolerance percentage defective no more than 10 percent of the time.

Alternatively, *power curves* illustrate the probability of rejecting a good lot given various levels of incoming quality. Mathematically, power curves are one minus the OC curve. In other words, the probability of rejecting a good lot is simply one minus the probability of accepting a good lot. Sampling procedures can be determined using either OC curves or power curves. The choice depends on the preferences of the quality specialist.

Exercises

20.1 Find a textbook that includes information on the American British Canadian Sampling Plan 105. Use the worksheets in this chapter to create the operating characteristic curve for a selected plan. (For a list of texts refer to the reference section on page 422.)

20.2 Complete the worksheet example in this chapter by adding the power curve calculations.

20.3 Given that you know your outgoing (incoming to the plan selected) quality is 0.003 defectives and that you want to have the lowest probability of rejection at that quality level, which plan should you select: $n = 10$ with an acceptance number of one or $n = 20$ with an acceptance number of two?

20.4 Create a side-by-side graph of the two plans in question 20.3.

20.5 Given the family of plans $c = 2$, $n = 10$, 12, 14, and 16, create a graph comparing the plans.

20.6 Use the worksheet template created in this chapter for the binomial distribution and create a graph of the probability of acceptance versus acceptance numbers (zero to five) for percent defectives of 0.01, 0.05, 0.10, and 0.15.

20.7 Redo the binomial distribution operation characteristic template so you can graph the probability of acceptance versus sample size for a family of curves with acceptance numbers zero through four.

21

Average Outgoing Quality

KEY TERMS

Incoming quality   Sampling plan

Outgoing quality

OUTLINE

Outgoing Quality

Creating the Average Outgoing Quality Worksheet

    Entering Worksheet Text

    Formatting Column Headings

    Calculating the Average Outgoing Quality Limit

Creating the Average Outgoing Quality Graph

Real Life

Summary

Exercises

Prior Knowledge

From previous chapters, you should know how to open and save worksheets, enter text, copy the contents of a cell or group of cells to another worksheet, and create and edit charts and graphs using the Chart Wizard. You should also know under what conditions it is most appropriate to use the binomial and hypergeometric distributions presented in chapter 19.

Outgoing Quality

Outgoing quality is the quality of a lot after it has been through the incoming inspection procedure. The outgoing quality is a function of the *sampling plan* and the incoming quality. The *incoming quality* is the quality of the product when it arrives at the plant. If the incoming quality is near perfect, then no matter what plan is selected, near perfect product will be outgoing. If the incoming quality is poor, the sampling plan will improve the outgoing quality, but it will not make it perfect.

Developing a sampling plan consists of the following steps:

1. Decide on the appropriate acceptable quality level.

2. Decide on the appropriate sample size n, given the probability of type I and type II errors.

3. Consult a table to determine the acceptance level (the maximum number of defective items that will allow the lot to be accepted).

4. Take a sample of n items from a lot.

5. If the number of defective items in the sample is less than the maximum number acceptable, then accept the lot; if the number of defective items in the sample is greater than the maximum number of acceptable items, then reject the lot.

The calculations are based on the assumption that a rejected lot is subjected to 100 percent inspection, which results in perfect product after the inspection. For any inspection plan there is an upper limit on average outgoing quality. No matter what the incoming quality, the average of the outgoing quality will be no greater than that limit.

Using these assumptions, the calculation of the average outgoing quality is simply the product of the incoming quality times the probability of acceptance. The worksheet to calculate outgoing quality may be built on the operating characteristic worksheet constructed in chapter 17.

Outgoing quality: The quality of products after lots have completed the inspection process.

Incoming quality: The quality of products before lots have completed the inspection process.

Sampling plan: The specification of how a lot is identified, the size of the lot, how a sample is selected from the lot, the sample size, the basis according to whether a lot is accepted or rejected, and what happens to the lot when the sample is accepted or rejected.

Creating the Average Outgoing Quality Worksheet

To create the average outgoing quality worksheet using the operating characteristic worksheet created in chapter 17, start by opening the Ocbin-01.xls worksheet. Follow these steps to create a new worksheet:

1. Click on Insert and click on Worksheet.

2. Double-right-click on the Sheet1 tab at the bottom of the worksheet

   .

3. When the text on the tab is highlighted, type the name of the new worksheet, *AOQ-Curve*, on the tab and press Enter.

4. Click on cell A1 and type *AOQbi-01.xls* and press Enter.

5. Click on File, Save As and save the worksheet as *AOQbi-01.xls* .

Entering Worksheet Text

To transfer the contents of the Ocbin-01.xls worksheet to the new worksheet, follow these steps:

1. In cell A9 type + and click on the OC-Curve tab.

2. Click on cell A9 in the OC-Curve worksheet and press Enter. Excel returns you to the AOQ-Curve worksheet.

3. In the AOQ-Curve worksheet, click on A9.

4. Copy the contents of cell A9 into the *range* A10:A11 by pointing to the + on the bottom right corner of the cell and dragging the + symbol into cells A10 and A11. When you release the mouse button the contents of the cells appear.

5. In cell A12 type *No inspection* and press Enter.

6. In cell C10 type *Average outgoing quality calculations* and press Enter.

7. In cell C11 type + and click on the OC-Curve tab.

8. Click on cell C11 in the OC-Curve worksheet and press Enter.

9. Copy the contents of cell C11 in the AOQ-Curve worksheet into the *range* D11:V11.

10. Click on cell C12 and type *+C11* and press Enter.

11. Copy the contents of cell C12 into the *range* D12:V12.

12. In cell A13 type + and click on the OC-Curve tab.

13. Click on cell A12 in the OC-Curve worksheet and press Enter.

14. Copy the contents of cell A13 in the AOQ-Curve worksheet into the *range* A14:A23.

15. In cell C13 type +*C$11** and click on the OC-Curve tab.

16. Click on cell C12 in the OC-Curve worksheet and press Enter.

17. Copy the contents of cell C13 in the AOQ-Curve worksheet into the range C13:V23.

Formatting Column Headings

To make the worksheet easy to read, you may format rows 9, 10, 11, and 12 using a bold type of font size 12. Column A may also be formatted using a bold type of font size 12. Use the Cell options in the Format menu. Next, format the cell *range* C13:V23 using font size 8. Figure 21.1 illustrates the results.

Calculating the Average Outgoing Quality Limit

The average outgoing quality (AOQ) limit for each acceptance number is calculated as the maximum probability that a lot that does not meet quality standards will be sent. AOQ is determined by the maximum value in the average outgoing quality calculations, given the sampling plan, which

Figure 21.1   Average outgoing quality worksheet.

includes the sample size and the acceptance level. This number signifies the worst quality level that could be sent out regardless of the incoming quality. For example, if the sampling plan has an acceptance of one, an acceptance quality of 95 percent, and sample size five, the probability of sending a lot that does not meet minimum standards is .1595 percent. See Figure 21.2.

To calculate the average outgoing quality limit:

1. In cell W9 type *Average outgoing* and press Enter.

2. In cell W10 type *quality limit* and press Enter.

3. In cell W13 type *=max(C13:V13)* and press Enter.

4. Copy the formula in cell W13 into the *range* W14:W23.

Figure 21.2 illustrates the results.

Creating the Average Outgoing Quality Graph

The steps for creating the average outgoing quality graphs are similar to the steps for creating the operating characteristic curves in chapter 17. Only acceptance levels of zero, one, two, and three are graphed in this exercise.

Figure 21.2 Average outgoing quality limits.

To create the graph for the AOQ-curves, follow these steps:

1. Identify the graphing *range* C11:V16 (remember, only no inspection and acceptance numbers 0, 1, 2, and 3 are included in the sample graph).

2. Click on the Chart Wizard icon .

3. Select the XY Scatter chart and select the sub-graph type (scatter with data points connected by smoothed lines without markers) and click on <u>N</u>ext>.

4. In step 2 of 4, click on the Series tab at the top of the screen and enter the following series labels by clicking on each series, and then typing the text in the box to the right: Series1: *No inspection*, Series2: ($c = 0$), Series3: ($c = 1$), Series4: ($c = 2$), and Series5: ($c = 3$) and click on <u>N</u>ext>.

5. In step 3 of 4, enter the chart title *Average Outgoing Quality*, the *x*-axis title *Incoming Quality*, the *y*-axis title *Outgoing Quality*, and click on <u>N</u>ext>.

6. Click on <u>F</u>inish.

7. Locate and size the graph as desired.

Examine Figure 21.3. The straight line labeled *No Inspection* shows the outgoing quality as the incoming quality goes from good to bad. Each of

Figure 21.3   Graph of outgoing quality.

the tests shows an improvement in the probability of outgoing quality. The higher the acceptance number, the better the outgoing quality. Even though the assumptions on which these calculations are made limit the application of the charts, it is useful to examine these charts to show the effect of a sampling plan.

Real Life

In an attempt to control the quality of the raw material being purchased, the manager decided to install an inspection system. Each lot of 1000 items would have a sample of 50 items taken. If one or more defective parts were found, the lot would be subject to 100 percent inspection. Figure 21.4 illustrates the results of the sampling plan. If the incoming quality was in the neighborhood of 0.07, then the average outgoing quality limit would be 0.037. The production history shows that the incoming quality is in the neighborhood of 0.01. The managers were advised that the plan was not providing much protection since the incoming quality was so much better than the average outgoing quality limit. This sampling plan simply ensures that incoming quality does not deteriorate.

Summary

Outgoing quality curves illustrate the probability of sending out products that do not meet minimum quality standards. *Outgoing quality* is a function of incoming quality and the sampling plan. When *incoming quality* is poor, a sampling plan should improve the quality of the outgoing products. As the acceptable quality level is increased, the probability of sending out a lot that does not meet specifications is substantially reduced.

Figure 21.4   Average outgoing quality.

Exercises

21.1 Find a textbook that includes information on the American British Canadian Sampling Plan 105. Use the worksheets in this chapter to create the average outgoing quality curve for a selected plan. (For a list of texts refer to the reference section on page 422.)

21.2 Given a family of sampling plans: $n = 20$, $c = 1$, $c = 2$, $c = 3$, $c = 4$, draw the family of average outgoing quality curves.

21.3 Given a family of sampling plans $c = 2$, $n = 10$, $n = 20$, $n = 30$, and $n = 40$, draw the family of average outgoing quality curves.

21.4 Given that you know that the outgoing (incoming to the plan selected) quality is 0.003 defective and that you want to have the lowest average outgoing quality limit at that quality, which plan should you select: $n = 10$ with an acceptance number of one or $n = 20$ with an acceptance number of two? Explain.

22

Comparing Control Chart Performance

Prior Knowledge

From previous chapters, you should know how to open and save worksheets, enter text and formulas, copy the contents of a cell or group of cells to another part of the worksheet, and create and edit graphs using the Chart Wizard. A basic understanding of macros in Excel is beneficial (see chapter 13).

You should have an understanding of type I and type II errors, operating characteristic curves and conditional probability curves. You should have knowledge of X-bar and CuSum control charts (discussed in chapters 10, 11, and 16).

Introduction

There are two ways to measure control chart performance:

1. The average run length (ARL)

2. The operating characteristic (OC) curve or the power curve

The *average run length* (ALR) shows on average how many runs of successive subgroups will be taken before a subgroup parameter shows that the parameter is beyond the control limits, indicating that a change has occurred, when in fact there is no change. The *operating characteristic* (OC) *curve* is a graph of the probability of acceptance that no change has occurred in the process average versus a given level of quality input.

The OC curve is a conditional probability curve that shows the distribution of relative frequencies that represent the probability of obtaining a particular value or outcome. For OC curves, in this experiment, it shows the probability of accepting the sample as within limits, given the various levels of input quality.

Because of the ease of simulating OC curves using Excel, we prefer to use OC curves to compare chart performance. Some statisticians prefer to use power curves which are simply one minus the values of the OC curve. Figure 22.1 illustrates the comparisons of OC curves for an X-bar chart and a CuSum chart.

Average run length (ARL): The average number of successive samples required before a type I error occurs.

Conditional probability curve: Shows the distribution of relative frequencies that represents the probability of obtaining a particular value or outcome. For normally distributed data, the curve is bell-shaped.

Operating characteristic curve (OC): Plots the probability of accepting a process as in control for various levels of quality.

Figure 22.1 Operating characteristic curves.

The operating characteristic curves for the X-bar and CuSum charts are close. The type I error, looking for a change (from 100) when no change has occurred is 6.0 percent (1.00–0.940) for the X-bar chart and 0.5 percent (1.00–0.995) for the CuSum chart. At one standard deviation from the mean (up or down) the probability of acceptance is 0.815 and 0.845 for the X-bar chart while the results are 0.835 and 0.830 for the CuSum chart. The simulated values indicate that the CuSum chart is better than the X-bar chart and the results are close.

A simulation experiment requires careful design and execution. The experiment to compare control chart performance consists of the following steps:

1. Generate 20 subgroups of five (5) observations each using an average of 100 and a standard deviation of 10, calculate the average, sample standard deviation, and control limits based on these 20 subgroups.

2. Generate three (3) additional subgroups with five (5) observations each with an average of 75 to 125 in steps of 5 with the standard deviation held constant at 10.

3. Create a template for the X-bar process control chart.

4. Create a template for the CuSum chart.

5. Run the model 200 times at each level to simulate values.

6. At each of the 200 cycles, include a counter for each model to count the number of subgroups with parameters beyond the control limits, by creating an IF statement outputting zero (0) if the parameter is within the control limits, or one (1) if no parameters are outside the control limits.

7. Create macros to keep a record of the number of parameters beyond the control limits at each level.

8. Create the conditional probability graphs for both the X-bar and CuSum data.

The reason for selecting a run of 20 plus three additional subgroups is that the X-bar chart needs approximately 20 subgroups to function. Later you may replicate the experiment with fewer subgroups in the base period to compare the two control charts' performance with small samples. This chapter shows how to create the worksheet illustrated in Figure 22.1 and then shows additions to the worksheet.

Creating an Operating Characteristic Curves Workbook

There are four worksheets contained in this Excel workbook: Data Generation, X-bar, CuSum, and Simulation. Each worksheet is created in this order.

Creating the Data Generation Worksheet

To label the Data Generation worksheet, double-click on the Sheet1 tab near the bottom of the screen. When the text is highlighted, type *Data Generation* and press Enter.

Entering Text for the Data Generation Worksheet

The Data Generation worksheet starts with entry of the text from Table 22.1 into a new workbook. Save the workbook using the Save <u>A</u>s option in the <u>F</u>ile menu.

Number the subgroups using the following procedures:

1. In cell A11 type *1* and press Enter.

2. In cell A12 type *=A11+1* and press Enter.

3. Copy the formula in cell A12 in the *range* A13:A33.

The subgroups are now numbered 1 through 33.

Table 22.1 Text Cells.

Cell	Text	Description
A1	Compare01.xls	Name of workbook
A5	Average:	Label
A6	Std Dev:	Label
A10	Subgroup	Column head
B3	Subgroups	
B4	Base	
B5	100	
B6	10	
B9	Subgroup Observations	
B10	1	
C4	Additional	
C5	110	
C6	10	
C10	2	
D10	3	
E10	4	
F10	5	
H10	Average	
I10	Std Dev	

Generating Sample Data

As discussed in chapter 13, Excel offers several methods for generating random numbers. For this simulation we elected to use a normal process generator based on the uniform random number function RAND(). In cell B11, type the formula

=round(rand()+rand()+rand()+rand()+rand()
+rand()+rand()+rand()+rand()–5,0)*$B$6+$B$5

and copy the formula into the *range* B12:F33.
    Change the formula in cell B31 to

=round(rand()+rand()+rand()+rand()+rand()
+rand()+rand()+rand()+rand()–5,0)*$C$6+$C$5

by pressing F2 and then editing the formula by changing the cell reference from B6 and B5 to C6 and C5. Copy the revised formula into the *range* B31:F33.

Entering Formulas for the Data Generation Worksheet

To enter the formulas to calculate the subgroup averages and standard deviations, follow these steps:

1. Average of each subgroup

    a. In cell H11 type =AVERAGE(B11:F11)

    b. Copy the formula into the *range* H12:H33.

2. Standard deviation of each subgroup

    a. In cell I11 type =STDEV(B11:F11)

    b. Copy the formula into the *range* I12:I33.

    This completes the calculations for the Data Generation worksheet. Figure 22.2 illustrates the Data Generation worksheet.

Creating the $\overline{X}$ Worksheet

To label the $\overline{X}$ worksheet, double-click on the Sheet2 tab near the bottom of the screen. When the text is highlighted, type *Xbar* and press Enter.

Entering Text for the $\overline{X}$ Worksheet

Table 22.2 shows the text needed for this worksheet. Type the text in the appropriate cells.
    The control chart factors in cells F3 (1.43), F4 (0), and F5 (2.09) are from the tables in the appendix.

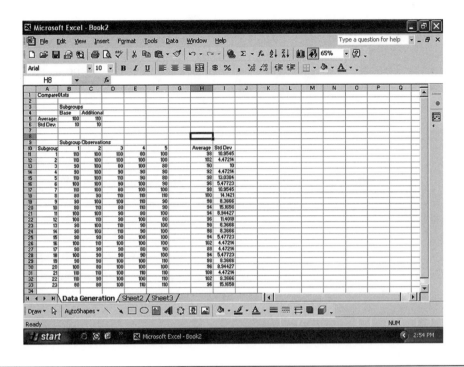

Figure 22.2 Data generation worksheet.

Table 22.2 X-bar text.

Cell	Text
E2	Control Chart Factors
E3	A3:
E4	B3:
E5	B4:
F3	1.43
F4	0
F5	2.09
F10	LCLx
G10	Xxbar
H10	UCLx
J10	Sbar
M9	Outliers

Linking Values from the Data Generation to the $\overline{X}$ Worksheet

The easiest way to create the X-bar worksheet is to link the cells to the Data Generation worksheet by following the steps below:

1. Select cell A10 and type +

2. Click on the Data Generation worksheet tab.

3. In the Data Generation worksheet click on cell A10 and press Enter.

4. Copy the formula in cell A10 into the *range* A11:A33.

5. Click on cell C10 and type +

6. Click on the Data Generation worksheet tab.

7. In the Data Generation worksheet click on cell H10 and press Enter.

8. Copy the formula in cell C10 into the *range* C11:D33.

Entering Formulas for the X-Bar Worksheet

To enter the formulas to calculate the upper and lower control limits and X-bar, type the following formulas:

1. In cell G11 type =AVERAGE($C$11:$C$30) (which is the average of each subgroup average for the base period).

2. In cell J11 type =AVERAGE($D$11:$D$30) (which is the average of the standard deviations of each subgroup for the base period).

3. In cell F11 type =$G$11–$F$3*$J$11

4. In cell H11 type =$G$11+$F$3*$J$11

5. Copy the formulas in the *range* F11:H11 into the *range* F12:H33.

The control chart calculations are complete, however, an outlier counter is needed.

Entering an Outlier Counter

In order to count the number of times the subgroup average exceeds the upper or lower control limit, type the following formulas in column M and N:

1. In cell M11 type =IF(C11<=F11,1,0) (which places a 1 in cell M11 if the observation is less than the lower control limit or a zero if the observation is greater than the lower control limit).

2. Copy the formula in cell M11 into the *range* M12:M33.

3. In cell N11 type =IF(C11>=H11,1,0) (which places a 1 in cell N11 if the observation is above the upper control limit).

4. Copy the formula in cell N11 into the *range* N12:N33.

5. In cell M10 type =*SUM(M11:M33)*

6. Copy the formula in cell M10 to cell N10.

7. In cell N9 type =*N10+M10* (which is the sum of outliers beyond both the lower and upper control limits).

If the value in cell N9 is greater than zero, an outlier has occurred; if the value is zero, no outliers have occurred.

Graphing the $\overline{X}$ Control Chart

We recommend that you create a graph of the X-bar control chart. The creation of the graph is a visual check of your work. Creation of the graph is left as an exercise. Figure 22.3 illustrates the X-bar worksheet and the control chart.

Creating the CuSum Worksheet

To label the CuSum worksheet, double-click on the Sheet3 tab near the bottom of the screen. When the text is highlighted, type *CuSum* and press Enter.

Entering Text for the CuSum Worksheet

Table 22.3 shows the text needed in the CuSum worksheet. Type the text in the appropriate cells.

Figure 22.3   X-bar worksheet and control chart.

Table 22.3   Text for the CuSum worksheet.

Cell	Text	
E7	Xo:	
F10	Xi-Xo	
G9	CuSum	
G10	sum(Xi-Xo)	
I13	Using Standard Calculations	
I14	SD(base):	
I15	F1:	
I16	F2:	
I17	K=F1*SD (Slope):	
I18	h=F2*SD:	
I19	Lead (d)=h/K:	
I20	y value:	
I21	x value:	
I22	Intercept (LCL):	
I23	Intercept (UCL):	
J43	Notice equal-------------------->	A place to check your work
K15	0.5	Factor F1
K16	5	Factor F2
L10	LCLcs	
M10	UCLcs	
N9	Outliers	
O8	Total	

Linking Values from the Data Generation to CuSum Worksheet

The easiest way to create the CuSum worksheet is to link the cells to the Data Generation worksheet by following the steps below:

1. Select cell A10 and type +

2. Click on the Data Generation worksheet tab.

3. In the Data Generation worksheet click on cell A10 and press Enter.

4. Copy the formula in cell A10 into the *range* A11:A33.

5. Click on cell C10 and type +

6. Click on the Data Generation worksheet tab.

7. In the Data Generation worksheet click on cell H10 and press Enter.

8. Copy the formula in cell C10 into the *range* C11:D33.

Entering Formulas in the CuSum Worksheet

Table 22.4 lists the formulas required to calculate the CuSum worksheet. Type these formulas into the appropriate cells and copy into the *ranges* indicated in Table 22.4. The completed worksheet is shown in Figure 22.4.

Graphing the CuSum Control Chart

We recommend you create a graph of the CuSum control chart. The creation of the graph is valuable for checking your work. This is left as an exercise. Figure 22.5 illustrates the CuSum Chart.

Table 22.4 Formulas for CuSum chart.

Cell	Formula	Description
A34	=A33+1	Copied into the *range* A35:A43
F7	=AVERAGE(C11:C30)	Average for the base period
F11	=C11–$F$7	Copied into the *range* F12:F33
G11	=+F11	
G12	=G11+F12	Copied into the *range* G13:G33
K14	=STDEV(C11:C30)	We simulated STDEV (sample) and STDEVP (population). Results were similar.
K17	=K15*K14	
K18	=K16*K14	
K19	=K18/K17	
K20	=G33	
K21	=A33+K19	
K22	=K20+K17*K21	
K23	=K20–K17*K21	
L11	=$K$22-$K$17*$A11	Copied into the *range* L12:L43
M11	=$K$23+$K$17*$A11	Copied into the *range* M12:M43
N11	=IF(G11>=L11,1,0)	Copied into the *range* N12:N43
O11	=IF(G11<=M11,1,0)	Copied into the *range* O12:O43
N10	=SUM(N11:N33)	Copied into cell O10
O9	=O10+N10	

Figure 22.4   CuSum worksheet.

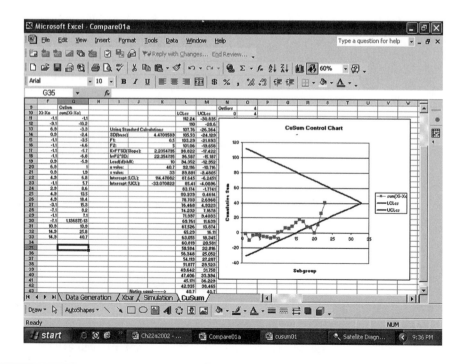

Figure 22.5   CumSum worksheet and control chart.

Creating the Simulation Worksheet

Create a fourth worksheet in the Compare01.xls workbook by clicking on Insert in the menu bar and then selecting Worksheet. Double-click on the Sheet4 tab at the bottom of the page and type *Simulation* to label the worksheet.

Entering Text for the Simulation Worksheet

Number the observations in column B by typing *1* in cell B13. In cell B14 type *=B13+1* and press Enter. Copy the formula into the *range* B14:B212.

Table 22.5 shows the text needed to create the Simulation worksheet. Type the text into the appropriate cells.

Table 22.5 Text for the Simulation worksheet.

Cell	Text	
B3	Xbar	
B4	CuSum	
C2	75	
C9	Xbar	
D10	Outlier (1=yes):	
D11	Formula:	
I7	Input	
I8	Average	
I9	SD:	
J7	Additional	
J8	75	Location where average for simulated additional cells is entered.
J9	10	Location where standard deviation for simulated additional cells is entered.
M9	CuSum Chart	
N10	Outlier (1=yes):	
N11	Formula:	
R2	Set security level to low	

Linking Number of Outliers to the Simulation Worksheet

To link the values for the number of outliers in the other worksheets to the Simulation worksheet, type the following formulas:

1. In cell G10 type =+*IF(Xbar!N9>0,0,1)* and press Enter.

2. In cell Q10 type =+*IF(CuSum!O9>0,0,1)* and press Enter.

The number of outliers for each run from both worksheets is transferred to the Simulation worksheet.

Linking the Sample Average to the Data Generation Worksheet

To run the simulation, the values for the averages in the simulation sheet must be linked to the values in the data generation sheet. To link the sample averages:

1. Click on C5 in the Data Generation worksheet.

2. Type +

3. Click on J8 in the Simulation worksheet and press Enter.

As you change the averages in J8 to run the simulation, these values are linked to the random number generator in the Data Generation worksheet to generate appropriate random numbers.

Entering Formulas in the Simulation Worksheet

Table 22.6 lists the numbers entered into the Simulation worksheet.

Every time function key F9 is pressed, the numbers in *range* C13:M212 and Q13:Y212 change. A macro is needed to stop the numbers from changing as parts of the simulation are completed.

Table 22.6   Numbers and formulas in the Simulation worksheet.

Cell	Formula	Copy Range
D2	=5+C2	Copied into the range E2:M2
C3	=SUM(C13:C212)/200	Copied into the range D3:M3
C4	=SUM(O13:O212)/200	Copied into the range D4:M4
C12	=C2	Copied into the range D12:M12
O12	=C2	Copied into the range O12:Y12
G11	=$G$10	Copied into range C13:M212
Q11	=$Q$10	Copied into range O13:Y212

Creating the Macro to Simulate Observations

The Simulation spreadsheet requires the use of a simple macro. Macros will not operate unless the security level is set to low. The steps for setting the security level, which are described in detail in chapter 13, are listed below:

1. Select Options from the Tools menu.

2. Click the Security tab.

3. Click the Macro Security button.

4. In the Security Level dialog box, click on the radio button to select the desired security level (Medium security is recommended).

The macro created in this workbook uses relative addressing. The concepts of absolute versus relative addressing were discussed in chapter 13. To display the stop recording and relative reference button, follow these steps:

1. Click on Tools in the menu bar.

2. Click on Customize.

3. Click on Toolbars.

4. Place a check mark on the Stop Recording option by clicking in the box.

5. Click on the Close button.

The relative reference box on the right side of the stop recording button

toggles between relative addressing on and relative addressing off. Clicking on the right side of the button changes addressing from absolute to relative.

To record the Macro, follow the steps below:

1. Make sure the relative reference button is toggled to the on position.

2. Type *75* in cell J8 and press Enter.

3. Place the cursor on cell C13.

4. Click on Tools.

5. Click on Macro.

6. Select Record New Macro.

For this macro we used Ctrl+c because we can execute the macro with one hand. To complete the macro:

1. Click on Edit in the menu bar.

2. Click on Copy.

3. Click on Edit.

4. Click on Paste Special.

5. Click on Values.

6. Click on OK.

7. Press Enter.

8. Press Enter again.

9. Move the cell pointer to O13.

10. Click on Edit.

11. Click on Copy.

12. Click on Edit.

13. Click on Paste Special.

14. Click on Values.

15. Click on OK.

16. Press Enter.

17. Press Enter again.

18. Move the cell pointer to cell C14.

19. Click on the square on the Stop Recording button [icon].

Click in C13 and press Ctrl-c to run the macro. Hold the Ctrl and the c keys down until you have changed all the formulas in column C and column O to numbers.

Type *80* in cell J8 and press Enter. Place the cell point on D13 and hold the Ctrl and the c keys down until you have changed all the formulas in columns D and P to numbers. Replicate the process by incrementally changing the values in J8 in increments of five (from 85 to 125) and running the macro in each column until all the columns of numbers have been changed. *Be careful to press the Enter key every time after you change the values in J8.*

Creating the Comparison Operating Characteristic Curves

To create the simulation control chart, follow these steps:

Depress and hold the left mouse button and drag to define the *range* B2:M4 and follow these steps:

1. Click on the Chart Wizard icon [icon].

2. In Step 1 of 4, select the XY(Scatter) and the straight line with data points Chart subtype and click on Next>.

3. In Step 2 of 4 click on Next>.

4. Enter the chart name *OC Curves Xbar vs CuSum*, *x*-axis name *Input Quality*, and the *y*-axis name *Probability of acceptance for a given input*, and click N̲ext>.

5. Select As O̲bject In to place the graph on the worksheet and click on F̲inish.

The OC curves comparing the performance of the $\overline{X}$ and CuSum charts are shown in Figure 22.6. The CuSum chart does have a higher probability of acceptance when the input quality is equal to the expected results and does fall off faster than the $\overline{X}$ chart; however, in the authors' opinions the improvement is minimal.

Summary

This chapter provides a structure for comparing the performance of two or more process control charts. For a data collection situation where there are 20 subgroups of five (5) in the base period and an additional three periods not in the base period, the CuSum chart had a type I error of 0.5 percent compared with the X-bar's chart type I error of 6.0 percent. Results were closer than expected for the number of simulations performed in the experiment.

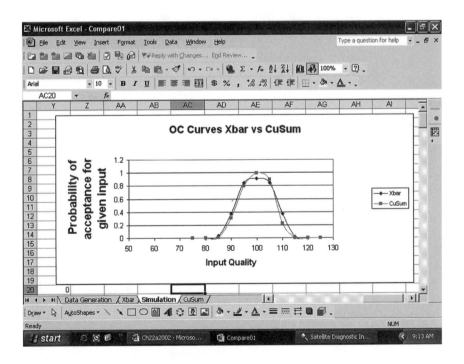

Figure 22.6 OC curves for X-bar versus CuSum.

Now that you have created a model workbook for comparing process control chart performance, you can add more control chart options such as EWMA charts. Another issue is comparing control charts for controlling changes in variation. In this chapter we did not simulate the range or sigma charts. In one of the exercises at the end of the chapter you have the opportunity to examine what happens to the CuSum chart when the standard deviation changes.

Exercises

22.1 Add a standard deviation chart to Compare01.xls. With the input average of the last three subgroups equal to the base period average, change the standard deviation from 10 to 11 to 12 to 13 and then create an OC curve for the CuSum chart. Explain the results.

22.2 Add a flat EWMA chart to Compare01.xls. How does the OC curve for the EWMA compare the X-bar and CuSum charts? Explain.

22.3 Redo the experiment in the text example for a base period of 10 subgroups and three additional subgroups. Do the results match using a base of 20 subgroups with three additional subgroups?

22.4 Redo the experiment of your choice with a base of three subgroups and with two additional subgroups.

22.5 Literature tells us that the probability of "false alarms" will double for the X-bar chart when the number of subgroups (of size $n = 5$) is reduced from 20 to 15. Run an experiment and explain your results.

Appendix

Tables of Factors and Formulas

Table A.1 Factors for determining from R the 3-sigma control limits for $\overline{X}$ and R charts.

Number of Observations in Subgroup (n)	Factor for $\overline{X}$ Chart (A_2)	Factors for R Chart	
		LCL (D_3)	UCL (D_4)
2	1.88	0.00	3.27
3	1.02	0.00	2.57
4	0.73	0.00	2.28
5	0.58	0.00	2.11
6	0.48	0.00	2.00
7	0.42	0.08	1.92
8	0.37	0.14	1.86
9	0.34	0.18	1.82
10	0.31	0.22	1.78
11	0.29	0.26	1.74
12	0.27	0.28	1.72
13	0.25	0.31	1.69
14	0.24	0.33	1.67
15	0.22	0.35	1.65
16	0.21	0.36	1.64
17	0.20	0.38	1.62
18	0.19	0.39	1.61
19	0.19	0.40	1.60
20	0.18	0.41	1.59

Upper control limit for $X = UCL_x = \overline{\overline{X}} + A_2\overline{R}$

Lower control limit for $X = LCL_x = X - A_2\overline{R}$

(If targeted or standard value (μ), $\overline{X}_0$, $\overline{X}'$ is used rather than $\overline{\overline{X}}$ as the central line on the control chart, substitute $\overline{X}'$ for $\overline{\overline{X}}$.)

Upper control limit for $R = UCL_R = D_4\overline{R}$

Lower control limit for $R = LCL_R = D_3\overline{R}$

Table A.2   Factors for determining from $\overline{\sigma}$ and $\overline{\sigma}_{RMS}$ the 3-sigma control limits for $\overline{X}$ and s or $\overline{\sigma}_{RMS}$ charts.

Number of Observations in Subgroup (n)	Factor X Chart Using σ_{RMS} (A_1)	Factor X Chart Using σ (A_3)	Factors s or $\overline{\sigma}_{RMS}$ Charts	
			LCL (B_3)	UCL (B_4)
2	3.76	2.66	0.00	3.27
3	2.39	1.95	0.00	2.57
4	1.88	1.63	0.00	2.27
5	1.60	1.43	0.00	2.09
6	1.41	1.29	0.03	1.97
7	1.28	1.18	0.12	1.88
8	1.17	1.10	0.19	1.81
9	1.09	1.03	0.24	1.76
10	1.03	0.98	0.28	1.72
11	0.97	0.93	0.32	1.68
12	0.93	0.89	0.35	1.65
13	0.88	0.85	0.38	1.62
14	0.85	0.82	0.41	1.59
15	0.82	0.79	0.43	1.57
16	0.79	0.76	0.45	1.55
17	0.76	0.74	0.47	1.53
18	0.74	0.72	0.48	1.52
19	0.72	0.70	0.50	1.50
20	0.70	0.68	0.51	1.49

All factors based on the normal distribution.

Upper control limit $X = UCL_X = \overline{\overline{X}} + A_3\overline{\sigma} = \overline{\overline{X}} + A_1\overline{\sigma}_{RMS}$

Lower control limit $X = LCL_X = \overline{\overline{X}} - A_3\overline{\sigma} = \overline{\overline{X}} - A_1\overline{\sigma}_{RMS}$

(If aimed-at or standard value (μ), $\overline{X}_0$, $\overline{X}'$ is used rather than $\overline{\overline{X}}$ as the central line on the control chart, substitute $\overline{X}'$ for $\overline{\overline{X}}$.)

Glossary

acceptance number: In an attribute acceptance sampling plan, an acceptance number is a nonnegative value that represents the maximum number of defective items that should be found in a sample. If the number of defective items found in a sample is less than or equivalent to the acceptance number, then the lot is accepted.

acceptable quality level: A fraction of defective items specified by the producer and/or customer as the maximum percentage of defective items considered acceptable in a sampling plan.

acceptance sampling: The procedure of taking a sample of observations from a lot of product or material and making a decision about whether to accept or reject the lot.

analysis of variance: A statistical technique for estimating the relationships among the variables when the independent variables are categorical.

animate: To animate means to add special visual or sound effects to the text, graphics, or any object on a slide as a way of directing attention to important elements of a presentation or making a presentation more interesting.

assignable causes of variation: Influences that can be identified.

attribute data: Measurements of the characteristics of items (components or products) that are classified as either meeting or not meeting specifications (accept or reject; go or no-go).

autocorrelation: An observation is related to or a function of previous data behavior.

average run length (ARL): The average number of successive samples required before a type I error occurs.

binomial distribution: A distribution based on attribute measures that assume only two values of outcomes are possible (for example, good–bad, on–off, or small–large). This distribution is for large populations in which sampling does not affect the probability of obtaining a given result.

c chart: A control chart for controlling an operation using the number of defects per inspection unit.

central tendency: The value where most of the observations in a sample are concentrated.

Chi-square distribution: The distribution of variances when the population is normally distributed. The Chi-square distribution is used to conduct goodness-of-fit tests to determine how well a sample distribution conforms to a theoretical Chi-square distribution.

classical probability: Statistical analysis based on knowledge of the process.

conditional probability curve: Shows the distribution of relative frequencies that represents the probability of obtaining a particular value or outcome. For normally distributed data, the curve is bell-shaped.

control: Reproducibility within limits.

correlation coefficient: A value between –1.0 and +1.0 that shows the degree of linear association between two variables.

cumulative distribution function (cdf): Shows the cumulative probability of all events from negative infinity up to the point specified.

defect: An occurrence of lack of conformity to one or more specifications.

defective item: A part that is considered unsatisfactory.

dialog box: An area on the screen that shows status information and allows the user to select among options and enter additional information.

distribution: The pattern or shape in which the observation values are distributed.

embedded object: An object such as a chart, picture, text, *range* of cells, or a file that is created in a source file, such as Word, Excel, or Photo Editor and inserted into a destination file, for example PowerPoint. Changes made in the source file are *not* reflected in the destination file.

fishbone diagram: A graph illustrating the relationships between inputs and outputs that is used to identify possible sources of quality problems.

fraction defective: The value derived by dividing the number of occurrences of a defective item by the total number of observations.

frequency distribution: The pattern formed by a group of values when the measurements are arranged according to the number of times each event (outcome) occurs.

goodness-of-fit test: Statistical procedure to test if observations could have come from a specified distribution.

histogram: A bar graph showing the spread of values in a sample and the frequency of each value.

hypergeometric distribution: A distribution based on attribute measures that assume only two values of outcomes are possible (for example, good–bad, on–off, or small–large). This distribution is for small populations in which taking a sample affects the probability of selecting an item with a particular value.

incoming quality: The quality of products before lots have completed the inspection process.

individual control chart: A control chart for controlling central tendency (average) using individual measurements.

inspection: Act of comparing material, products, and performance against the established specification standards and limits.

LCL_r: Lower control limit for the subgroup range.

LCL$_s$: Lower control limit for the subgroup standard deviation.

LCL$_{\bar{x}}$: Lower control limit for the subgroup average.

linked object: Is an object such as a chart, picture, text, *range* of cells, or a file that was created in a source file, such as Word, Excel, or Photo Editor and inserted into a destination file, for example, PowerPoint. The linked object in the destination file may be updated whenever the information in the source file is updated.

lot tolerance percent defective: A fraction of defective items specified as the poorest level of quality that the customer is willing to accept in a given lot.

lower natural tolerance limit (LNTL): The normal lower limit of the output of a process.

mean: The arithmetic mean is the sum of the values in a sample divided by the number of values in the sample.

median: The median is the middle value in the sample, which has an equal number of values above and below.

mode: The mode is the most frequently occurring value in the data set.

moving average and moving range charts: A pair of control charts for controlling both the central tendency (average) and variation of a process using variable limits.

nonconformities: Defects.

np control chart: Control chart for attribute data that uses a count.

open: Windows term for reading a worksheet from a disk.

operating characteristic curve: Graph of the probability of accepting a lot given various levels of incoming quality.

outgoing quality: The quality of products after lots have completed the inspection process.

outlier: A point above the upper control limit or below the lower control limit.

p control chart: Control chart for attribute data that uses fractions or percentages.

parameters: Descriptive statistics computed from a population.

Pareto analysis: Analysis for identifying the sources (types) of defects and ordering the sources according to cost or frequency of occurrence so that corrective action may be taken.

Pareto diagram: A combination bar and line graph illustrating the frequency of sources (types) of defects.

percent defective: The value derived by multiplying the fraction defective by 100.

power curve: Graph of the probability of rejecting a lot given various levels of incoming quality.

probability density function: Shows the probability that the value of any random variable will fall between any two points. Frequently shown with a histogram for discrete values and a curve for continuous values.

process capability study: Analysis of the capability of a process to produce results in terms of percent defective.

process generator: A computer procedure that uses a random number generator to produce numerical values that fit a specific distribution.

$\bar{R}$: The average of the subgroup ranges, a measure of dispersion.

range (cell): A cell *range* is defined by a cell in the upper left position and a cell in the lower right position. All the cells between are in the cell *range*.

range (statistical): The difference between the largest and smallest values in a data set; a measure of variation.

regression analysis: A statistical technique for investigating and describing the relationships among variables.

relative frequency: Shows the probability of an outcome given all possible outcomes.

residual: A residual is the difference between the value of an observation and the value of the previous observation.

$\overline{S}$: The average of subgroup standard deviations, a measure of dispersion.

sampling plan: The specification of how a lot is identified, the size of the lot, how a sample is selected from the lot, the sample size, the basis according to whether a lot is accepted or rejected, and what happens to the lot when the sample is accepted or rejected.

save: Windows term for recording a worksheet on disk.

sigma: The standard deviation of a subgroup.

significance test: A test that uses statistical information to aid in making a decision.

specification limit: The results required.

specifications: Characteristics of a product or service that are represented by measurements that define whether the product or service meets minimum standards.

stable system: A system working in an environment in which only normal random variation is present.

standard deviation: A measure of a distribution's dispersion that is measured by the square root of the sum of the squared deviations from the mean for each value, divided by $n - 1$.

statistical process control: Using statistical analytical methods to measure the performance of a process to ensure that the output meets customer needs.

statistical quality control: Activities associated with ensuring that goods and services satisfy customer needs.

statistics: Descriptive statistics computed from a sample.

template: A worksheet model recorded on disk, CD, or tape for future use.

trendline: A line that predicts new values based on previous values.

type I error: Numbers indicate a change when there is none and time and money are wasted looking for the change.

type II error: Numbers do not indicate a change when one has occurred and we miss an opportunity to improve the process.

u chart: A control chart for controlling an operation using the average number of defects over a selected number of inspection units.

UCL_r: Upper control limit for the subgroup range.

UCL_s: Upper control limit for the subgroup standard deviation.

$UCL_{\overline{x}}$: Upper control limit for the subgroup average.

unstable system of chance causes: A system working in an environment in which some source of variation, in addition to normal random variation, is present.

upper natural tolerance limit (UNTL): The normal upper limit of the output of a process.

variable data: Data representing a quality characteristic that is measured.

variance: A measure of a distribution's dispersion that is calculated by summing the squared differences between each observed value and the sample mean, and then dividing the sum by the number of observations minus one.

variation: The dispersion among values in a data set.

visual test: Comparing the graphs of two or more data sets to determine if the data sets are from the same type of distribution.

V-mask: The V-shaped control chart that graphs the cumulative sum. The upper control limit is the bottom line of the V and the lower control limit is the upper line of the V. The V-mask must be recalculated every time a new observation is collected.

worksheet: Another term for a spreadsheet.

worksheet program: A program for creating, editing, calculating, saving, and opening computer files, and for graphing and printing worksheets using cells identified by their row and column position.

$\bar{X}$: The subgroup average; a measure of central tendency.

$\bar{X}$ *and R charts:* A pair of control charts for controlling the central tendency and variation of a process using the range.

$\bar{X}$ *and sigma control charts:* A pair of control charts for controlling the central tendency and variation of a process using the standard deviation.

$\bar{\bar{X}}$: The average of subgroup averages.

Reference List

Abbott, James C. *Practical Understanding of Capability: Implementing Statistical Process Control (SPC).* Easley, SC: Robert Houston Smith Publishers, 1999.

Abraham, Bovas, ed. *Quality Improvement Through Statistical Methods.* Boston: Birkhauser, 1998.

Aft, Lawrence S. *Quality Improvement Using Statistical Process Control.* Philadelphia, PA: Saunders College Publishing, 1988.

American Society for Quality Control. *Glossary & Tables for Statistical Quality Control.* Milwaukee: ASQC Quality Press, 1983.

Burr, John T. *SPC Tools for Everyone.* Milwaukee: ASQC Quality Press, 1993.

Derman, Cyrus. *Statistical Aspects of Quality Control.* San Diego, CA: Academic Press, 1996.

Doty, Leonard A. *Statistical Process Control.* New York: Industrial Press, 1996.

Duncan, Acheson J. *Quality Control and Industrial Statistics.* Burr Ridge, IL: Richard D. Irwin, 1974.

Farnum, Nicholas R. *Modern Statistical Quality Control & Management.* Belmont, CA: Wadsworth Publishing, 1993.

Grant, Eugene L. *Statistical Quality Control.* New York: McGraw-Hill, 1988.

Keats, J. Bert. *Statistical Applications in Process Control.* New York: Marcel Dekker, 1996.

King, Dennis W. *Statistical Quality Control Using the SAS System.* Cary, NC: SAS Institute, 1996.

Klippel, Warren H., ed. *Statistical Quality Control.* Dearborn, MI: Society of Manufacturing Engineers, 1984.

Mitra, Amitava. *Fundamentals of Quality Control & Improvement.* Englewood Cliffs, NJ: Prentice-Hall, 1998.

Montgomery, Douglas C. *Introduction to Statistical Quality Control.* New York: John Wiley & Sons, 1996.

Pyzdek, Thomas. *An SPC Primer: Programmed Introduction to Statistical Process Control Techniques.* Milwaukee: ASQC Quality Press, 1984.

––––––. *Pyzdek's Guide to SPC: Fundamentals.* Tucson, AZ: Quality America, 1989.

––––––. *Pyzdek's Guide to SPC, Vol. II: Applications & Special Topics.* Tucson, AZ: Quality America, 1991.

Resource Engineering. *SPC Workout Workbook: The Official Companion Guide to the SPC Workout.* Tolland, CT: Resource Engineering, 1996.

Smith, Gerald. *Statistical Process Control & Quality Improvement.* Paramus, NJ: Macmillan Publishing, 1994.

Trietsch, Dan. *Statistical Quality Control: A Loss Minimization Approach.* River Edge, NJ: World Scientific Publishing, 1998.

Thompson, James R and Jacek Koronacki. *Statistical Quality Control for Quality Improvement.* Boca Raton, FL: Chapman & Hall, 2001.

Wheeler, Donald J. *Advanced Topics in Statistical Process Control: The Power of Shewhart's Charts.* Knoxville, TN: SPC Press, 1995.

Whitehouse, Gary E. *IIE Microsoftware: Statistical Quality Control—IBM.* Norcross, GA: Engineering & Management Press, 1984.

Index